TEACHINGS OF PRESIDENTS OF THE CHURCH

GEORGE ALBERT SMITH

Published by
The Church of Jesus Christ of Latter-day Saints
Salt Lake City, Utah

Books in the *Teachings of Presidents of the Church* Series

Teachings of Presidents of the Church: Joseph Smith (item number 36481)

Teachings of Presidents of the Church: Brigham Young (35554)

Teachings of Presidents of the Church: John Taylor (35969)

Teachings of Presidents of the Church: Wilford Woodruff (36315)

Teachings of Presidents of the Church: Joseph F. Smith (35744)

Teachings of Presidents of the Church: Heber J. Grant (35970)

Teachings of Presidents of the Church: George Albert Smith (36786)

Teachings of Presidents of the Church: David O. McKay (36492)

Teachings of Presidents of the Church: Harold B. Lee (35892)

Teachings of Presidents of the Church: Spencer W. Kimball (36500)

To order these books, go to your local distribution center or visit store.lds.org.

Your comments and suggestions about this book would be appreciated. Please submit them to Curriculum Development, 50 East North Temple Street, Room 2404, Salt Lake City, UT 84150-3220 USA.

Or e-mail your comments and suggestions to:

cur-development@ldschurch.org

Please list your name, address, ward, and stake. Be sure to give the title of the book. Then offer your comments and suggestions about the book's strengths and areas of potential improvement.

Contents

George Albert Smith

Introduction

The First Presidency and the Quorum of the Twelve Apostles have established the *Teachings of Presidents of the Church* series to help you deepen your understanding of the restored gospel and draw closer to the Lord through the teachings of latter-day prophets. As the Church adds volumes to this series, you will build a collection of gospel reference books for your home. The volumes in this series are designed to be used for personal study and for Sunday instruction. They can also help you prepare other lessons or talks and answer questions about Church doctrine.

This book features the teachings of President George Albert Smith, who served as President of The Church of Jesus Christ of Latter-day Saints from May 21, 1945, to April 4, 1951.

Personal Study

As you study the teachings of President George Albert Smith, prayerfully seek the inspiration of the Spirit. The questions at the end of each chapter will help you understand President Smith's teachings and apply them in your life. As you study these teachings, you may want to think about how you could teach them to family members and friends. This will strengthen your understanding of what you read.

Teaching from This Book

You can use this book to teach at home or at church. The following guidelines can help you.

Prepare to Teach

Seek the guidance of the Holy Ghost as you prepare to teach. Prayerfully study the chapter to become confident in your understanding of President Smith's teachings. You will teach with greater sincerity and power when his words have influenced you personally (see D&C 11:21).

If you are teaching a Melchizedek Priesthood or Relief Society lesson, you should not set this book aside or prepare lessons from other materials. Prayerfully select from the chapter those teachings that you feel will be most helpful to those you teach. Some chapters contain more material than you will be able to discuss during class time. Allow good discussions to continue rather than trying to cover all the teachings.

Encourage participants to study the chapter before the lesson and to bring the book with them. When they do so, they will be better prepared to participate in a discussion and edify one another.

Introduce the Chapter

As you introduce the chapter, and throughout the lesson, try to create an atmosphere where the Spirit can touch the hearts and minds of those you teach. To start the lesson, help those you teach focus on the teachings of the chapter. To do this, you could:

- Read and discuss the section titled "From the Life of George Albert Smith" at the beginning of the chapter.
- Discuss a picture or scripture from the chapter.
- Sing a related hymn.
- Briefly share a personal experience about the topic.

Lead a Discussion about President Smith's Teachings

As you teach from this book, invite others to share their thoughts, ask questions, and teach one another. They will learn best when they actively participate. This is also a good way to help them receive personal revelation. To encourage discussion, use the questions at the end of the chapter. These questions are referenced at various places in the chapter to show which section of teachings they refer to. You could also develop your own questions especially for those you are teaching. For example, you could ask participants how they can apply President Smith's teachings in their responsibilities as parents or as home teachers or visiting teachers.

The following options may give you additional ideas:

- Ask participants to share what they have learned from their personal study of the chapter. It may be helpful to contact a few participants during the week and ask them to come prepared to share what they have learned.

• Assign participants to read selected questions from the end of the chapter (either individually or in small groups). Ask them to look for teachings in the chapter that relate to the questions. Then invite them to share their thoughts and insights with the rest of the group.

• Read together a selection of President Smith's statements from the chapter. Ask participants to share examples from the scriptures and from their own experience that illustrate what President Smith taught.

• Ask participants to choose a section they are interested in and read it silently. Invite them to gather in groups of two or three people who chose the same section and discuss what they learned.

Conclude the Discussion

Briefly summarize the lesson or ask one or two participants to do so. Encourage those you teach to share with others what they have learned from President Smith's teachings. Testify of the teachings you have discussed. You may also want to invite others to share their testimonies.

Information about the Sources Quoted in This Book

The teachings of President Smith in this book are direct quotations from a variety of sources. These excerpts have retained the punctuation, spelling, capitalization, and paragraphing of the original sources unless editorial or typographic changes have been necessary to improve readability. For this reason, you may notice minor inconsistencies in the text. For example, the word *gospel* is lowercased in some quotations and capitalized in others.

Also, President Smith often used terms such as *men, man,* or *mankind* to refer to all people, both male and female. He frequently used the pronouns *he, his,* and *him* to refer to both genders. This was common in the language of his era. Despite the differences between these language conventions and more current usage, President Smith's teachings apply to both women and men.

Historical Summary

The following chronology provides a brief historical framework for the teachings of President George Albert Smith presented in this book.

1870, April 4	Born in Salt Lake City, Utah, to John Henry and Sarah Farr Smith.
1874–75	His father, John Henry Smith, serves a mission in Great Britain. George Albert is four years old when he leaves.
1880, October 27	John Henry Smith is ordained an Apostle.
1882–85	John Henry Smith serves as president of the European Mission.
1883	George Albert Smith begins working in a clothing factory at age 13.
1888	Begins working for a railroad company. He suffers permanent damage to his eyes because of his work.
1891, September–November	Serves a mission in southern Utah for the Young Men's Mutual Improvement Association.
1892, May 25	Marries Lucy Emily Woodruff in the Manti Utah Temple.
1892–94	Serves a mission in the southern United States, beginning just a few weeks after his marriage. Lucy joins him four months into the mission.
1903, October 8	Ordained an Apostle by President Joseph F. Smith.

1904	Writes his "personal creed," a list of 11 ideals that he commits to live by (see pages 1–2 of this book).
1909–12	Suffers from serious health problems.
1919–21	Presides over the European Mission.
1921–35	Serves as general superintendent of the Young Men's Mutual Improvement Association.
1922	Elected vice president of the National Society of the Sons of the American Revolution. He serves in this office until 1925 and then again in 1944 and 1946.
1930, September	Helps organize the Utah Pioneer Trails and Landmarks Association to locate and mark Church historic sites. He is elected as the organization's first president.
1933, July 27	Becomes president of the Society for the Aid of the Sightless in Utah.
1934, May 31	Receives the Silver Buffalo, the highest award given by the Boy Scouts of America.
1935–36	Supervises the publication of the Book of Mormon in braille.
1937, November 5	Lucy dies at the age of 68 after an extended illness.
1938, January–July	Visits the missions of the Church in the South Pacific, including stops in Hawaii, Samoa, Tonga, Tahiti, New Zealand, and Australia.
1943, July	Set apart as President of the Quorum of the Twelve Apostles.
1945, May 21	Set apart as President of The Church of Jesus Christ of Latter-day Saints.

1945, September 23	Dedicates the Idaho Falls Idaho Temple.
1945, November 2	Meets with United States president Harry S Truman to discuss efforts to send aid to Europe after World War II.
1946, May	Visits members of the Church in Mexico, the first President of the Church to do so. Presents a copy of the Book of Mormon to Mexican president Manuel Ávila Camacho.
1947, July 24	Dedicates This Is the Place Monument and commemorates the centennial of the pioneers' arrival in the Salt Lake Valley.
1947	Church membership reaches one million.
1949, September 30– October 2	Participates in the first-ever televised broadcast of general conference.
1951, April 4	Dies in Salt Lake City, Utah, on his 81st birthday.

The Life and Ministry of George Albert Smith

One day during his service as President of the Church, George Albert Smith was sent a photograph with a note that read, "I am sending you this picture because it is a graphic illustration of the man we believe you are." It was a picture of President Smith visiting with a mother and her four young children. On that particular day, President Smith had been rushing to catch a train when the mother stopped him, hoping her children could have the opportunity to shake hands with a prophet of God. An observer captured the moment in the photograph.

The note continued, "The reason we treasure [this picture] so is because, as busy as you were, in spite of the fact you were being hurried into your car and then to your waiting train, you still took time out to shake the hand of each child in this family."[1]

Acts of kindness like this one characterized the life and ministry of George Albert Smith. Whether by offering love and encouragement to a neighbor struggling with his faith or by organizing vast welfare efforts to feed thousands of people, George Albert Smith lived by the commandment of the Savior, "Thou shalt love thy neighbour as thyself" (Mark 12:31).

Early Years, 1870–90

About age 4

George Albert Smith was born on April 4, 1870, to John Henry and Sarah Farr Smith in a humble home in Salt Lake City. The Smith family had a great legacy of service in the kingdom of God. George Albert's father would later serve in the Quorum of the Twelve Apostles and in the First Presidency. His grandfather and namesake,

George A. Smith, was a cousin to the Prophet Joseph Smith and was among the first Latter-day Saint pioneers to enter the Salt Lake Valley in 1847; George A. Smith was also an Apostle and a counselor to President Brigham Young. George Albert's great-grandfather John Smith served as Patriarch to the Church and as the first stake president in Salt Lake City. And his maternal grandfather, Lorin Farr, was the first mayor of Ogden, Utah, and the first stake president in that city.

John Henry Smith

George Albert Smith loved and admired his parents. He credited his father for teaching him to reach out to those in need,[2] and he praised his mother for the sacrifices she made to raise her family in the gospel. "Although we were very poor," he recalled, "and my father was on a mission when I was five years old, I never remember of hearing my mother complain, and I never saw her shed a tear because of conditions that surrounded her. She could make a dollar go as far as anybody I ever knew. . . .

". . . When father was absent from home on a mission, mother took his place, and she was really the head of the house in his absence. We attended to our prayers, and had a blessing on the food, and in case of sickness, she called in the elders, for she had great faith in the ordinances of the gospel. She has always been a strict tithe-payer, and as far as I have been able to discover, there has never entered her mind a thought that perhaps there might be a mistake and 'Mormonism' not be true. She believes it with all her soul."[3]

Sarah Farr Smith

In particular, George Albert Smith remembered his mother teaching him to pray and trust that God would answer: "When I think of the influence of my mother when I was a little [boy] I am moved to reverence and tears. . . . I remember as though it were yesterday, she took me by the hand and we walked up a flight of stairs to the second story. There I knelt before her and held her hand as she taught me to pray. Thank God for those mothers who have in their hearts the spirit of the Gospel

Children of John Henry and Sarah Farr Smith.
George Albert Smith is on the left.

and a desire to bless. I could repeat that prayer now and it is a great many years since I learned it. It gave me an assurance that I had a Heavenly Father, and let me know that He heard and answered prayer. When I was older we still lived in a two story frame house and when the wind blew hard it would rock as if it would topple over. Sometimes I would be too frightened to go to sleep. My bed was in a little room by itself, and many a night I have climbed out and got down on my knees and asked my Father in Heaven to take care of the house, preserve it that it would not break in pieces and I have got back into my little bed just as sure that I would be safeguarded from evil as if I held my Father's hand."[4]

Looking back on his childhood, George Albert Smith said:

"My parents were living in very humble circumstances, but I praise my Maker and thank him with all my heart for sending me into their home.

". . . I learned when I was a boy that this is the work of the Lord. I learned that there were prophets living upon the earth. I learned that the inspiration of the Almighty would influence those who lived to enjoy it.

". . . I am thankful for my birthright, thankful for parents who taught me the gospel of Jesus Christ and set the example in their home."[5]

Young George Albert was known as a happy, playful boy. Friends appreciated his cheerful nature, and he enjoyed entertaining them with the harmonica, banjo, and guitar and a repertoire of funny songs. Yet he also had experiences that helped him develop a strong sense of responsibility that was remarkable for his young age. When he was 12 years old, George Albert attended Brigham Young Academy, where he received some counsel that was to have a profound effect upon his life. He later recalled:

"It was fortunate that part of my instruction came under Dr. Karl G. Maeser, that outstanding educator who was the first builder of our great Church schools. . . . I cannot remember much of what was said during the year that I was there, but there is one thing that I will probably never forget. I have repeated it many times. . . . Dr. Maeser one day stood up and said:

"'Not only will you be held accountable for the things that you do, but you will be held responsible for the very thoughts that you think.'

"Being a boy, not in the habit of controlling my thoughts very much, it was quite a puzzle to me what I was to do, and it worried me. In fact, it stuck to me just like a burr. About a week or ten days after that it suddenly came to me what he meant. I could see the philosophy of it then. All at once there came to me this interpretation of what he had said: Why, of course, you will be held accountable for your thoughts because when your life is complete in mortality, it will be the sum of your thoughts. That one suggestion has been a great blessing to me all my life, and it has enabled me upon many occasions to avoid thinking improperly because I realize that I will be, when my life's labor is complete, the product of my thoughts."[6]

Young George Albert assumed great responsibilities at home in 1882 when his father, who had been serving in the Quorum of the Twelve for two years, was called as president of the European

Mission. John Henry's absence required that George Albert help provide for the family. When he was 13, he applied to work at a Church-owned manufacturing plant and department store in Salt Lake City, but the manager said they could not afford to hire anyone. George Albert replied that he had not asked to be paid, only to work. He added, "I know that if I'm worth anything I'll get paid."[7] His positive attitude earned him a position as a factory worker for $2.50 a week, and his strong work ethic soon helped him advance to better positions in the company.

When he was 18, he found work with a railway surveying party. While working this job, the glare from the sun on the desert sands damaged his eyes. This left George Albert's vision permanently impaired, making it difficult for him to read and causing him discomfort throughout his life.

Missionary Service and Marriage, 1891–94

In September 1891 President Wilford Woodruff called George Albert Smith to serve a short-term mission in southern Utah. His specific assignment was to work with the youth of the Church in the area. For the next four months he and his companion helped set up youth organizations in the stakes and wards, spoke in numerous meetings, and encouraged the young people to live the standards of the Church.

Upon returning from his mission, George Albert continued courting his childhood sweetheart, Lucy Woodruff, the granddaughter of President Wilford Woodruff. They had grown up as neighbors, and Lucy had noticed the character traits George Albert was developing. She recorded her admiration for him in her diary: "Tonight I retire with a thankful heart to God . . . and pray that he may give me strength to be more deserving of the love of one whom I firmly believe to be one of the best young men that was ever placed on the earth. His goodness and kindness causes tears to come to my eyes."[8]

Lucy Emily Woodruff Smith

But Lucy had many admirers of her own, and some of them were very well-to-do and offered her extravagant gifts. George Albert, on the other hand, attracted Lucy with his dedication to the Lord. He wrote to her, "If you are interested in marrying someone for money it would not be me, because I have long ago decided that I will not devote myself or my life or my time to making money but toward serving the Lord and toward helping His children in this world."[9] Lucy made her choice, and on May 25, 1892, she and George Albert were married in the Manti Utah Temple. George Albert's father performed the ceremony. On that day Lucy gave her husband a small locket with her picture inside. He kept the locket on the chain of his pocket watch, where it hung close to his heart, and wore it nearly every day for the rest of his life.[10]

The newlyweds had less than a month together before George Albert departed for another mission, this one a proselyting assignment to the southern United States. Even though they had known his departure was imminent—the call had come three weeks before they were married—the separation was still difficult. They were both overjoyed when, four months later, Lucy was called to serve by her husband's side in the mission office, where Elder Smith had recently been assigned to serve as mission secretary.

The president of the Southern States Mission was J. Golden Kimball, who at the same time was serving as a member of the Seventy. Twice during the period of Elder Smith's service, President Kimball had to leave the mission to take care of important matters back in Salt Lake City—once shortly after Elder Smith became the mission secretary and again about one year later. On both occasions, President Kimball left the tremendous responsibility for leading and

Missionaries in the Southern States Mission.
Newly married Lucy (third from left) and George Albert Smith
(seated next to her) served together in the mission home.

administering the mission with Elder Smith, offering support and counsel through numerous letters. In all, Elder Smith served as acting president of the mission for approximately 16 months. It worried President Kimball to be away so long, but he trusted his young assistant. He wrote in a letter to Elder Smith, "I think my discernment and intelligence, however limited it may be, enables me to value your integrity and worth, which I assure you I do."[11] In another letter he wrote, "Always let this one idea stand uppermost: that I appreciate your labors, zeal, and good spirit."[12]

President Kimball had many opportunities to witness Elder Smith's zeal and good spirit. On one occasion the two were traveling together and had been invited to spend the night in a small log home. George Albert Smith later recalled:

"About midnight we were awakened with a terrible shouting and yelling from the outside. Foul language greeted our ears as we sat up in bed to acquaint ourselves with the circumstances. It was a bright moonlit night and we could see many people on the outside. President Kimball jumped up and started to dress. The men pounded on the door and used filthy language ordering the Mormons to come out, that they were going to shoot them. President Kimball asked me if I wasn't going to get up and dress and I told him no, I was going to stay in bed, that I was sure the Lord would take care of us. In just a few seconds the room was filled with shots. Apparently the mob had divided itself into four groups and were shooting into the corners of the house. Splinters were flying over our heads in every direction. There were a few moments of quiet, then another volley of shots was fired and more splinters flew. I felt absolutely no terror. I was very calm as I lay there, experiencing one of the most horrible events of my life, but I was sure . . . that the Lord would protect me, and he did.

"Apparently the mob became discouraged and left. The next morning when we opened the door, there was a huge bundle of heavy hickory sticks such as the mob used to beat the missionaries in the South."[13]

Years later George Albert Smith shared this experience with his grandchildren to teach them to trust the Lord. "I want to impress on you," he said, "that the Lord will take care of you in times of danger, if you will give him the opportunity."[14]

Family Life

George Albert and Lucy were released from their mission in June 1894. A few months after their return to Salt Lake City, Lucy received a blessing from her grandfather, President Wilford Woodruff, promising her that she would bear children. On November 19, 1895, she gave birth to a daughter they named Emily, and four years later another daughter, Edith, was born. Their last child, George Albert Jr., was born in 1905.

George Albert Smith was an affectionate father, adored by his children. Edith wrote of him: "To me my Father had all of the attributes that endear a father to his daughter. He fulfilled all of my expectations of fatherhood." Especially impressive to the children was the way George Albert treated his beloved wife. "Father's affection and consideration for mother were beautiful," Edith wrote. "He never lost an opportunity to show his appreciation of her. Everything they did, they did together, after well-laid plans and teamwork. She was precious to him. . . . While we all adored Mother, I am sure that his thoughtfulness and tenderness toward her made her even more beloved by us children."[15]

As a father, George Albert Smith tried earnestly to help his children experience the joy he felt by living the gospel. One Christmas Day, after the gifts had been opened, he asked his young daughters how they would feel about giving away some of their toys to children who had not received any Christmas presents. Since they had just received new toys, the girls agreed that they could give away some of their old toys to the needy children.

"Wouldn't you like to give them some of the new ones, too?" George Albert gently suggested.

His daughters were hesitant, but eventually they agreed to give up one or two of their new toys. George Albert then took the girls to the home of the children he had in mind, and they delivered the gifts. The experience was so uplifting that as they left, one of the girls said with excitement in her voice, "Now let's go and get the rest of the toys for them."[16]

Quorum of the Twelve Apostles, 1903–45

On Tuesday, October 6, 1903, George Albert Smith had a busy day at work and was unable to attend the sessions of general conference that day. By the time he left the office, the afternoon session of conference was nearly over, so he started for home with plans to take his children to the fair.

When he arrived at his house, he was surprised to find a crowd of visitors, one of whom stepped forward and congratulated him warmly.

"What is all this about?" he asked.

"Don't you know?" she responded.

"Don't I know what?"

The Quorum of the Twelve Apostles in 1921. Standing, left to right: Joseph Fielding Smith, James E. Talmage, Stephen L Richards, Richard R. Lyman, Melvin J. Ballard, and John A. Widtsoe. Seated, left to right: Rudger Clawson, Reed Smoot, George Albert Smith, George F. Richards, Orson F. Whitney, and David O. McKay.

"Why, you've been sustained as a member of the Quorum of the Twelve Apostles," the visitor exclaimed.

"That couldn't be right," George Albert said. "There must be some mistake."

"I heard it myself," she countered.

"It must have been some other Smith," he said. "Not a word has been said to me about it, and I can't believe it is true."

Confused, the visitor returned to the Tabernacle to find out whether she was mistaken. There she was informed that she was right—George Albert Smith was the newest member of the Quorum of the Twelve Apostles. [17]

His daughter Emily later recalled the scene at the Smith home: "It seemed like the whole Tabernacle was streaming across the lawn into our house, crying and kissing mother. They were all saying that

Father was an apostle, and we thought that being an apostle must be the worst thing that could possibly happen to you."

Even after the report had been verified, George Albert determined that he would still take his daughters to the fair as promised, "although he didn't see much of it," Emily remembered. "He spent the whole time with his back to the wall talking to people."[18]

Two days later, on October 8, 1903, George Albert Smith was ordained an Apostle in an upper room of the Salt Lake Temple by President Joseph F. Smith. After the ordination he was invited to share his feelings with the members of the Quorum of the Twelve present. "I feel weak and lack judgment compared with men of maturer years," he said, "but my heart is right, and I desire sincerely the onward progress of the work of the Lord. . . . I have a living testimony of the divinity of this work; I know that the gospel has come to earth under the direction and guidance of the Lord himself, and that those chosen to preside were and are His servants in very deed. I desire and pray that I may live pure and humble, so that I may be entitled to the promptings and admonitions of the Spirit to guide me throughout my life."[19]

George Albert Smith served in the Quorum of the Twelve for nearly 42 years, including 2 years as President of the Quorum. During this time he filled many assignments and blessed people around the world in numerous ways.

Sharing the Gospel and Making Friends for the Church

Elder Smith had a natural talent for putting people at ease and turning enemies into friends. A local businessman, not a member of the Church, said of him at his funeral: "He was an easy man to know. He was a man you would just like to know. His friendly smile, his hearty handclasp, and the warmth of his greeting made you feel inwardly, in your heart, the sincerity of his friendship for you and for his fellow man."[20]

This talent was valuable at a time when the Church was still largely unknown throughout the world and held in suspicion by many. Once, while fulfilling an assignment in West Virginia, he learned that city officials had threatened to arrest anyone caught preaching Mormonism. Elder Smith met with the city clerk, Mr. Engle, to try to change the policy. He later wrote in his journal: "When I first called on Mr. Engle he was very sharp in his manner and curtly informed me that we would not be tolerated in that city. . . . I told him I believed he was misinformed and would like to sit down with him and have a chat. . . . We spent some time discussing Mormonism. He melted down considerable before I left and shook hands with me and gave me his card. I left feeling sure I had removed some prejudice." [21] Three days later Elder Smith paid him another visit and this time left a copy of the Book of Mormon with him. [22]

Elder Smith was always looking for opportunities to talk to people about the Church. Whenever his assignments required him to travel, he took with him copies of the Book of Mormon, Church magazines, and other Church literature that he hoped to give away. Because the Book of Mormon bears powerful witness of Jesus Christ, Elder Smith considered it an ideal Christmas gift and often mailed copies to friends of other faiths and even to prominent people he had never met. [23] In a letter accompanying one such Christmas gift he wrote: "In a few days the Christian world will celebrate the birth of the Saviour and it is customary at that time to remember our friends. I trust therefore that you will accept from me a copy of the Book of Mormon. . . . Believing that you will be glad to have this in your library I am sending it to you as a Christmas present."

He received the following response: "The book will have place on our shelves and will be read [from cover to cover] with open-minded thoroughness. It cannot fail to broaden the views and increase the spirit of tolerance of all who read it thoughtfully." [24]

Civic Involvement

Elder Smith encouraged Church members to be involved in their communities and to use their influence to improve conditions in the world. He himself was involved in several civic organizations despite his demanding calling as a General Authority. He was elected president of the International Irrigation Congress and Dry Farming Congress, and he was elected to six terms as vice president of the National Society of the Sons of the American Revolution. A strong proponent of aviation as a way for General Authorities to fulfill their travel assignments more efficiently, Elder Smith served on the board of directors of Western Air Lines. He was also actively involved in the Boy Scouts of America and in 1934 was awarded the Silver Buffalo, the highest honor given in Scouting. In the years after World War I he served as Utah state chairman of the Armenian and Syrian Relief campaign and as the state representative at the International Housing Convention, whose purpose was to find shelter for those left homeless by the war. [25]

Before his call as an Apostle, George Albert had been active in politics, earnestly campaigning for causes and candidates that he felt would improve society. Once he became a General Authority, his involvement in politics declined, but he continued to advocate causes he believed in. For example, in 1923 he helped introduce a bill in the Utah State Legislature that led to the construction of a sanatorium for tuberculosis patients. [26]

Elder Smith's compassion for others was particularly evident in his service as president of the Society for the Aid of the Sightless, an office he held from 1933 to 1949. As one who suffered from visual impairment himself, Elder Smith felt a special sympathy for those who are blind. He supervised the publication of the Book of Mormon in braille, and he instituted a program to help people who are blind learn to read braille and adapt to their disability in other ways. His efforts endeared him to those he served. One member of the Society for the Aid of the Sightless expressed her appreciation through a poem that was presented to Elder Smith on his 70th birthday:

> When Life beats hard with stormy hands,
> And bitter teardrops fall;
> When friendless Winter chills my soul,
> And empty echoes call—
> 'Tis then I turn, with eager hope,
> My steps though spent and lame,
> To find an understanding heart,
> Where burns a friendly flame—
> A heart where gentle Wisdom dwells,
> Compassionate and kind,

*Elder George Albert Smith supervised the publication
of the Book of Mormon in braille.*

Whose faith in God and man has taught
A like faith to the Blind. . . .

Although his tender loving face
From us is shut apart,
We see the gracious wisdom
Of his understanding heart;
We feel a peace within his soul
And know a peace our own;
We hear his silent prayer that tells
We do not walk alone;
His faith in us will give us strength,
As unseen paths we plod;
Our souls uplifted by a man
In partnership with God.[27]

Personal Illness and Other Trials

For most of his life, George Albert did not have particularly good health. Though he enjoyed swimming, horseback riding, and other physical activities, his body was frail and often weak. Besides his chronic eye problems, Elder Smith suffered from stomach and back pain, constant fatigue, heart trouble, and many other ailments throughout his life. The stress and pressure of his many responsibilities also took a toll on him, and at first he was unwilling to slow his busy pace in order to preserve his health. As a result, from 1909 to 1912 he fought an illness so severe that it kept him bedridden and prevented him from fulfilling his duties in the Quorum of the Twelve. It was a very trying time for Elder Smith, who wanted desperately to resume his service. The death of his father in 1911 and a serious bout of influenza afflicting his wife made Elder Smith's recovery even more difficult.

Years later he shared the following experience he had had during this period:

"A number of years ago I was seriously ill. In fact, I think everyone gave up on me but my wife. . . . I became so weak as to be scarcely able to move. It was a slow and exhausting effort for me even to turn over in bed.

"One day, under these conditions, I lost consciousness of my surroundings and thought I had passed to the Other Side. I found myself standing with my back to a large and beautiful lake, facing a great forest of trees. There was no one in sight, and there was no boat upon the lake or any other visible means to indicate how I might have arrived there. I realized, or seemed to realize, that I had finished my work in mortality and had gone home. . . .

"I began to explore, and soon I found a trail through the woods which seemed to have been used very little, and which was almost obscured by grass. I followed this trail, and after I had walked for some time and had traveled a considerable distance through the forest, I saw a man coming towards me. I became aware that he was a very large man, and I hurried my steps to reach him, because I recognized him as my grandfather [George A. Smith]. In mortality he weighed over three hundred pounds, so you may know he was a large man. I remember how happy I was to see him coming. I had been given his name and had always been proud of it.

George A. Smith

"When Grandfather came within a few feet of me, he stopped. His stopping was an invitation for me to stop. Then—and this I would like the boys and girls and young people never to forget—he looked at me very earnestly and said:

"'I would like to know what you have done with my name.'

"Everything I had ever done passed before me as though it were a flying picture on a screen—everything I had done. Quickly this vivid retrospect came down to the very time I was standing there. My whole life had passed before me. I smiled and looked at my grandfather and said:

"'I have never done anything with your name of which you need be ashamed.'

"He stepped forward and took me in his arms, and as he did so, I became conscious again of my earthly surroundings. My pillow was as wet as though water had been poured on it—wet with tears of gratitude that I could answer unashamed.

"I have thought of this many times, and I want to tell you that I have been trying, more than ever since that time, to take care of that name. So I want to say to the boys and girls, to the young men and women, to the youth of the Church and of all the world: Honor your fathers and your mothers. Honor the names that you bear."[28]

Eventually Elder Smith began to regain his strength, and he emerged from this trial with a renewed sense of gratitude for his testimony of the truth. He told the Saints during a subsequent general conference: "I have been in the valley of the shadow of death in recent years, so near the other side that I am sure that [if not] for the special blessing of our Heavenly Father I could not have remained here. But, never for one moment did that testimony that my Heavenly Father has blessed me with become dimmed. The nearer I went to the other side, the greater was my assurance that the gospel is true. Now that my life has been spared I rejoice to testify that I know the gospel is true, and with all my soul I thank my Heavenly Father that he has revealed it to me."[29]

Various physical ailments and other adversities continued to afflict Elder Smith in the coming years. Perhaps his greatest trial came in the years 1932 to 1937, when his wife, Lucy, suffered from arthritis and neuralgia. She was in great pain and by 1937 required almost constant care. Then a heart attack in April 1937 nearly took her life and left her even weaker than before.

Though he worried about Lucy constantly, Elder Smith continued to perform his duties as best he could. On November 5, 1937, he spoke at the funeral of a friend, and as he sat down after his address, someone handed him a note telling him to return home immediately. He later wrote in his journal: "I left the chapel at once but my Darling wife had breathed her last before I arrived at home. She was passing while I was talking at the funeral. I am of course bereft of a devoted helpmeet and will be lonely without her."

Lucy and George Albert had been married a little more than 45 years at the time of her death. She was 68 years old. Though he deeply missed his wife, Elder Smith knew that the separation was only temporary, and this knowledge brought him strength. "While my family are greatly distressed," he wrote, "we are comforted by the assurance of a reunion with mother if we remain faithful. She has been a devoted, helpful, considerate wife and mother. She has been a sufferer for six years in one way or another and I am sure she is happy with her mother and other dear ones over there. . . . The Lord is most kind and has taken away every feeling of death, for which I am exceedingly grateful."[30]

President of the European Mission

In 1919 President Heber J. Grant, who had recently been sustained as President of the Church, called Elder Smith to preside over the European Mission. During a general conference address just days before his departure, Elder Smith said:

"I would like to say to you, my brothers and sisters, that I esteem it an honor—nay, more than an honor, I esteem it a very great blessing—that the Lord has raised me from the feeble condition that I was in a short time ago, restoring me to such a condition of health that the brethren have felt that it will be possible for me to fill a mission in a foreign land. . . .

". . . Next Wednesday I expect to take the train to the coast and then across the ocean to the field to which I have been called. Thank God for the opportunity of going. I am grateful that the knowledge of this truth has come into my soul."[31]

At this time Europe was still recovering from World War I, which had ended just a few months before. Because of the war, the number of missionaries in Europe was very low, and one of Elder Smith's tasks was to increase that number. The strained economic conditions in postwar Europe, however, made governments unwilling to grant the necessary visas. To make matters worse, there was still a lot of misunderstanding about and prejudice against the Latter-day Saints. To improve the Church's image, Elder Smith met with numerous government officials and other prominent figures. In explaining the purpose of the missionaries in Europe and throughout the world, he would often say, "Keep all the good things that you have, keep all that God has given you that enriches your life, and then let us share something with you that will add to your happiness and increase your satisfaction."[32] According to one of the missionaries who served under him, "through his masterful, kind way he won their esteem and friendship and secured concessions concerning the missionaries which had been denied before."[33]

By the end of his service in 1921, Elder Smith had succeeded in raising the number of missionaries serving in Europe and changing some misconceptions about the Latter-day Saints. He had also made friends for the Church, and he kept in contact with them through letters for many years to come.

Preserving Church Historic Sites

Elder Smith loved to tell others about the Church and the great events in its history. Throughout his ministry he did much to help preserve that history by creating monuments and otherwise marking sites of interest in Church history. As one of his associates wrote, "He has believed that by calling attention of the younger generation to the accomplishments of their forebears he would be rendering an important service."[34]

As a young Apostle he went to Palmyra, New York, and negotiated the purchase of the Joseph Smith Sr. farm in the name of the Church. While in New York he also visited with a man named Pliny Sexton, who owned the Hill Cumorah, the place where Joseph Smith obtained the gold plates. Mr. Sexton was unwilling to sell the land to the Church, but he and Elder Smith nevertheless became friends. Due in part to the good relationship Elder Smith maintained with Mr. Sexton, the Church was eventually able to purchase the property and dedicate a monument there.

In 1930, the centennial year of the organization of the Church, Elder Smith helped establish the Utah Pioneer Trails and Landmarks Association and was elected as the group's first president. Over the next 20 years, this organization placed more than 100 monuments and markers, many of them memorializing the pioneers' trek to the Salt Lake Valley. Elder Smith officiated at the dedications of most of these monuments.[35]

Explaining the Church's interest in historic sites, he wrote: "It has been customary to build monuments to individuals that their memories might be retained. Great events have also been permanently established in the minds of people by building monuments. . . . There are many points of interest that are being forgotten and the people have felt that it was desirable to mark them in a substantial way so that those who follow will have their attention called to important events."[36]

As one whose grandfather had walked to Utah with the pioneers, Elder Smith felt deep respect for those early Church members who had sacrificed so much for their faith. In an address to the Relief Society, he shared the following experience he had while retracing the route of the handcart pioneers:

"We came to the part of the trail where the Martin Handcart Company had lost so many lives. We found, as near as we could, the place where they camped. Those who were descendants of that party were there to assist in placing a marker. Then we came to Rock Creek; a temporary marker had been placed there by us the

*Monument on the Hill Cumorah, where the angel Moroni
delivered the gold plates to Joseph Smith.*

year before. At that particular time of the year beautiful wild flowers were growing everywhere, the wild iris was plentiful, and members of the party gathered some of these flowers and laid them tenderly upon a mound of stone that had been piled up the year before. . . . Here 15 members of this Church had been buried in one grave, they having died from hunger and exposure.

"You know there are times and places when we seem to come nearer to our Heavenly Father. As we sat around the camp fire in that little valley of Rock Creek, where the Willie Handcart Company had met disaster,—we who were descendants of the pioneers, of those who had crossed the plains in the heat of the summer and the cold of the winter—stories were told of the experiences of our ancestors. . . . It was a delightful occasion. History was being repeated for our benefit.

". . . It seemed to me that we were in the very presence of those who had given their all that we might have the blessings of the Gospel. We seemed to feel the presence of the Lord.

"As we walked away, after we had shed our tears—for I doubt if there was a dry eye in the group of about 30 or 40 people—the influence that came as a result of that little gathering had touched our hearts, and one of the good sisters took me by the arm and said, 'Brother Smith, I am going to be a better woman from now on.' This woman . . . is one of the best of women but I believe she was touched as probably most of us were, by the fact that in some particulars we felt we had not measured up to the ideals that should have been in our souls. The people buried here had not only given days of their lives but they gave life itself as evidence of their belief in the divinity of this work. . . .

"If the members of this organization [the Relief Society] will be as faithful as were those who lie buried on the plains, who met their problems with faith in the Lord, you will add to your many accomplishments and the favor of a loving Father will flow to you and yours."[37]

President of the Church, 1945–51

Early in the morning of May 15, 1945, while riding a train in the eastern United States, Elder Smith was awakened by a railroad official with a message: President Heber J. Grant, who was President of the Church at the time, had passed away. Elder Smith changed trains as soon as he could and returned to Salt Lake City. Just a few days later George Albert Smith, as the senior member of the Quorum of the Twelve Apostles, was set apart as the eighth President of The Church of Jesus Christ of Latter-day Saints.

In his first general conference address as President of the Church, he said to the Saints who had just sustained him, "I wonder if anyone else here feels as weak and humble as the man who stands before you."[38] He expressed similar feelings to members of his family: "I have not wanted this position. I have not felt equal to it. But it has come to me, and I will fill it to the best of my ability. I want you all

President Smith and his counselors,
J. Reuben Clark Jr. (left) and David O. McKay (right)

to know that, whatever you are doing in the church, from [home] teaching to presiding over a stake, if you do it to the best of your ability, your position is just as important as mine."[39]

There were many who felt that President Smith's talents were uniquely suited to this calling. One of the General Authorities expressed this confidence shortly after President Smith was sustained: "It is frequently said that the Lord has raised up a particular man to perform a particular mission. . . . It is not for me to say what particular mission President George Albert Smith has ahead of him. This I do know, however, that at this particular time in the world's history, never was the need for love among brethren so desperately needed as it is needed today. Furthermore, I do know this, that there is no man of my acquaintance who loves the human family, collectively and individually, more profoundly than does President George Albert Smith."[40]

Helping the Needy in the Aftermath of World War II

World War II ended just months after George Albert Smith became President of the Church. The war had left thousands of people homeless and destitute in Europe, and President Smith quickly mobilized the Church's welfare resources to provide aid. President Gordon B. Hinckley later said of this effort: "I was among those who worked nights at Welfare Square here in Salt Lake City loading commodities onto rail cars which moved the food to the port from which it was shipped across the sea. During the time of the Swiss Temple dedication [in 1955], when many of the Saints of Germany came to the temple, I heard some of them, with tears running down their cheeks, speak with appreciation for that food which had saved their lives."[41]

President Smith also knew that there were great spiritual needs among the people of the world in the aftermath of such a devastating war. In response, he took steps to reorganize missions in countries where the war had interrupted missionary work, and he encouraged the Saints to live the gospel of peace in their personal lives. "The best evidence of gratitude at this time," he said shortly after the close of the war, "is to do all we can to bring happiness to this sad world, for we are all our Father's children, and we are all under the obligation of making this world a happier place for our having lived in it.

"Let us extend kindness and consideration to all who need it, not forgetting those who are bereft; and in our time of rejoicing for peace, let us not forget those who have given their loved ones as part of the price of peace. . . .

"I pray that men may turn to God, and give obedience to his ways, and thereby save the world from further conflict and destruction. I pray that the peace that comes only from our Heavenly Father may abide in the hearts and in the homes of all who mourn."[42]

Increased Opportunities to Share the Gospel

President Smith continued to share the gospel with others at every opportunity, and these opportunities increased with his new position. In May 1946 President Smith became the first President of the

Church to visit the Saints in Mexico. Besides meeting with members of the Church and speaking at a large conference, President Smith also called on several high-ranking officials in Mexico and talked to them about the restored gospel. During a visit with Mexican president Manuel Ávila Camacho, President Smith and his party explained: "We come with a special message for you and your people. We are here to tell you of your forefathers and of the restored Gospel of Jesus Christ. . . . We have a book that . . . tells of a great prophet who with his family and others, left Jerusalem 600 years before Christ, and came to . . . this great land of America, known to them as a 'land of promise, choice above all other lands.' This Book of Mormon tells also of the visit of Jesus Christ to this continent, and that He organized His Church and chose His twelve disciples."

President Ávila, who expressed respect and admiration for the Latter-day Saints living in his country, became very interested in the Book of Mormon and asked, "Would it be possible for me to get a copy of the Book of Mormon? I have never before heard about it." President Smith then presented him with a leather-bound copy in Spanish, with passages of particular interest listed at the front of the book. President Ávila said, "I shall read the entire book, for this is of great interest to me and to my people."[43]

Celebrating the Centennial of the Pioneers' Arrival

One of the highlights of George Albert Smith's six years as President of the Church came in 1947, when the Church celebrated the centennial of the arrival of the pioneers in the Salt Lake Valley. President Smith oversaw the celebration, which gained national attention and culminated in the dedication of This Is the Place Monument in Salt Lake City, near the location where the pioneers first entered the valley. Since 1930 President Smith had been involved in planning a memorial to honor the accomplishments and the faith of the pioneers. He was careful, however, to make sure the monument also honored early explorers, missionaries from other faiths, and important American Indian leaders from that era.

At the dedication of This Is the Place Monument, George Q. Morris, then the president of the Eastern States Mission, noted a spirit of goodwill, which he attributed to President Smith's efforts:

This Is the Place Monument, which commemorates the pioneers' arrival in the Salt Lake Valley, was dedicated by President Smith in 1947.

"President Smith's contributions to brotherhood and tolerance were reflected in the dedicatory service. . . . The monument itself had honored in sculpture—as far as possible in individual portrait sculpture—the men who had made history in the intermountain west preceding the Mormon Pioneers, regardless of race or religion. When the program for the dedicatory service was being prepared, it was President Smith's desire that all the major religious groups be represented in addition to state, county, and city officials. A Catholic priest, a Protestant bishop, a Jewish rabbi, and representatives of the Church of Jesus Christ of Latter-day Saints were prominent speakers. An eastern visitor, after the program, made this remark, 'Today I have had a spiritual rebaptism. What I have witnessed could not have happened anywhere else in the world. The spirit of tolerance that was manifest today was magnificent.'"[44]

Though the 60-foot monument was impressive, President Smith taught that the best way to honor the pioneers was to follow their example of faith and devotion. In the prayer dedicating the monument, he said: "Our Father which art in heaven, . . . we stand in thy presence this morning on this quiet hillside and look at a great monument that has been erected in honor of thy sons and daughters and their devotion. . . . We pray that we may be blessed with the same spirit that characterized those faithful ones who believed in thee and thy Beloved Son, who came to this valley because they desired to live here and worship thee. We pray that the spirit of worship and of gratitude may continue in our hearts."[45]

Reflections on Life at Age 80

Despite his advancing years, for most of his presidency President Smith was able to fulfill his responsibilities without the physical ailments that had limited him in the past. In an article published in April 1950, near his 80th birthday, President Smith looked back on his life and noted how God had sustained and blessed him:

"In these eighty years, I have traveled more than a million miles in the world in the interest of the gospel of Jesus Christ. I have been in many climes and in many lands and in many nations, and from my childhood people have been kind and helpful to me, members of the Church and non-members as well. Wherever I have gone, I have found noble men and women. . . .

". . . When I think of what a weak, frail individual I am, to be called to be the leader of this great Church, I realize how much I need help. Gratefully I acknowledge the help of my Father in heaven, and the encouragement and companionship during my life of many of the best men and women that can be found anywhere in the world, both at home and abroad."

He went on to express love for the people he had served for so many years:

"Surely it is a blessed thing to be associated with such people, and from the depths of my soul I take this occasion to thank you all for your kindness to me, and I also take this occasion to say to all of you: You will never know how much I love you. I have not the words to express it. And I want to feel that way toward every son and every daughter of my Heavenly Father.

"I have lived a long time, as compared with the average of human beings, and I have had a happy life. It will not be many years, in the natural course of events, till the summons to the other side will reach me. I look forward to that time with pleasant anticipation. And after eighty years in mortality, traveling in many parts of the world, associating with many great and good men and women, I witness to you, that I know today better than I ever knew before that God lives; that Jesus is the Christ; that Joseph Smith was a prophet of the Living God; and that the Church that he organized under the direction of our Heavenly Father, the Church of Jesus Christ of Latter-day Saints . . . is operating under the power and authority of the same priesthood that was conferred by Peter, James, and John upon Joseph Smith and Oliver Cowdery. I know this, as I know that I live, and I realize that to bear this testimony to you is a very serious matter and that I shall be held accountable by my Heavenly Father for this and all other things that I have taught in his name. . . . With love and kindness in my heart for all, I bear this witness in the name of Jesus Christ our Lord."[46]

One year later, on his 81st birthday, April 4, 1951, George Albert Smith passed away quietly in his home with his son and daughters at his bedside.

Simple Acts of Loving Service

George Albert Smith accomplished much during his 81 years—in the Church, in his community, and throughout the world. But those who knew him personally remembered him best for his many simple, humble acts of kindness and love. President David O. McKay, who officiated at President Smith's funeral, said of him, "Truly he was a noble soul, happiest when he was making others happy."[47]

Elder John A. Widtsoe, a member of the Quorum of the Twelve Apostles, recounted an experience he had while trying to resolve a weighty, difficult issue:

"I sat in my office rather tired after the day's work. . . . I was weary. Just then there was a knock upon the door, and in walked George Albert Smith. He said, 'I am on the way home after my day's

President Smith in his office.

work. I thought of you and the problems that you are expected to solve. I came in to comfort you and to bless you.'

"That was the way of George Albert Smith. . . . I shall never forget it. We talked together for awhile; we parted, he went home. My heart was lifted. I was weary no longer.

"You see, love . . . is not a mere word or a sensation within. To be a worthy love, it must be brought into action. President Smith on that occasion did that. He gave of his own time, his own strength, to me."[48]

Elder Matthew Cowley, also a member of the Quorum of the Twelve and a close friend of President Smith, paid tribute at the funeral service in this way:

"Everyone in distress, everyone beset with illness or other adversity, whoever came within the presence of this son of God, drew virtue and strength from him. To be in his presence was to be healed, if not physically, then indeed spiritually. . . .

". . . God attracts the godly, and I am sure that the shortest journey this man of God ever made in all of his travels has been the journey which he has just taken. God is love. George Albert Smith is love. His is godly. God has taken him unto himself.

". . . We can't honor a life like this with words. They are not adequate. There is only one way to honor his virtue, his sweetness of character, his great qualities of love, and that is with our deeds. . . .

"Let us all be a little more forgiving, a little more tender in our associations with each other, a little more considerate of one another, a little more generous of each other's feelings."[49]

On George Albert Smith's gravestone is the following inscription. It provides a fitting summary of his life of loving service:

"He understood and disseminated the teachings of Christ and was uncommonly successful in putting them into practice. He was kindly, patient, wise, tolerant, and understanding. He went about doing good. He loved Utah and America, but was not provincial. He had faith, without reservation, in the need for and in the power of love. For his Church and his family he had unbounded affection and served them passionately. Yet his love was not limited; it included all men, regardless of race, faith, or station. To them and of them he frequently said: 'We are all our Father's children.'"

Notes

1. In D. Arthur Haycock, "A Day with the President," *Improvement Era,* Apr. 1950, 288.

2. See "Pres. Smith's Leadership Address," *Deseret News,* Feb. 16, 1946, Church section, 6.

3. "Mothers of Our Leaders," *Relief Society Magazine,* June 1919, 313–14.

4. "To the Relief Society," *Relief Society Magazine,* Dec. 1932, 707–8.

5. "After Eighty Years," *Improvement Era,* Apr. 1950, 263.

6. "Pres. Smith's Leadership Address," 1.

7. In Merlo J. Pusey, *Builders of the Kingdom* (1981), 209.

8. Lucy Woodruff's journal, Feb. 5, 1888, George Albert Smith Family Papers, University of Utah, box 138, book 1.

9. In Emily Stewart Smith, "Some Notes about President George Albert Smith," May 1948, George Albert Smith Family Papers, University of Utah, box 5, page 3.

10. See Emily Stewart Smith, "Some Notes about President George Albert Smith," 5.

11. J. Golden Kimball, letter dated Mar. 18, 1893, George Albert Smith Family Papers, University of Utah, box 72, folder 12.

12. J. Golden Kimball, letter dated June 30, 1893, George Albert Smith Family Papers, University of Utah, box 72, folder 15.

13. "How My Life Was Preserved," George Albert Smith Family Papers, University of Utah, box 121, scrapbook 1, pages 43–44.

14. "How My Life Was Preserved," 43.

15. Edith Smith Elliott, "No Wonder We Love Him," *Relief Society Magazine,* June 1953, 366, 368.

16. See *Builders of the Kingdom,* 240.

17. See *Builders of the Kingdom,* 224–25.

18. Emily Smith Stewart, in "Pres. Smith Mementos At Y." *Deseret News,* Oct. 14, 1967, Church section, 6–7.

19. George Albert Smith Family Papers, University of Utah, box 100, folder 23, page 11.

20. John F. Fitzpatrick, in Conference Report, Apr. 1951, 172.

21. George Albert Smith's journal, Oct. 27, 1906, George Albert Smith Family Papers, University of Utah, box 73, book 3, page 70.

22. See George Albert Smith's journal, Oct. 30, 1906, George Albert Smith Family Papers, University of Utah, box 73, book 3, page 72.

23. See Francis M. Gibbons, *George Albert Smith: Kind and Caring Christian, Prophet of God* (1990), 208–9.

24. In Glenn R. Stubbs, "A Biography of George Albert Smith, 1870 to 1951" (PhD diss., Brigham Young University, 1974), 295.

25. See Bryant S. Hinckley, "Greatness in Men: Superintendent George Albert Smith," *Improvement Era,* Mar. 1932, 270, 271.

26. See "A Biography of George Albert Smith," 283.

27. Irene Jones, "The Understanding Heart," *Improvement Era,* July 1940, 423.

28. "Your Good Name," *Improvement Era,* Mar. 1947, 139.

29. In Conference Report, Oct. 1921, 42.

30. George Albert Smith's journal, Nov. 5, 1937, George Albert Smith Family Papers, University of Utah, box 74, book 11, pages 83–84.

31. In Conference Report, June 1919, 42, 44.

32. In Conference Report, Oct. 1950, 8.

33. James Gunn McKay, in "A Biography of George Albert Smith," 141.

34. George Q. Morris, "Perpetuating Our Ideals through Markers and Monuments," *Improvement Era,* Apr. 1950, 284.

35. See "Markers and Monuments," 284.

36. Letter to Leslie O. Loveridge, Mar. 15, 1937, George Albert Smith Family Papers, University of Utah, box 67, folder 25.

37. "To the Relief Society," *Relief Society Magazine,* Dec. 1932, 705–6.

38. In Conference Report, Oct. 1945, 18.

39. In *Builders of the Kingdom,* 315–16.

40. Joseph F. Smith, in Conference Report, Oct. 1945, 31–32; Joseph F. Smith was Patriarch to the Church and the grandson of President Joseph F. Smith, sixth President of the Church.

41. Gordon B. Hinckley, in Conference Report, Apr. 1992, 75; or *Ensign,* May 1992, 52.

42. "Some Thoughts on War, and Sorrow, and Peace," *Improvement Era,* Sept. 1945, 501.

43. See Arwell L. Pierce, in Conference Report, Apr. 1951, 112–13.

44. "Markers and Monuments," 284–85.

45. "Dedicatory Prayer," *Improvement Era,* Sept. 1947, 571.

46. "After Eighty Years," 263–64.

47. David O. McKay, in Conference Report, Apr. 1951, 3.

48. John A. Widtsoe, in Conference Report, Apr. 1951, 99.

49. Matthew Cowley, in Conference Report, Apr. 1951, 168–69.

Living What We Believe

*Our religion must find expression
in our everyday lives.*

From the Life of George Albert Smith

When he was 34 years old, George Albert Smith made a list of resolutions that he called his "personal creed"—11 ideals that he committed to live by:

"I would be a friend to the friendless and find joy in ministering to the needs of the poor.

"I would visit the sick and afflicted and inspire in them a desire for faith to be healed.

"I would teach the truth to the understanding and blessing of all mankind.

"I would seek out the erring one and try to win him back to a righteous and a happy life.

"I would not seek to force people to live up to my ideals but rather love them into doing the thing that is right.

"I would live with the masses and help to solve their problem that their earth life may be happy.

"I would avoid the publicity of high positions and discourage the flattery of thoughtless friends.

"I would not knowingly wound the feelings of any, not even one who may have wronged me, but would seek to do him good and make him my friend.

"I would overcome the tendency to selfishness and jealousy and rejoice in the successes of all the children of my Heavenly Father.

"I would not be an enemy to any living soul.

1

"Knowing that the Redeemer of mankind has offered to the world the only plan that will fully develop us and make us really happy here and hereafter, I feel it not only a duty but also a blessed privilege to disseminate this truth."[1] [See suggestion 1 on page 9.]

Those who knew President Smith declared that he truly did live by his creed. Ezra Taft Benson, then a member of the Quorum of the Twelve Apostles, shared an experience in which President Smith was true to his resolution to "visit the sick and afflicted and inspire in them a desire for faith to be healed":

"I shall never cease to be grateful for the visits he made to my home while I was [away] serving as a humble missionary. . . . Particularly I am thankful for a visit in the still of the night when our little one lay at death's door. Without any announcement, President Smith found time to come into that home and place his hands upon the head of that little one, held in her mother's arms as she had been for many hours, and promise her complete recovery. This was President Smith, he always had time to help, particularly those who were sick, those who needed him most."[2]

Spencer W. Kimball noted another instance in which President Smith's actions demonstrated his conviction to do good to "one who may have wronged [him]":

"It was reported to [President Smith] that someone had stolen from his buggy the buggy robe. Instead of being angry, he responded: 'I wish we knew who it was, so that we could give him the blanket also, for he must have been cold; and some food also, for he must have been hungry.'"[3]

Another observer wrote of George Albert Smith: "His religion is not doctrine in cold storage. It is not theory. It means more to him than a beautiful plan to be admired. It is more than a philosophy of life. To one of his practical turn of mind, religion is the spirit in which a man lives, in which he does things, if it be only to say a kind word or give a cup of cold water. His religion must find expression in deeds. It must carry over into the details of daily life."[4]

One of his counselors in the First Presidency, President J. Reuben Clark Jr., summed up President Smith's personal integrity with these words: "He was one of those few people of whom you can say he lived as he taught."[5]

Teachings of George Albert Smith

Our obedience to the gospel—not just our Church membership—qualifies us to be called Saints.

Worship in the Church of Jesus Christ of Latter-day Saints is a devoted life, a desire to be worthy of him in whose image we have been created and who has given us all . . . that is worth while—the gospel of Jesus Christ.[6]

What a fine thing it is to feel that we belong to a church that is or should be composed of saints. It is not sufficient that we have our names upon the records. It is important that we live the lives that entitle us to be called Saints, and if you will do that, you will be happy. . . .

When Jesus of Nazareth came into the world and began preaching the Gospel of the Kingdom, there were many, particularly the self-righteous Pharisees, who rejected His message, claiming that they were the descendants of Abraham and indicated that their lineage would save them in the Kingdom of God.

The Savior informed them that if they were children of Abraham, they would do the works of Abraham. [See John 8:33–39.] I would like to say to the Latter-day Saints, if we are worthy to be called Latter-day Saints, it will be because we are living the lives of saints, and it is the purpose of the Gospel to qualify us in that way. The world has gotten into such a condition and has been deceived by the adversary for such a long time and has declared that the mere belief in God is all that is necessary, that I am fearful for it. That is only a trick of the adversary.[7] [See suggestion 2 on page 9.]

"Mormonism," so-called, is the Gospel of Jesus Christ, consequently it is the power of God unto salvation to all those who believe and obey its teachings. It is not those who say, "Lord, Lord," who enjoy the companionship of His spirit but those who do His will [see Luke 6:46].[8]

"Whosoever heareth these sayings of mine, and doeth them, I will liken him unto a wise man, which built his house upon a rock."

Referring to the 7th chapter of Matthew and the 24th verse, I find the following:

"Therefore, whosoever heareth these sayings of mine, and doeth them, I will liken him unto a wise man, which built his house upon a rock:

"And the rain descended, and the floods came, and the winds blew, and beat upon that house; and it fell not; for it was founded upon a rock.

"And everyone that heareth these sayings of mine and doeth them not, shall be likened unto a foolish man, which built his house upon the sand:

"And the rain descended, and the floods came, and the winds blew, and beat upon that house; and it fell: and great was the fall of it." [Matthew 7:24–27.]

How many of us, learning the will of the Father, are doing it? How many of us day by day are laying a foundation and building a structure that shall conform to the dignity of the stature of our Master? 'Yea, man is the tabernacle of God, even temples; and whatsoever temple is defiled, God shall destroy that temple.' [D&C 93:35.] He has given us intelligence and wisdom above our fellowmen. A knowledge of pre-existence has been given to the Latter-day Saints; a knowledge that we are here because we kept our first estate, and that we have been given the opportunity of gaining eternal life in the presence of our Heavenly Father, by keeping our second estate. We will not be judged as our brothers and sisters of the world are judged, but according to the greater opportunities placed in our keeping. We will be among those who have received the word of the Lord, who have heard His sayings, and if we do them it will be to us eternal life, but if we fail condemnation will result.[9]

Let us do better than we have ever done before. Let us renew our determination to be real Latter-day Saints, and not just make-believe. . . . I do not know anybody who can not do a little better than he has been doing, if he makes up his mind.[10]

Our Heavenly Father expects us to prepare for and live worthy of His promised blessings.

I have opened to the twenty-second chapter of St. Matthew's account of the Savior's teaching, and will read this particular parable:

"And Jesus answered and spake unto them again by parables, and said,

"The kingdom of heaven is like unto a certain king, which made a marriage for his son,

"And sent forth his servants to call them that were bidden to the wedding. . . .

"And when the king came in to see the guests, he saw there a man which had not on a wedding garment:

"And he saith unto him, Friend, how camest thou in hither, not having a wedding garment? And he was speechless.

"Then saith the king to the servants, Bind him hand and foot, and take him away, and cast him into outer darkness; there shall be weeping and gnashing of teeth.

"For many are called, but few are chosen." [See Matthew 22:1–3, 11–14.] . . .

. . . Here was a man who came into the wedding feast, and when the time came the king or the master saw that he didn't have a wedding garment on. He had ignored the importance of it, apparently. He had come in, not prepared, expecting to participate. He had come to the feast—they had all been bidden to the feast, but I assume that they were supposed to know that only those would be admitted who were properly clothed, and this man was amazed when the question was asked him why he was there in that condition.

The world seems to think that they can come whenever they are ready. Our Father's children do not understand that there is some preparation to be made. The adversary has so deceived them as to make them believe that no preparation is necessary, anything will do, but in this message that the Savior gave in a parable to his associates we are informed that there must be some preparation, and without that preparation no one will be permitted to partake of the more precious gifts of our Heavenly Father. That applies to the membership of this Church who have an idea that because they have been invited, and because their names appear upon the record among those who have been called, there is nothing more for them to do. . . . They have forgotten the Lord and are not preparing for the feast to which he has invited them.

Our Heavenly Father intends that we shall prepare for the wedding feast or we will be excluded. He expects us to continue to store our minds with the truth, and to disseminate that truth as opportunity offers among all his children. The fact that our names appear upon the Church records is no guarantee that we will find our place in the celestial kingdom. Only those who live worthy to be members of that kingdom shall find place there.

In the midst of the unsettled condition, the uncertainty that is in the world, if there ever was a time when we should examine ourselves, to find out if we are doing what the Lord would have us do, it is today; if there ever was a time when we should be sure that we are in the pathway of eternal life, it is now. We can't slight these opportunities. God will not be mocked. When he has offered to us a gift, when he has placed within our reach a blessing, when he has invited us to partake of a feast and we ignore it, we may be sure that we shall suffer the distress that will come to those who refuse the blessings of the Lord when they are offered.[11]

We cannot live like the world and expect to obtain our rightful place in the Kingdom. The Lord tells us in the first section of the Doctrine and Covenants, referring to evil: that he cannot look upon sin with the least degree of allowance [see D&C 1:31]. This is hard medicine, because some of us in the Church have the idea that we can trifle with the Gospel of our Lord and with fundamentals of Eternal Life, and yet gain the place we want. This is not true. The Lord will be merciful, but he will be just, and if we want any blessing there is only one way we may obtain it, and that is to keep the commandments that will entitle us to the blessing.[12] [See suggestion 3 on page 9.]

If we are doing our full duty, our lives give evidence of our belief in the gospel.

Within the last year, I have had the privilege of meeting and conversing on the gospel with some men who live in this community [Salt Lake City], not members of our Church. One man had resided here for twenty years, a man whose life is above reproach, a good citizen, a splendid business man, one who has kindly feelings towards our people. He told me that he had lived here twenty years, and he had come to the conclusion that we were just as good as our neighbors who are members of other churches; he could not see any difference in us.

I want to say to you, my brethren and sisters, that is no compliment to me. If the gospel of Jesus Christ does not make me a better man, then I have not developed as I should, and if our neighbors not in this Church can live among us from year to year and see no evidence of the benefits that come from keeping the

"If we are reaching out in all directions to do good to the children of our Father, then we will . . . rejoice in the good that we accomplish here."

commandments of God in our lives, then there is need for reform in Israel. . . .

. . . Are you doing your duty? are we performing the labor that the Lord has entrusted to our care? do we sense the responsibility that is upon us? or are we idly floating down stream, going with the tide taking it for granted that in the last day, we will be redeemed?[13]

We are called a peculiar people [see 1 Peter 2:9] because, perchance, we thoroughly believe the gospel of Jesus Christ. . . .

If our peculiarity went to the extent that we lived by every word that proceeds from the mouth of our Heavenly Father [see D&C 84:44], then we would indeed be a blessed people. We do, to a large degree, live by the testimony that has been given to us by our Redeemer, and thus far we are a blessed people; but we would be yet more greatly blessed and prospered if we could bring ourselves to do our full duty.

I pray that the spirit which will enable us to serve faithfully may be with us, that the desire to do good may overcome the temptations that are placed in our way, and that, wherever we go, others observing our good works may be constrained to glorify our Father who is in heaven [see Matthew 5:16].[14]

Now let us examine ourselves. Are we doing as much as we should? And if we are not, let us turn around and do better. If we are doing as we should, if we are reaching out in all directions to do good to the children of our Father, then we will bring to ourselves the blessing of an all wise Father, and we will rejoice in the good that we accomplish here. . . .

Let us be humble and prayerful, living near to our Heavenly Father, and evidence our belief in the Gospel of Jesus Christ by living up to its principles. Let us evidence our faith in God, and in the work He has given to the earth, by a correct and consistent life, for after all that is the strongest testimony that we will be able to bear of the truth of this work.[15] [See suggestion 4 on page 10.]

Suggestions for Study and Teaching

Consider these ideas as you study the chapter or as you prepare to teach. For additional help, see pages v–vii.

1. As you review President Smith's creed (pages 1–2), think of some ideals or principles that you would like to follow in your own life. Consider recording them in a personal journal.

2. Read the last three paragraphs on page 3. What does it mean to be a Latter-day Saint? What can parents do to help their children learn to live the life of a saint?

3. As you read the section that begins on page 5, think about how the parable of the wedding feast might apply to your life (see also Matthew 22:1–14). For example, what do you think the wedding feast represents? Whom do the invited guests represent? Ponder what you can do to "prepare for the wedding feast" (page 6).

4. Read the last paragraph of teachings (on page 9) and think of someone you know who has a strong testimony of the gospel. How does that person's life give evidence of his or her testimony? Consider what you can do to give evidence of your testimony.

Related Scriptures: Matthew 7:16–23; James 1:22–25; 2:15–18; 1 John 2:3–6; Moroni 7:3–5; Doctrine and Covenants 41:5

Teaching help: "To help us teach from the scriptures and the words of latter-day prophets, the Church has produced lesson manuals and other materials. There is little need for commentaries or other reference material" (*Teaching, No Greater Call: A Resource Guide for Gospel Teaching* [1999], 52).

Notes

1. "President George Albert Smith's Creed," *Improvement Era,* Apr. 1950, 262.
2. Ezra Taft Benson, in Conference Report, Apr. 1951, 46.
3. Spencer W. Kimball, *The Miracle of Forgiveness* (1969), 284.
4. Bryant S. Hinckley, "Greatness in Men: Superintendent George Albert Smith," *Improvement Era,* Mar. 1932, 270.
5. J. Reuben Clark Jr., in Doyle L. Green, "Tributes Paid President George Albert Smith," *Improvement Era,* June 1951, 405.
6. In Conference Report, Apr. 1949, 8.
7. "The Church with Divine Authority," *Deseret News,* Sept. 28, 1946, Church section, 1, 6.
8. In Conference Report, Apr. 1913, 28–29.
9. In Conference Report, Oct. 1906, 47.
10. In Conference Report, Apr. 1941, 27.
11. In Conference Report, Oct. 1930, 66–68.
12. Seventies and stake missionary conference, Oct. 4, 1941, 6.
13. In Conference Report, Oct. 1916, 49.
14. "Some Points of 'Peculiarity,'" *Improvement Era,* Mar. 1949, 137.
15. In Conference Report, Apr. 1914, 13.

CHAPTER 2

"Love Thy Neighbour as Thyself"

Reaching out to others in love and compassion is essential to the gospel of Jesus Christ.

From the Life of George Albert Smith

George Albert Smith was well known for his capacity to love others. President J. Reuben Clark Jr., one of his counselors in the First Presidency, said of him: "His real name was Love. . . . He gave his love to everyone he met. He gave his love to all whom he did not meet."[1]

President Smith's love for others grew from his sincere conviction that we are all brothers and sisters, children of the same Heavenly Father. Near the end of his life, he said to the Saints:

"I do not have an enemy that I know of, and there is no one in the world that I have any enmity towards. All men and all women are my Father's children, and I have sought during my life to observe the wise direction of the Redeemer of mankind—to love my neighbor as myself. . . . You will never know how much I love you. I have not words to express it. And I want to feel that way toward every son and every daughter of my Heavenly Father."[2]

President Smith demonstrated his love for others through countless acts of compassion. One observer noted: "It is characteristic of President Smith to go out of his way on errands of personal comfort and blessing to many who are sick, who are down-hearted, and who have cause to be grateful for his cheerful encouragement. It is not uncommon to see him, before and after office hours, walking hospital halls, visiting room after room, blessing, encouraging, and cheering with his unexpected appearances in those places where his comforting and reassuring presence is so gratefully

"The gospel teaches us to have charity for all and to love our fellows."

welcome. . . . It is characteristic of him to go wherever he feels that he can give help and encouragement."[3]

President Thomas S. Monson shared a specific example of President Smith going out of his way to show love for someone in need:

"On a cold winter morning, the street cleaning crew [in Salt Lake City] was removing large chunks of ice from the street gutters. The regular crew was assisted by temporary laborers who desperately needed the work. One such wore only a lightweight sweater and was suffering from the cold. A slender man with a well-groomed beard stopped by the crew and asked the worker, 'You need more than that sweater on a morning like this. Where is your coat?' The man replied that he had no coat to wear. The visitor then removed his own overcoat, handed it to the man and said, 'This coat is yours. It is heavy wool and will keep you warm. I just work across the street.' The street was South Temple. The good Samaritan who walked into the Church Administration Building to his daily work and without his coat was President George Albert Smith of The Church of Jesus Christ of Latter-day Saints. His selfless act of generosity revealed his tender heart. Surely he was his brother's keeper."[4] [See suggestion 1 on page 18.]

Teachings of George Albert Smith

All people are our brothers and sisters, children of our Heavenly Father.

We look upon all men as our brothers, all women as our sisters; we look upon the face of every human being that is in the world as a child of our Father, and believe that as each is in the image of the Father, so also each possesses a spark of divinity that if developed will prepare us to return to His presence. . . .

That is our understanding of the purpose of our existence in the world, and explains our interest in our fellowmen. Many have supposed that we were exclusive in our lives, and some have thought that we were clannish. The fact is, we look upon every child that is born into the world, as a son or daughter of God, as our brother or our sister, and we feel that our happiness will not be complete in the kingdom of heaven unless we enjoy the companionship of our families and those of our friends and associates with whom we have become acquainted and in whose interest we give so much of our time on earth.[5]

As I think of my regard and my affection for my Father's family, the human family, I remember something my earthly father said, and I think probably I inherited that in part from him. He said, "I have never seen a child of God so deep in the gutter that I have not had the impulse to stoop down and lift him up and put him on his feet and start him again." I would like to say I have never seen one of my Father's children in my life that I have not realized he was my brother and that God loves every one of his children.[6]

What a happy world it would be if men everywhere recognized their fellowmen as brothers and sisters, and then followed that up by loving their neighbors as themselves.[7] [See suggestion 2 on page 18.]

The gospel of Jesus Christ teaches us to love all of God's children.

The gospel teaches us to have charity for all and to love our fellows. The Savior said:

"Thou shalt love the Lord thy God with all thy heart, and with all thy soul, and with all thy mind, this is the first and great commandment.

"And the second is like unto it, Thou shalt love thy neighbor as thyself. On these two commandments hang all the law and the prophets." [Matthew 22:37–40.]

Brethren and sisters, if the gospel of Jesus Christ, as delivered to you, has not planted that feeling of love in your hearts for your fellow men, then I want to say that you have not enjoyed the full fruition of that wonderful gift that came to earth when this Church was organized.[8] [See suggestion 3 on page 19.]

Our ministry is one of love. Our service is one which enriches our lives. . . . If we are living as God intends that we should live,

"Let us evidence by our conduct . . . that we do keep that great commandment . . . , 'Thou shalt love thy neighbor as thyself.'"

if we are ministering as he desires that we should minister, every day of our lives is enriched by the influence of his Spirit, our love of our fellowmen increases and our souls are enlarged until we feel that we could take into our arms all of God's children, with a desire to bless them and bring them to an understanding of the truth.[9]

As members of the Church of Christ, we should keep His commandments and love one another. Then our love should pass beyond the border lines of the Church with which we are identified, and reach out after the children of men.[10]

Let us evidence by our conduct, by our gentleness, by our love, by our faith, that we do keep that great commandment that the Savior said was like unto the first great commandment, "Thou shalt love thy neighbor as thyself."[11]

We exercise charity by reaching out to those who need help and encouragement.

The measurement of the result of what love and charity may bring into the world is impossible. Opportunity is offered in every branch and ward and mission field to go about radiating sunshine, developing happiness and lifting up those who are discouraged, and bringing joy and comfort to those who are in distress. [12]

The Lord says this:

"See that ye love one another; cease to be covetous; learn to impart one to another as the gospel requires. . . .

"And above all things, clothe yourselves with the bond of charity, as with a mantle, which is the bond of perfectness and peace." [D&C 88:123, 125.] . . .

. . . Are you following his advice with reference to charity? I want to say that at this particular period of our lives we need to exercise charity, not only in imparting of our substance to those who are in need, but we need to have charity for the weaknesses and failures and mistakes of our Father's children. [13]

If we find a man or a woman who has not succeeded in life, one who is weakening in his faith, let us not turn our backs upon him; let us make it a point to visit him, and go to him in kindness and love, and encourage him to turn from the error of his way. The opportunity to do individual work among us as a people is present everywhere; and there are few men and few women in this Church who could not, if they would, reach out a little farther from the circle with which they are identified, and say a kind word, or teach the truth to some of our Father's children. . . . This is our Father's work. It is the most important thing that we will be identified with in this life. [14]

I have only good will in my heart for mankind. I haven't any animosity in my heart toward any living human being. I know some that I wish would behave themselves a little better than they do, but that is their loss, not mine. If I can get my arm around them and help them back on the highway of happiness by teaching them the gospel of Jesus Christ, my happiness will be increased thereby. . . .

"Go about radiating sunshine, developing happiness and lifting up those who are discouraged, and bringing joy and comfort to those who are in distress."

You cannot drive people to do things which are right, but you can love them into doing them, if your example is of such a character that they can see you mean what you say. [15] [See suggestion 4 on page 19.]

True happiness comes from loving and serving others.

Do not forget no matter how much you may give in money, no matter how you may desire the things of this world to make yourselves happy, your happiness will be in proportion to your charity and to your kindness and to your love of those with whom you associate here on earth. Our Heavenly Father has said in very plain terms that he who says he loves God and does not love his brother is not truthful [see 1 John 4:20]. [16]

It isn't only what we receive that makes us happy; it is what we give, and the more we give of that which is uplifting and enriching to our Father's children, the more we have to give. It grows like a great fountain of life and bubbles up to eternal happiness. [17]

When our life here is ended and we return home, we will find credited to us there every good act we have performed, every kindness we have done, every effort we have put forth to benefit our fellows. . . .

. . . Let us evidence our appreciation of what the Lord has given us by serving Him, and we are serving Him when we do good to His children. Freely we have received, now freely give [see Matthew 10:8]. With hearts warmed with love and kindness for our fellow men, let us press steadily on until the final summons shall come, and we shall meet our record. Then, if we have improved our talents, if we have been honest, true, chaste, benevolent, and charitable, and have sought to uplift every soul with whom we have associated, if we have lived up to the light we have received, and disseminated that light whenever opportunity has presented, how happy we will be and how our hearts will swell with gratitude when we receive from the Maker of heaven and earth that welcome plaudit: "Well done, good and faithful servant; thou hast been faithful over a few things; I will make thee ruler over many things; enter thou into the joy of thy Lord." [Matthew 25:21.][18] [See suggestion 5 on page 19.]

Suggestions for Study and Teaching

Consider these ideas as you study the chapter or as you prepare to teach. For additional help, see pages v–vii.

1. Consider ways you can demonstrate love President Smith as did (see pages 11–13). For example, how can we demonstrate love in fulfilling our home and visiting teaching assignments?

2. As you study the first section of teachings (pages 13–14), think about how applying these teachings might improve your relationship with your neighbors, co-workers, family members, and others.

3. Read the last full paragraph on page 14. What are some teachings or stories in the scriptures that inspire you to love and serve others?

4. Study the section that begins on page 16, particularly the last two paragraphs. Think of someone who may be outside "the circle with which [you] are identified." What is something specific you can do to reach out to such a person?

5. Ponder President Smith's teachings on pages 17–18. What experiences have you had that have taught you that true happiness comes from making others happy?

Related Scriptures: Matthew 5:43–44; 25:34–40; Luke 10:25–37; John 13:34–35; 1 John 4:7–8; 1 Nephi 11:16–25; Moroni 7:44–48

Teaching help: "Quite a bit of teaching that is done in the Church is done so rigidly, it's lecture. We don't respond to lectures too well in classrooms. We do in sacrament meeting and at conferences, but teaching can be two-way so that you can ask questions. You can sponsor questions easily in a class" (Boyd K. Packer, "Principles of Teaching and Learning," *Ensign,* June 2007, 87).

Notes

1. J. Reuben Clark Jr., "No Man Had Greater Love for Humanity Than He," *Deseret News,* Apr. 11, 1951, Church section, 10, 12.

2. "After Eighty Years," *Improvement Era,* Apr. 1950, 263.

3. Richard L. Evans, "Anniversary," *Improvement Era,* Apr. 1946, 224.

4. In Conference Report, Apr. 1990, 62; or *Ensign,* May 1990, 47.

5. "Mormon View of Life's Mission," *Deseret Evening News,* June 27, 1908, Church section, 2.

6. "Pres. Smith's Leadership Address," *Deseret News,* Feb. 16, 1946, 6.

7. In Conference Report, Oct. 1946, 149.

8. In Conference Report, Apr. 1922, 52.

9. In Conference Report, Oct. 1929, 24.

10. In Conference Report, Apr. 1905, 62.

11. In Conference Report, Apr. 1949, 10.

12. "To the Relief Society," *Relief Society Magazine,* Dec. 1932, 704.

13. "Saints Blessed," *Deseret News,* Nov. 12, 1932, Church section, 5, 8.

14. In Conference Report, Apr. 1914, 12–13.

15. In Conference Report, Apr. 1946, 184–85.

16. "To the Relief Society," 709.

17. *Sharing the Gospel with Others,* sel. Preston Nibley (1948), 214; address given Nov. 4, 1945, in Washington, D.C.

18. "Mormon View of Life's Mission," 2.

*"I know that my Redeemer lives and gladly yield my humble efforts
to establish His teachings."*

CHAPTER 3

Our Testimony of Jesus Christ

The restored gospel gives Latter-day Saints additional
witnesses that Jesus Christ is the Son of God.

From the Life of George Albert Smith

In his travels as a General Authority, George Albert Smith occasionally met those who thought that the Latter-day Saints do not believe in Jesus Christ. This misconception amazed and worried President Smith, and he tried to correct it by sharing his personal witness of the Savior.

On one occasion he spoke at a Church meeting in Cardston, Canada, about the life and mission of Christ. The next morning he went to the railway station to buy a train ticket. While he waited in line, he overheard a conversation between a woman and the ticket agent. The woman mentioned that the evening before she had decided to attend a Latter-day Saint worship service.

The ticket agent looked surprised. "My goodness," she said. "You do not mean to say you went to church there."

"Yes, I did," the woman answered. "Why not?"

The ticket agent said, "They do not even believe in Jesus Christ."

Then the woman replied, "Only last night I listened to one of the elders of the Church speaking of the life of Jesus of Nazareth, and I have never heard anybody who seemed more profoundly impressed with a knowledge that Jesus was indeed the Christ, than the speaker on that occasion."[1] [See suggestion 1 on page 30.]

George Albert Smith gained strength from his testimony of Jesus Christ, and he delighted in sharing it with others. At the age of 44, having served in his apostolic calling for 11 years, he said:

"I have been buoyed up and, as it were, lifted out of myself and given power not my own to teach the glorious truths proclaimed by the Redeemer of the world. I have not seen Him face to face but have enjoyed the companionship of His spirit and felt His presence in a way not to be mistaken. I know that my Redeemer lives and gladly yield my humble efforts to establish His teachings. . . . Every fibre of my being vibrates with the knowledge that He lives and some day all men will know it.

"The Savior died that we might live. He overcame death and the grave and holds out to all who obey His teachings the hope of a glorious resurrection. . . . I know this is the work of the Lord, that Jesus was indeed our Savior." [2]

President Smith passed away on his 81st birthday, April 4, 1951. During the final moments of his life, with his family close by, his son asked, "Father, is there something you'd like to say to the family—something special?"

With a smile, he reaffirmed the testimony he had shared numerous times throughout his life: "Yes, only this: I know that my Redeemer liveth; I know that my Redeemer liveth." [3]

Teachings of George Albert Smith

Jesus Christ is the Son of God, and He lives today as our resurrected Savior.

I have found many in the world who have not known that we believe in the divine mission of our Lord, and I have been led to say upon more than one occasion that there are no people in the world who so well understand the divine mission of Jesus Christ, who so thoroughly believe him to have been the Son of God, who are so sanguine [confident] that at the present time he is enthroned in glory at the right hand of his Father, as the Latter-day Saints. [4]

I know as I know that I live that he was the son of God, that through him and through him only will we gain exaltation in the celestial kingdom and all those who follow in his footsteps and live according to the teachings that he gave, will be happy in this life and will prepare for themselves a mansion in his celestial kingdom, where they will dwell with him forever. [5]

The Redeemer of mankind was more than a good man who came into the world to teach us ethics. The Redeemer of mankind possessed more than ordinary intelligence. He was indeed the Son of God, the only begotten of God in the flesh. . . . He came to call men to repentance, to turn them from the error of their way. He went among them representing God the Eternal Father, proclaiming that he was in the image of his Father, and that those who had seen him had seen the Father, and told them that he had been sent to do the will of his Father, and called on all men to turn from the error that had crept in among them, to repent of their sins and go down into the waters of baptism.[6]

In the time of the Savior the adversary whispered to [the] people, he is not the Son of God, surely you will not accept him, he is just an ordinary man, he is only the son of Mary and Joseph and he is not any more the Son of God than you are, and the people listened to that insidious, wicked one and crucified the Redeemer of mankind.[7]

He was indeed the Son of God. He labored among [the people] in love and kindness; but they cast His name out as evil. . . . He was the Son of God, and He did have the right to speak in the name of the Father. The truths He brought to the earth came from the Father; and though they nailed Him to the cross, though they placed upon His head the plaited crown of thorns, and put the mock scepter in His hands, though they spilled His blood with the cruel spear, yet the word that He delivered to them was the word of the Lord, and He was indeed the Son of God.[8]

Not only do we believe that Jesus of Nazareth lived upon the earth, but we believe that he still lives, not as an essence, not as something incorporeal or intangible, but we believe in him as an exalted man; for he arose with the same body that was laid in the tomb of Joseph of Arimathaea, the same body that was ministered to there by those who loved him. The same Jesus Christ who came forth from the tomb, brought with him that body which had been purified and cleansed, . . . and he took it with him when he disappeared from the gaze of humanity at Jerusalem when the two men in white raiment said: "As you see him go, so likewise will he return again." [See Acts 1:10–11.]

This is the Jesus of Nazareth that the Latter-day Saints believe in. We also believe that the promises that have been made concerning humanity will be fulfilled, that in due time, when the gospel shall have been preached in all the earth, to every nation, kindred, tongue and people, when men shall be left without an excuse with reference to it, we believe that through the power of our Heavenly Father mankind will receive that wonderful blessing of resurrection from the dead, and that the Redeemer of mankind will come in the clouds of heaven with power and with glory to dwell upon this earth. We believe that Jesus of Nazareth will come to dwell with those who are worthy of celestial glory.[9] [See suggestion 2 on page 30.]

We accept the Bible's testimony of the divine mission of Jesus Christ.

Jesus of Nazareth went down into the water and was baptized by John, and when he came up out of the water, the Holy Ghost came and descended upon him in the form of a dove. And a voice from heaven said, "This is my beloved Son, in whom I am well pleased." [See Matthew 3:13–17.]

Could there be anything more definite than that? Our wonderful Bible contains all that information and much more, of course. When people say or think that we do not believe in the divine mission of Jesus Christ, let them know that we believe all that the Bible teaches in reference to him. We believe the story of how he organized his people and taught them, and how eventually, . . . he was crucified.[10]

We accept without reservation the testimony of all of the evangelists contained in the New Testament with reference to the resurrection of the Redeemer of mankind. It is so plain that it seems to me that no thoughtful person can fail to comprehend it. The fact is that after the Savior was crucified and was laid in the tomb he came forth, and for forty days he associated with his disciples, he partook of fish and honeycomb with them, they felt the prints of the nails in his hands and the spear mark in his side. He declared to them while he stood among them, "Behold my hands and my feet that it is I myself: handle me and see for a spirit hath not flesh and bones as

"We accept without reservation the testimony . . . in the New Testament with reference to the resurrection of the Redeemer of mankind."

ye see me have." [See Luke 24:39–43.] Surely this is incontrovertible evidence and yet there are many of our Father's children who do not understand it.[11] [See suggestion 3 on page 30.]

The Book of Mormon and the testimony of Joseph Smith give us additional evidence of Christ's divinity.

The question has been raised in the old world that Jesus was not of divine origin, because He was born as a little child, cradled in a manger, His mother being Mary and his reputed father Joseph the carpenter. Many have admitted that He was a great and good man, but they have desired to rob Him of the divinity of His birth.

Fortunately, however, for the Latter-day Saints, we have received a witness that these things are true; and in addition to that, we have received the testimony that He came to [the] western hemisphere, as recorded in the Book of Mormon, and ministered unto the Nephites upon this continent. He did not come this time as a little child, but He came in the clouds of heaven; and His coming was proclaimed by a voice that penetrated to the very center of every person that dwelt in the land. He came this time as a man from heaven, and they saw Him come. They knew that He was the Christ, for His coming had been predicted by their prophets. He gave to them the same organization that existed in the Church at Jerusalem. He taught them that they must be baptized, as He had been, by those having authority to officiate in that ordinance. [See 3 Nephi 11:1–27.] This was not the word of an ordinary man; it was the word of the Son of God, who had ascended to His Father, and who had come back again, that the children of men might have another testimony added to the number that had already been given to them. [12]

What more direct evidence of resurrection from the dead could have been had than that he, in his resurrected body, came among [the Nephites] and taught them the same Gospel that he taught in Jerusalem? And he now fulfilled the promise he had made in Jerusalem when he said, "Other sheep I have which are not of this fold; them also I must bring and they shall hear my voice; and there shall be one fold and one shepherd." [John 10:16.] He came in his resurrected body to bring to them the information he had predicted should be given to those to whom he now ministered.

It was a wonderful experience for those people. After teaching them all day . . . he healed their sick and blessed their children and continued to instruct them in the beauty of his Gospel. There was no doubt in their minds that he was the Savior of the world. They saw him come from heaven and witnessed his marvelous power. . . . He came in glory. Angels came down from heaven as it were in the midst of fire and surrounded the little children so that they were encircled with fire. And the angels did minister unto them. [See 3 Nephi 17:6–24.]

Those were not hallucinations, but experiences of such marvelous character as to be remembered forever by those who experienced them. As Latter-day Saints we accept this record as evidence of the resurrection of Jesus Christ our Lord. [13]

Then in the day and age in which we live there arose another individual. . . . [Joseph Smith] not only had the witness of the Bible

When the resurrected Savior visited the Nephites, "angels came down from heaven as it were in the midst of fire and surrounded the little children."

that Jesus was the Christ, but he saw God the Father standing in the clouds of heaven, clothed with glory, and Jesus Christ, the Redeemer of the world, exalted at His right hand, and he heard the voice of the Lord, saying, "This is My Beloved Son, hear Him." [See Joseph Smith—History 1:16–17.] He bore testimony of this glorious vision to those with whom he associated. Others also received a witness from on high. Their testimony in the divinity of the Savior's mission had been increased and strengthened, so that it was no longer a matter of ancient history that God lived and that Jesus was the Christ; they knew it personally, because they had received a testimony themselves. [14]

To my mind one of the strongest testimonies of the divinity of the life of our Savior is the testimony of Joseph Smith who laid down his life as a witness of the truth of the gospel of Jesus Christ. [15] [See suggestion 3 on page 30.]

Each of us can gain a personal testimony that Jesus is the Christ.

We have another testimony, another evidence that is even more perfect and more convincing than the others, because it is a testimony that comes to the individual when he has complied with the requirements of our Father in Heaven. It is a testimony that is burned into our souls by the power of the Holy Ghost, when we have performed the work that the Lord has said must be performed if we would know that the doctrine be of God or whether it be of man.[16]

He Himself has said, "My doctrine is not mine, but his that sent me. If any man will do his will he shall know of the doctrine, whether it be of God, or whether I speak of myself." (John 7:16–17) That was His own promise. We as Christians in all [the] world accept that promise and should try to prove it to see whether it is workable or not. There are many who have done this. I realize that there are . . . many who have put that to the test, many who know that God lives and that Jesus is the Christ, that He is the Savior of the world.[17]

So, not only do we have the evidence of the records . . . , not only do we have the testimony of good men who have lived upon the earth in our day, but if we have complied with the requirements of our Heavenly Father, if we have had faith in God, if we have repented of our sins, if we have received baptism by immersion, if we have received the Holy Ghost under the hands of authorized servants of the Lord, I say, if we have done all these things then there is in each soul a sure knowledge that cannot be gainsaid [denied] that God lives and that Jesus Christ was the Redeemer of mankind. . . .

. . . As one of the humble members of this Church I bear you my witness that I know he lives as I know that I live. . . . Jesus is the Christ, and I know that the children of men must come to that knowledge, that they must receive it, and in the language of him who lives in heaven, "every knee shall bow and every tongue confess that Jesus is the Christ." [See D&C 88:104.][18] [See suggestion 4 on page 31.]

Our mission is to share with all people what we know about Jesus Christ.

I say to you Latter-day Saints, there are no other people in all the world who have all the information that we have with reference to the divinity of the Savior; and if we did not believe in Him we would be under greater condemnation than the others that have never had that information. And so we can say to the world without hesitation that we believe these things. . . .

I congratulate you that there has come into your lives this privilege and this blessing. And now I adjure you as your brother, plead with you as one of the humblest among you, do not hide your candle under a bushel. Do not conceal the knowledge God has bestowed upon you from your fellows.

Do not annoy them, but do not be unwise enough as to hide from them the gospel of Jesus Christ. That is the only power of God unto salvation in the celestial kingdom.[19]

The happiest men and the happiest women that you know in the world are those who are conforming their lives to the teachings of the gospel of Jesus Christ. They are those who have the assurance of eternal life; they are those who understand the purpose of our being. . . . As I have traveled to and fro in the world bearing this message, my soul has been filled with joy, and my eyes have been dimmed with tears, when I have seen how perfectly men's lives may be transformed by the gospel of Jesus Christ. I have seen those who were discouraged, those who were in darkness, those who questioned the purpose of their being, and when they have had taught to them the glorious truths of the gospel of Jesus Christ, they have changed, they have learned to be happy, to be contented, to be satisfied, to be enthusiastic in believing and teaching the gospel that was proclaimed by Jesus Christ when he dwelt upon this earth and traveled in Galilee.

Brethren and sisters, the world does not understand that, but it is our mission to assist them to understand it, and it is not with egotism, it is not with arrogance, but with charity for all, with loving tenderness, that this message is sent forth. . . .

As one of the humblest among you, I thank him with all my heart for the assurance that has come into my life. . . . Above all, I thank him for the knowledge that has been burned into my soul; I know that my Heavenly Father lives, I know that Jesus Christ is the Savior of mankind, and that there is no other name under heaven whereby men and women may be exalted, but the name of Jesus Christ, our Lord. I do know that he came into the world in this latter day, that he bestowed divine authority upon a humble boy who was seeking the truth, and the result of that has been the organization of the Church with which we are identified; and there is with it the power of God unto salvation to all those who believe. [20]

I pray that we may so live as to be worthy exemplars of His cause. I pray that our lives may be such that we may show by them that we are indeed believers in the Lord Jesus Christ. [21] [See suggestion 5 on page 31.]

Suggestions for Study and Teaching

Consider these ideas as you study the chapter or as you prepare to teach. For additional help, see pages v–vii.

1. Read the story on page 21. How would you respond to someone who says the Latter-day Saints do not believe in Jesus Christ?

2. President Smith taught, "Not only do we believe that Jesus of Nazareth lived upon the earth, be we believe that he still lives" (page 23). What reasons do Latter-day Saints have for believing that Jesus Christ lives today? What reasons do you personally have for believing this?

3. Briefly review pages 24–27. What are some stories or passages from the scriptures that have strengthened your testimony that Jesus Christ is the Son of God? Read 1 Nephi 10:17 and consider ways you can increase your understanding of the Savior's mission.

4. As you read page 28, think about how obedience to the principles and ordinances of the gospel has strengthened your testimony of Jesus Christ. What can parents do to help their children gain this testimony?

5. What thoughts or feelings do you have as you read President Smith's testimony on pages 29–30? Think about times when you have seen people's lives change because of the gospel of Jesus Christ. How has the gospel changed your life?

Related Scriptures: Matthew 16:15–17; 17:1–5; 2 Nephi 25:26; Alma 5:45–48; Doctrine and Covenants 76:22–24; 110:1–4

Teaching help: "[Avoid] the temptation to cover too much material. . . . We are teaching people, not subject matter per se; and . . . every lesson outline that I have ever seen will inevitably have more in it than we can possibly cover in the allotted time" (Jeffrey R. Holland, "Teaching and Learning in the Church," *Ensign,* June 2007, 91).

Notes

1. In *Deseret News,* Dec. 27, 1924, Church section, 6; see also *Sharing the Gospel with Others,* sel. Preston Nibley (1948), 201–2.
2. "Testimony of Elder George Albert Smith," *Liahona: The Elders' Journal,* Feb. 2, 1915, 502.
3. In Robert L. Simpson, *The Powers and Responsibilities of the Priesthood,* Brigham Young University Speeches of the Year (Mar. 31, 1964), 8.
4. In *Deseret News,* Dec. 27, 1924, Church section, 6.
5. In *Deseret News,* Jan. 15, 1927, Church section, 8.
6. In Conference Report, Oct. 1921, 39.
7. In Conference Report, Apr. 1918, 39.
8. In Conference Report, Apr. 1904, 63.
9. In *Deseret News,* Dec. 27, 1924, Church section, 6.
10. In Conference Report, Oct. 1950, 156.
11. In Conference Report, Apr. 1939, 120–21.
12. In Conference Report, Apr. 1905, 61.
13. In Conference Report, Apr. 1939, 121–22.
14. In Conference Report, Apr. 1905, 61–62.
15. In *Deseret News,* Jan. 15, 1927, Church section, 8.
16. In *Deseret News,* Dec. 27, 1924, Church section, 6.
17. *Sharing the Gospel with Others,* 206; address given Nov. 4, 1945, in Washington, D.C.
18. In *Deseret News,* Dec. 27, 1924, Church section, 6.
19. *Sharing the Gospel with Others,* 211, 214; address given Nov. 4, 1945, in Washington, D.C.
20. In Conference Report, Oct. 1927, 48–50.
21. In *Deseret News,* Jan. 12, 1907, 31.

On December 23, 1905, George Albert Smith participated with other Church leaders in the dedication of a monument at the birthplace of the Prophet Joseph Smith.

The Prophet Joseph Smith, God's Instrument in Restoring the Truth

*Through the Prophet Joseph Smith, God restored
the gospel of Jesus Christ in its purity.*

From the Life of George Albert Smith

Near the 100th anniversary of the Prophet Joseph Smith's birth, Elder George Albert Smith traveled with President Joseph F. Smith and others to visit places of importance in the life of the Prophet. On the morning of December 23, 1905, a monument to Joseph Smith was dedicated at his birthplace in Vermont. It was a moving experience for George Albert Smith and those in his company to be in a place of such significance in the Restoration of the gospel. "Our tears flowed freely," he recalled. "Under the influence of the Spirit, every soul was humbled, every heart was melted, and we rejoiced in the blessings of our Heavenly Father." [1] George Albert Smith was asked to give the benediction at the dedicatory services. After summarizing the day in his journal, he wrote: "Thus ended one of the most eventful days of my life. I am thankful to be one of the few of our people to assist in the task just completed." [2]

They later went to the site of the First Vision, in Palmyra, New York. Elder Smith recalled: "We went into the grove where Joseph had knelt down and asked the Lord to inform him which one of the churches he should join. We were impressed to sing, in that hallowed place, the beautiful . . . hymn, 'Joseph Smith's First Prayer.'" [3]

After visiting the Hill Cumorah, the Kirtland Temple, and other sites connected with the mission of the Prophet, the company was called together by President Joseph F. Smith on the final evening of the trip. "After singing several of the songs of Zion, each member of the party was permitted to testify of the goodness and mercy of our Father unto us. The Spirit of the Lord was poured out upon us, and we shed tears of joy and happiness."[4] [See suggestion 1 on pages 42–43.]

Several years later, while George Albert Smith was serving as President of the Church, some books were published that attempted to defame Joseph Smith. In a general conference of the Church, President Smith boldly defended the Prophet, bearing testimony of his mission in these words:

"Many of the benefits and blessings that have come to me have come through that man who gave his life for the gospel of Jesus Christ. There have been some who have belittled him, but I would like to say that those who have done so will be forgotten and their remains will go back to mother earth, if they have not already gone, and the odor of their infamy will never die, while the glory and honor and majesty and courage and fidelity manifested by the Prophet Joseph Smith will attach to his name forever."[5]

Elder Harold B. Lee, then a member of the Quorum of the Twelve Apostles, was so impressed with this statement that he kept a clipping of it in his wallet and quoted it often, desiring that President Smith's words "could be heard to all the ends of the earth."[6]

Teachings of George Albert Smith

Joseph Smith's First Vision demonstrated that the heavens are not sealed.

We believe that our Heavenly Father has spoken in our own day . . . , that he heard the humble prayer of a youth in Palmyra, and answered his prayer and blessed him with a knowledge of his personality, that all people might know the Lord, if they will.

It was a very natural thing that Joseph Smith should seek the Lord. He came of a . . . people who believed in our Heavenly Father, in the divine mission of the Savior, in the efficacy of prayer, and that God would hear and answer his people if they went before him with a proper spirit. It was easy for this young man to believe, because he had been born and reared in a believing household; and when he went out into the woods in response to the injunction of the scripture (James 1:5): "If any of you lack wisdom, let him ask of God, that giveth to all men liberally, and upbraideth not; and it shall be given him," he believed that his prayer would be answered, and our Heavenly Father has promised his children from the beginning, that, "by faith ye may know all things."[7]

His faith in God led him away from the belief, common in his day, that the Bible contained all the revelation possible for men to receive, and that the heavens were sealed over his head. He prayed to the Lord, and his prayer was answered. He beheld the Father and the Son descending to earth surrounded with glorious light. He received an indisputable knowledge that they had tabernacles like men, and that they were material personages; they spoke to him and he heard their voices.[8]

The result [of Joseph's prayer] was that wonderful manifestation, unlike any other that we have ever heard of in the history of the world. We have heard of instances where our Heavenly Father has manifested himself; we have read of instances where the Redeemer of mankind has manifested himself; but we have never read of any instance where the Father and the Son before have appeared to any living being and have spoken to that individual.

People of the world do not believe it. Men and women have been taught that the heavens are sealed . . . , and when this youth declared that in our day, at the very time when we needed light most of all, when men and women were running to and fro for the word of God and could not find it, as predicted by the old prophets [see Amos 8:11–12], the Lord had manifested himself, he [Joseph] was ridiculed. . . . His statement was rejected, and those who should have been his friends turned away from him and even said it was of the evil one. What was the boy's testimony?

". . . I had actually seen a light, and in the midst of that light I saw two personages, and they did in reality speak to me; and though I was hated and persecuted for saying that I had seen a vision, yet it was true; and while they were persecuting me, reviling me, and speaking all manner of evil against me falsely for so say-ing, I was led to say in my heart: Why persecute me for telling the truth? I have actually seen a vision, and who am I that I can with-stand God, or why does the world think to make me deny what I have actually seen? For I had seen a vision; I knew it, and I could not deny it, neither dared I do it, at least I knew that by so doing I would offend God, and come under condemnation." [See Joseph Smith—History 1:25.][9]

In the year 1830, when this Church was organized, there was not upon the earth a church organization that would announce that they believed that God would reveal himself to the children of men. The teachings of the churches were all contrary to that, and our Father saw the futility of trying to save his sons and daughters until they could be inspired to come to him with the belief that he would hear and answer their prayers. When the boy prophet, in the woods of Palmyra, saw the Father and the Son, and realized that they were indeed personages, that they could hear and reply to what he said, it began a new era in this world, and laid a foundation for the faith of the children of men. They could now pray to our Father in heaven and realize that he could hear and answer their prayers, that there was a connection between the heavens and the earth.[10] [See suggestion 2 on page 43.]

Though young and inexperienced, Joseph Smith was called to restore the true Church of Jesus Christ.

Faith prompted Joseph to seek God in prayer and ask which church he should identify himself with. What was the response? Did the Lord say, "My boy, they are all good, they are all striv-ing to keep my commandments, the men who are leaders of all these churches are approved of me, any church will do, they will all lead you back into the presence of our Heavenly Father?" The boy might have expected such an answer from the conditions that existed. But he wanted to know what to do, and he had full faith that the Lord would tell him. So when he prayed, he asked which of the churches he should join, and I presume he was astonished when [he was told], "Join none of them; they teach for doctrine

Joseph Smith's First Vision "began a new era in this world, and laid a foundation for the faith of the children of men."

the commandments of men; they draw near to me with their lips but their hearts are far from me; they have a form of godliness, but deny the power thereof." [See Joseph Smith—History 1:19.] Think of a boy fourteen years of age arising from his knees in the woods near his home and announcing to the world such a message as that! Can you imagine that a youth would have dared to do such a thing as that? But with the witness that had been given unto him by his Heavenly Father, with that commandment from the Lord himself, dared he do anything else than make the announcement that the Lord had spoken to him?[11]

Joseph Smith was only a boy when the hands of Peter, James and John were laid upon his head and he was ordained to the Melchizedek Priesthood,—he and Oliver Cowdery. A little later Joseph Smith was directed to organize a Church. He was only a young man, but he organized it under the direction of the Redeemer of mankind. And it is patterned after the Church which was organized by the Savior when he was upon the earth. I have no doubt there were many who looked upon this young man as an upstart, and thought it was ridiculous that one who had not been educated to become a leader should presume to lead. But he was like the other servants of our Heavenly Father who have lived upon the earth, who have been called by the Lord to perform a special labor, and the lack of knowledge pertaining to the things of this world did not preclude the possibility of the Lord's giving unto him information that made him equal and even superior in many respects to those who had possessed great earthly opportunities that were denied him. [12]

Abused and misrepresented though he was, despised by those who should have been his friends, opposed by the learned and scholarly men of the time, he succeeded in restoring the Gospel of life and salvation and establishing the Church of Jesus Christ of Latter-day Saints.

While the powers of evil were ever active for his destruction, he was preserved by the Lord until his work was finished and all the keys and ordinances necessary for the salvation of the human family had again been delivered to men. [13] [See suggestion 3 on page 43.]

The truths restored through Joseph Smith bring peace and joy to those who accept them.

From that boy who, at fourteen years of age, beheld the Father and the Son, there came that wonderful message that our Father in heaven and his Son Jesus Christ are glorified men; that the Savior of the world had been resurrected from the dead. That youth beheld what the world had known, but for some reason had forgotten, and he began bearing witness of it to the children of men. [14]

[In the early 1800s] there were few people in the world who believed in a personal God with a body. But a manifestation came at that time to the Prophet Joseph Smith, when he was only a boy, not yet fifteen years of age, and he saw the Father and the Son and so testified. He also received visitations from other heavenly beings, and the Lord, through them gave him additional information for the children of men, and he, in his own way, gave to us, or to those who preceded us in the Church, an understanding of the purpose of life. . . . His description of heaven inspires us with a desire to be worthy of a home there when our earthly lives are finished. A literal resurrection and a description of heaven and hell are made so plain that, to use a scripture, "a wayfaring man, though a fool, need not err therein." [See Isaiah 35:8.][15]

Through him was revealed temple building, the eternity of the marriage covenant, and salvation for the dead, bringing unspeakable joy to thousands of our Father's children.

The eternal truths enunciated by him are finding their way among the peoples of the earth, bringing peace and contentment to those who accept them.[16]

Our Heavenly Father knew what was coming when in this latter day he restored the gospel in its purity. He knew of the apostasy in the world among his children, and that they had departed from the plain truth, and in his great mercy, he revealed this latter-day work. From the country he chose a boy from among the people, and inspired him to begin the work that was destined to revolutionize the religious world. He knew that the world was groping in darkness, and in mercy restored the light. There is no other way that happiness may be enjoyed by the children of men but by lives of righteousness, and people cannot live righteous lives and be out of harmony with truth. There was much truth in the world but it was so mixed with error that the Lord himself told the Prophet Joseph Smith that the men who were the teachers and instructors in the churches taught for doctrine the commandments of men, and warned the boy that he was not to be identified with them. He then restored the gospel, the power of God unto salvation, unto all those who will believe and obey it.[17]

"I say to all men everywhere, examine the teachings of the Gospel of our Lord as revealed to the Prophet Joseph Smith, search them prayerfully."

I say to all men everywhere, examine the teachings of the Gospel of our Lord as revealed to the Prophet Joseph Smith, search them prayerfully, and you shall find the panacea for the ills of this world, and it will be discovered in no other way. [18] [See suggestion 4 on page 43.]

Joseph Smith was willing to give his life for his testimony.

As had been the case with prophets whom the Lord had raised up before, it seemed necessary in this case that the testimony of His servant should be sealed with his life's blood. No more [poignant] page will be found in the history of the world than that upon which is inscribed the last sayings of our beloved Prophet Joseph Smith. He knew that his time was near at hand; he realized that his life's mission had been fulfilled. . . . And when the time came that he was face to face with death, he said, "I am going like a lamb to the slaughter, but I am calm as a summer morning. I have a conscience void of offence toward God and toward all men. If they take my life, I shall die an innocent man, and my blood shall cry from the ground for vengeance, and it shall yet be said of me, 'He was murdered in cold blood.'" [See D&C 135:4.]

He was not afraid to stand before the pleasing bar . . . and answer for the deeds done in the body. He was not afraid to meet the charge that had been made against him, that he was deceiving the people and dealing unjustly with them. He was not afraid of the result of his life's mission, and of the final triumph of the work which he knew was of divine origin, and for which he gave his life. Yet the people of the world, as before, judge this work by the spirit of man. They do not have the Spirit of God, which would enable them to understand that it came from our Father in heaven.[19]

This youth was so sure of the revelation that he had received, and was so anxious that his Father's children, all of them, should know of the truth, that from the time he received the plates of the Book of Mormon from the angel Moroni he devoted his entire life to the organization of the Church and disseminating the truth. . . . There was burning in his soul a knowledge such as Stephen had [see Acts 7:54–60], such as the Redeemer had, that our Heavenly Father was at the helm, that it was his work that was upon the earth, that it was his power that would eventually control, that this life was but a part of eternity. He was prepared to give up a part of his earth-life, if need be, in order that he might enjoy eternally the companionship that he so sincerely loved, and the association of good men and women who have and do dwell upon the earth, and will again dwell upon the earth when it becomes the celestial kingdom.[20]

Joseph Smith taught that he knew there was a hereafter, and that he knew that God lived, and that God knew that he knew that God lived. He was willing to give his life in order that you, my brethren and sisters, might have your faith strengthened and that your confidence in him might not be shaken. He knew the purpose of this life. He knew that we were here to prepare for the future and a more glorious existence. And he was willing, if need be, to give his own life, not simply that he might lose it, for our benefit, but because he knew that the Father had said that he who would save his life should lose it, but he who would lose his life for His sake should find it, even life eternal [see Matthew 16:25]. It was this knowledge that made it possible for the Prophet and [the] Patriarch of the Church [Hyrum Smith] in early days to [leave behind] loved ones, to be incarcerated in prison, and to give all that they had in this world, that men can give for their brethren—their mortal life.[21]

In the year 1830, the Church was organized with six members. The adversary of all righteousness has from that day to the present sought to impede its progress and destroy it. I wonder if that great man, Joseph Smith, who gave his life that the Church might be organized and carried on as the Lord intended, can see the Church as it exists today, with its branches established in all parts of the world, and realize that each day since he was martyred, since he laid down his life and sealed his testimony with his blood, the Church has become stronger than the day before.[22] [See suggestion 5 on page 43.]

Suggestions for Study and Teaching

Consider these ideas as you study the chapter or as you prepare to teach. For additional help, see pages v–vii.

1. Think about the experiences President Smith describes in the first three paragraphs of "From the Life of George Albert Smith"

(pages 33–34). What experiences in your life have strengthened your testimony of the Prophet Joseph Smith? As you read this chapter, identify statements from President Smith's teachings that strengthen your testimony, and consider sharing them with members of your family, priesthood quorum, or Relief Society.

2. Review the first section of teachings (pages 34–36) and review Joseph Smith's own account of the First Vision (see Joseph Smith—History 1:10–19). How has the First Vision influenced your faith in God? How have you seen it influence the faith of others?

3. Study the section that begins on page 36 and read Doctrine and Covenants 1:17–19. What can we learn about service in the Church from Joseph Smith's example? Think of a time when you were given an assignment from the Lord and did not feel qualified. How did the Lord help you?

4. What are some of the truths that the Lord revealed through Joseph Smith? (For some examples of these truths, see the section that begins on page 38.) How has your life been blessed because you know these truths?

5. As you ponder the last paragraph of teachings (page 42), consider what you can do to help the Church continue to become stronger.

Related Scriptures: Isaiah 29:13–14; 1 Corinthians 1:26–27; 2 Nephi 3:5–9, 11–15; Doctrine and Covenants 135

Teaching help: "To encourage discussion, use the questions at the end of the chapter. . . . You could also develop your own questions especially for those you are teaching. For example, you could ask participants how they can apply President Smith's teachings in their responsibilities as parents or as home teachers or visiting teachers" (from page vi of this book).

Notes

1. In Conference Report, Apr. 1906, 54.

2. Journal entry dated Dec. 23, 1905, George Albert Smith Family Papers, University of Utah, box 73, book 2, page 160.

3. In Conference Report, Apr. 1906, 56.

4. In Conference Report, Apr. 1906, 57–58.

5. In Conference Report, Apr. 1946, 181–82.

6. Harold B. Lee, in Conference Report, Oct. 1947, 67.

7. In Conference Report, Oct. 1921, 158–59.

8. "The Latter-day Prophet," *Millennial Star,* Dec. 7, 1905, 822.

9. In Conference Report, Oct. 1921, 159–60.

10. In Conference Report, Apr. 1917, 37.

11. In Conference Report, Oct. 1921, 159–60.

12. In Conference Report, Apr. 1927, 83.

13. "The Latter-day Prophet," 823.

14. In Conference Report, Oct. 1921, 160.

15. In Conference Report, Apr. 1934, 26.

16. "The Latter-day Prophet," 823.

17. In Conference Report, Oct. 1916, 46–47.

18. In Conference Report, Oct. 1931, 121.

19. In Conference Report, Apr. 1904, 63–64.

20. In Conference Report, Oct. 1927, 48.

21. In Conference Report, Apr. 1905, 62–63.

22. In Conference Report, Oct. 1945, 18.

The Holy Priesthood—for the Blessing of God's Children

The priesthood is the authority of God.
Those who hold the priesthood must be worthy
and use it to bless others.

From the Life of George Albert Smith

During the priesthood session of general conference on October 2, 1948, President George Albert Smith said:

"I wonder sometimes if as fathers we take pains to explain to our boys the seriousness of the obligation assumed when a boy becomes a deacon. I wonder if when the boy is ordained a deacon the father lets him feel that he has something now that is eternally important. . . .

"I remember, as if it were yesterday, when John Tingey placed his hands on my head and ordained me a deacon. I had the matter so presented to me and the importance of it, that I felt it was a great honor. The result was, it was a blessing to me, and then after awhile other ordinations came to me. But in each case the foundation was laid in my mind that here was an opportunity for another blessing."[1]

In the same talk, President Smith taught that one of the blessings that come from ordination to the priesthood is the opportunity to bless the lives of others. As an example, he told about an influential priesthood holder—a home teacher—from his youth:

"Rodney Badger was a teacher in my father's home for years, and a great man. Whenever he came the family met and he sat and asked us questions and told us the things that he thought we ought

*"I wonder if when [a] boy is ordained a deacon the father lets him feel
that he has something now that is eternally important."*

to understand. And I want to tell you that when he came into our home he brought the spirit of the Lord with him. And when he went out we felt we had had a visit from a servant of the Lord."[2]

President Smith concluded by expressing his desire that priesthood holders serve the members of their wards and stakes and "not lose an opportunity to help uplift and develop and bring them to be what our Father would have them be."[3] [See suggestion 1 on page 54.]

Teachings of George Albert Smith

Jesus Christ restored divine authority to the earth during His mortal ministry.

When the Savior came in the meridian of time, He found that great city of Jerusalem teeming with evil. The inhabitants were living in such a way that they had lost divine authority, so [God] sent His Son into the world and began again a Church possessing divine power. . . . There were those in His line who were good people, . . . and there were others who were still officiating in the Priesthood, but it was necessary for the Savior to come to restore divine authority. . . .

. . . When He began His ministry, He did not call to His aid the kings and rulers and priests and those who were high in authority, but He called the humble fishermen, and the result was that He gathered around Him men who could be taught, and not men who would not believe Him. He organized a Church under the direction of our Heavenly Father. He conferred divine authority upon His associates and directed them as to what they should do. . . . He had divine authority, and the righteous ones recognized Him to be the Son of God. Some think Him only to be a good man. We believe He came upon the earth not alone to teach the people what to do, but to confer on His associates divine authority to administer the ordinances of His Church. . . .

In the days of the Savior, He was the presiding authority. Next to Him came a quorum of twelve men, chosen by Him. When He passed away, the Quorum of Twelve, not a number of ordinary men who called themselves disciples, but a quorum of twelve men who possessed divine authority and had received it from Jesus Christ, became the leadership of the Church.[4] [See suggestion 2 on page 54.]

The priesthood was restored in our day by men who held it anciently.

It is recorded and recognized in heaven and on earth that creeds and denominations multiplied after [Jesus Christ] left the earth, and the churches increased in number upon the earth, until in the days of Joseph Smith, our beloved prophet, there were many denominations. There were many men who pretended to possess divine authority, and I think some of them thought they had received it. . . .

When the time came and the world had lost the authority or Priesthood, the Lord called a humble boy and gave him a heavenly manifestation and talked to him, told him what he should do, and sent other messengers and heavenly beings from time to time, the result of which was the organization of the Church of Jesus Christ of Latter-day Saints, and in that Church was deposited divine authority. . . .

When Joseph Smith was a young man the Lord directed him to translate the Book of Mormon. On one occasion when Joseph and Oliver Cowdery were translating, the Lord sent a holy being to answer their questions about baptism. Who was he that came? John the Baptist, who held the Aaronic Priesthood. Where did he come from? He came from heaven. . . . He appeared to Joseph Smith and Oliver Cowdery as a glorious resurrected being. He came directed by our Heavenly Father to confer the Aaronic Priesthood upon Joseph and Oliver, for it was not to be found any place in all the world. It was necessary that the heavens open and a man who had held the Priesthood, and still held it, should come and confer it.

Following that, Peter, James and John, who held the Melchizedek Priesthood, conferred that Priesthood upon Joseph and Oliver, and the Lord directed the organization of the Church, with a Presidency, consisting of a president and two counselors; also a Quorum of

"Men who held the Priesthood formerly came and conferred that Priesthood upon humble men."

Twelve Apostles, a Patriarch, High Priests, Seventies, Elders, Priests, Teachers and Deacons; the same kind of an organization that existed in the primitive church, as far as authority was concerned.[5]

The same authority that [Joseph Smith] had has been conferred upon your sons, and they will be required by our Father in heaven to minister in the ordinances of the Gospel. The responsibility that came to Joseph Smith has not been lost by his departure, it has fallen upon other shoulders. Our Father in heaven has raised up from time to time those who have had the authority to speak in His name, to administer in the ordinances of the Gospel, and to bless the children of men. They have shared that honor with you and with your children.[6]

I am grateful that in this day and age the Lord has revealed the Gospel again. The Father and the Son appeared; men who held the Priesthood formerly came and conferred that Priesthood upon humble men and they in turn were commanded to confer it upon others. So the Gospel and the Priesthood have been made available to all who will qualify to receive the same, and that is the Lord's way.[7]

Your mission is a very remarkable one, you men who bear the Priesthood. Upon you has been conferred divine authority. You did not obtain your right to preach and teach the gospel and officiate in its ordinances as a result of training in a college or university. You received your authority from men divinely commissioned to act as servants of the Lord, and it was conferred upon you by those who received it direct from Jesus Christ our Lord.[8] [See suggestion 3 on page 54.]

The power and authority of God can be found only in His true Church.

I have had men ask me: "Of what benefit is your church more than some other church?" I have tried, in a tactful way, to explain to them the difference. Any organization may band together for worship, but that does not give them divine authority. Any group of churches may mass together and organize community churches. That does not confer divine authority. Men may unite for good purposes, but authority from our Heavenly Father is only obtained in his way, and his way in former days was by calling and ordaining men and setting them apart for the work. The same thing is true in our day. . . .

People should be made to understand that just to bow before the Lord in prayer does not give them divine authority. To live up to the requirements that are made of honesty, virtue, truth, etc., does not give them divine authority. . . . It is not sufficient that we pray, that we attend church. It is necessary that we possess divine authority, and it is the claim that we possess that authority that has brought upon this Church much of the persecution that has followed it from the beginning. But it is the truth and many of our Father's children are beginning to observe the effect of divine authority in this Church. They see the development that is made in the lives of men and women.[9] [See suggestion 4 on page 54.]

I personally do not desire to be understood to be finding fault and criticizing the people who belong to the various denominations of the world. I am thankful that there are in so many of them good men and good women who believe in him and with the light that they have serve God; but the fact remains that our Father has established in this world, his Church. He has conferred upon men in this day his authority, and there is no other authority in the world that he will recognize but that which he himself has instituted.[10] [See suggestion 5 on page 54.]

Priesthood ordinances are essential for us to enter the celestial kingdom.

If we were like all other denominations, we might seek the Lord and receive his blessings, because every man that does good in this world receives a blessing; we might have all the cardinal virtues and make them our own, but without the power of God and the authority of the holy Priesthood it is not possible for men to attain to the celestial kingdom.[11]

The only plan that will prepare men for the Celestial kingdom is the plan that has been given by Jesus Christ, our Lord; and the only authority that will qualify men to teach and to officiate in the ordinances of the Gospel properly is the authority of Jesus Christ, our Lord.[12]

Joseph Smith, Jr. was called by God to be His prophet and through him was restored to the earth the Holy Melchizedek Priesthood which is the power of God delegated to man to act in His name. Through this Priesthood every ordinance of the Gospel of our Lord, Jesus Christ, necessary for the salvation of the children of man, is authoritatively administered.[13]

How would it affect us if we had to part with the authority that God has conferred upon us? It would mean that there had been closed to us the doors of the celestial kingdom. It would mean that the crowning blessing toward which I have been taught to look since I was a child would not be realized. . . . The companionship of my loved ones, . . . who are dear to me almost as life itself, could not be enjoyed in the celestial kingdom.[14]

The priesthood . . . is a blessing that, if we are faithful, will open the doors of the celestial kingdom and give us a place there to live throughout the ages of eternity. Do not trifle with this priceless blessing.[15] [See suggestion 6 on page 54.]

Priesthood holders have a responsibility to live exemplary lives and use the priesthood to bless others.

How beautiful it is to realize that men who are worthy may receive [the] priesthood, and in the authority that is given them, do so many things that are a blessing to our Father's other children.[16]

You cannot go out into the world in any other Church or in all other Churches and find . . . men holding divine authority. Do not forget that. You belong to a choice body of men, . . . having had hands laid upon them, and receiving divine authority, making you partners with the Master of Heaven and Earth. I do not mean that you can't laugh, smile, and enjoy life, but I do mean that there should be deep in every soul a consciousness that "I am my brother's keeper. I hold authority from the Lord Jesus Christ—I am a bearer of the Holy Priesthood." If we will do this we will not be found trifling with sacred things as some have done in the past.[17]

The fact that they hold the Priesthood will be to many men a condemnation, because of the manner in which they have treated it, regarding it as though it were something very ordinary.[18]

Some men think that because they hold the Priesthood that that gives them a special way in which they may conduct themselves in their homes. I want to tell you that you men who hold the Priesthood will never get into the Celestial Kingdom, unless you honor your wives and your families and train them and give them the blessings that you want for yourselves.[19]

The authority of our Heavenly Father is upon the earth for the blessing of mankind, not to make those who receive that authority arrogant, but to make them humble; not to make those who have received special privileges feel that they are greater than others, but to make us humble in our souls, prayerful in our hearts, and considerate of all men in all that we do, and thus exemplify by upright lives that which our Heavenly Father desires us to teach.[20]

Being a member of the Church and holding the Priesthood will not get us anywhere unless we are worthy. The Lord has said that every blessing that we desire is predicated upon obedience to His commandments. We may deceive our neighbors, and we may deceive ourselves with the idea that we are going through all right, but unless we keep the commandments of our Heavenly Father, unless we bear worthily this holy Priesthood that is so precious, we will not find our place in the celestial kingdom.[21]

You brethren . . . have had conferred upon you a sacred opportunity, a sacred trust. You have received the blessings of the holy Priesthood. Divine authority has been conferred upon you, and with that authority there has come the responsibility of raising your voice and living your life so that the people of the world may know the difference between the Gospel of Jesus Christ and other organizations of the world.[22]

Wherever you go, keep in mind the fact that you represent him who is the author of our being. The priesthood that you hold is not the priesthood of Joseph Smith, or Brigham Young, or any other men who have been called to leadership of the Church at home or abroad. The priesthood that you hold is the power of God, conferred upon you from on high. Holy beings had to be sent to earth . . . in order to restore that glorious blessing that had been lost to the earth for hundreds of years. Surely we ought to be grateful for our blessings.[23]

I pray that the Lord will bless us all, that we will be worthy to bear the priesthood that He has offered to us and conferred upon us, that wherever we go people will be able to say, "That man is a servant of the Lord."[24] [See suggestion 7 on page 54.]

Suggestions for Study and Teaching

Consider these ideas as you study the chapter or as you prepare to teach. For additional help, see pages v–vii.

1. Think about the experiences President Smith describes on pages 45–47. What can we do to help young men prepare to be ordained to priesthood offices? What can we do to help young women understand the importance of priesthood power in their lives? Why is it important for men and women to learn about the priesthood?

2. Why was it "necessary for the Savior to . . . restore divine authority" (page 47) during His earthly ministry, in addition to teaching the gospel?

3. Read page 49 and the first paragraph on page 50. Why do you think the Lord makes His authority available to all worthy men instead of restricting it to a few men with formal training?

4. President Smith spoke of the "development that is made in the lives of men and women" because of the priesthood (page 50). What does this statement mean to you? What can you do to nurture the power and influence of the priesthood in your life?

5. As you review the section that begins on page 50, think about how you would respond if someone asked you the question posed to President Smith: "Of what benefit is your church more than some other church?"

6. Study the section that begins on page 51. What are some of the "priceless blessings" you have received because of the priesthood?

7. As you study the last section of teachings (pages 52–53), look for the responsibilities that President Smith says come with the priesthood. What can priesthood quorum members do to support each other in their responsibilities? How can women help priesthood holders stay true to these responsibilities? What can priesthood holders do to support women in their divine roles?

Related Scriptures: John 15:16; Alma 13:1–3, 6–10; Doctrine and Covenants 84:19–22; Joseph Smith—History 1:68–72; Articles of Faith 1:5

Teaching help: "Testify whenever the Spirit prompts you to do so, not just at the end of each lesson. Provide opportunities for those you teach to bear their testimonies" (*Teaching, No Greater Call,* 45).

Notes

1. In Conference Report, Oct. 1948, 180–81.
2. In Conference Report, Oct. 1948, 186.
3. In Conference Report, Oct. 1948, 190.
4. "The Church with Divine Authority," *Deseret News,* Sept. 28, 1946, Church section, 6.
5. "The Church with Divine Authority," 6.
6. In Conference Report, Apr. 1904, 64.
7. In Conference Report, Apr. 1934, 28–29.
8. In Conference Report, Apr. 1927, 83.
9. In Conference Report, Apr. 1934, 28–29.
10. In Conference Report, Apr. 1917, 37–38.
11. In Conference Report, Oct. 1926, 106.
12. In Conference Report, Apr. 1934, 30.
13. "Message to Sunday School Teachers," *Instructor,* Nov. 1946, 501.
14. In Conference Report, Apr. 1925, 65.
15. In Conference Report, Apr. 1949, 191–92.
16. In Conference Report, Oct. 1950, 6.
17. Seventies and stake missionary conference, Oct. 4, 1941, 7.
18. In Conference Report, Apr. 1948, 184.
19. In Conference Report, Apr. 1948, 184.
20. In Conference Report, Oct. 1928, 94.
21. In Conference Report, Apr. 1943, 91–92.
22. In Conference Report, Oct. 1933, 25.
23. In Conference Report, Oct. 1945, 118.
24. In Conference Report, Oct. 1950, 182.

"I am only a man, one of the humblest among you, but I have been called to this service . . . by the authority of our Heavenly Father."

Sustaining Those Whom the Lord Sustains

Our leaders are chosen by the Lord, and He expects us to sustain them in word and action.

From the Life of George Albert Smith

George Albert Smith was sustained as President of the Church in general conference in October 1945. Near the end of the conference, President Smith expressed gratitude for the sustaining vote of the Saints: "I thank you for the confidence that has been manifested, my brothers and sisters, in hoping that I may succeed, and promising as some of you have, that you will help me to succeed, because I am only a man, one of the humblest among you, but I have been called to this service—and I would not be here if I did not know I had been called—by the authority of our Heavenly Father."

He then added this request: "I will need the help of every man and every woman and every child, not for my blessing, but for your blessing, and for the blessing of the children of men wherever they may be. That is not *my* responsibility, that is *our* responsibility."[1]

As the teachings in this chapter demonstrate, George Albert Smith understood the heavy burdens carried by the First Presidency, even before he became President of the Church. He taught the Saints that their loyalty and faithfulness can help ease those burdens, and he exemplified this principle during his service in the Quorum of the Twelve Apostles.

In 1946, while conducting a session of general conference, President Smith introduced the sustaining of Church officers by explaining that it is more than just a passive act: "We now have one order of business that is customary with these Conferences; that is, the presentation of the Authorities of the Church to be sustained by the vote of the people. I hope that you will realize, all of you, that this is a sacred privilege. . . . It will not be just a symbol but it will be an indication that, with the help of the Lord, you will carry your part of the work."[2] [See suggestion 1 on page 65.]

Teachings of George Albert Smith

Those who preside over the Church are prepared, chosen, and inspired by the Lord.

This great Church has been presided over by men who have been specially prepared, specially taught, specially equipped for that high honor that has been conferred upon each as he has taken his place. Our Heavenly Father in his wisdom has surrounded these leaders of Israel with others who like themselves have faith and who do not bow to the individual because of his personality or individuality as president of the Church, but who recognize him as the mouthpiece of our Heavenly Father and sustain him and uphold him and pray for him, and love him, in order that they, too, may receive the blessings of our Heavenly Father.

There is no other organization like this in the world. There are no other people [who are] led as this people are led. It is truly said that those who preside are just men. It is through them that our Heavenly Father will perform his work. It is through them that the gospel must be taught. . . . The man who presides over us today is not presiding because of his own native ability. He is not presiding because he is the son of some great potentate, but he is in the position he occupies because our Father in heaven knows the integrity of his soul. Realizing the determination he would have to carry this message to all the nations of the earth, he prepared him for the high calling that has been conferred upon him. He presides as a representative of our Heavenly Father.[3]

I have been thinking today of the humble but great men who have led this Church from its organization. . . . I have been well acquainted with [many of the] Presidents [of the Church] and believe that they were all men of God. It is inconceivable that our

Heavenly Father would choose any other kind to preside over his Church.[4]

What happened when [Joseph Smith] died? . . . [The Saints] didn't hold a conclave, choose a chairman and pick a new leader. The leader had already been chosen by the Lord. He was the senior member of the Quorum of the Twelve, Brigham Young. . . . The Church as a body in all its sessions sustained him as President. When he died, his counselors did not say they were the President, but the Quorum of the Twelve presided for a long time, and then their senior member was sustained as President of the Church. Perfect order prevailed. . . .

I have traced some of these things in order that there may be no mistake. Joseph Smith did not choose himself to be President of the Church. Neither did any who followed him. . . . The appointment comes from our Heavenly Father through His inspiration, and men receive all the power that comes with an appointment.[5]

How grateful we ought to be to know that this work is not the work of man, but it is the work of the Lord; that this Church, that bears the name of Jesus Christ, is directed by him, and he will permit no man or group of men to destroy it. He will not permit the men who preside over his Church to lead the people into error, but he will sustain them with his almighty power. He will magnify them in the eyes of good and great men and women. He will bless their ministry and it will be fraught with success. Those who oppose and find fault will not find joy in their opposition. Those who criticize and seek to destroy the influence of the leaders of the Church will suffer the result of their wrong-doing.[6]

There is need for us to have thanksgiving in our hearts that we are led by holy men who are inspired by our Father in heaven to teach us day by day.[7] [See suggestion 2 on pages 65–66.]

Through His servants, the Lord teaches us the pathway to happiness and safety.

From the time of Father Adam until the present the Lord has admonished the people through his servants. He has inspired them to better living when they have listened to him, and from age to age, as his children have required it, he has sent holy men into the world, to impart instruction tending to happiness, has inspired them to teach the glorious truths that ennoble and enrich mankind.[8]

I know of nothing of great importance that has happened in the world that the Lord through his prophets has not advised the people of beforehand, so that they have not been left in ignorance of what was to develop, but could plan their lives, if they would, to their advantage. . . .

The case of Noah is in point. He was commanded of the Lord to build an ark in which the righteous might be preserved from the flood which was to come. Noah built the ark and preached repentance to his generation for a period of one hundred and twenty years, thus fully warning them. The people, however, were so wicked that they failed to heed the warning. Having their agency, they chose evil rather than righteousness. The rains descended, and the floods came, and only Noah and his family of eight souls were saved. All had been fully warned, but because of their wilfulness and their refusal to repent they were drowned. [See Moses 8:13–30.][9]

The Lord wants us to be happy. That is why he gave us the gospel of Jesus Christ. That is why he conferred the priesthood upon us. He wants us to have joy. That is why he organized this church and set in it the various offices, and all these things are in order. . . . If you will follow the leadership of the Lord, and those whom the Lord sustains, you will not fall away into darkness, lose the light, transgress the laws of God, and forfeit your privileges that he is so anxious that all of us should enjoy.[10]

There is only one pathway of safety for me in this day and that is to follow those whom the Lord has appointed to lead. I may have my own ideas and opinions, I may set up my own judgment with reference to things, but I know that when my judgment conflicts with the teachings of those that the Lord has given to us to point the way, I should change my course. If I desire salvation I will follow the leaders that our Heavenly Father has given to us, as long as he sustains them.[11] [See suggestion 3 on page 66.]

Those who are humble and faithful sustain and defend the Lord's servants.

I have known thousands of the rank and file of this great Church, men and women of many nations who in humility and faithfulness have accepted the gospel to become identified with the Church of Jesus Christ of Latter-day Saints. . . . [They] have prayed for and sustained their leaders . . . , and during my experience in the Church I have yet to know of one person who has been observing the commandments of the Lord who has raised his or her voice against those who were called to preside over this Church. That is really remarkable. . . .

One of the greatest testimonies to me of the divinity of this work is that a multitude of people . . . having the opportunity in Stake Conference . . . to express themselves by voting either to sustain or refuse to sustain those who preside over them (every one exercising free agency) continue to uphold their leaders. Surely the Spirit of the Lord prompts the faithful, humble people to sustain his chosen servants.[12]

When Moses led Israel from Egypt through the wilderness and into the promised land, Amalek attacked Israel at Rephidim. Moses directed Joshua to choose fighting men to protect Israel. Moses, Aaron, and Hur went to the top of a hill overlooking the battlefield. While Moses held the rod of God above his head, Israel prevailed, but when he let his hands down because of weakness, Amalek prevailed. A stone seat was provided and Aaron and Hur held up his hands in order that the blessings of God could flow to Israel that their warriors might prevail and the battle was won. The power of God was upon Moses and remained with him until he had finished his work. [See Exodus 17:8–13.] When he had the support of the people they too were blessed, and so it has been with every servant of the Lord who has presided over Israel. . . .

. . . Just as long as [the President] presides over this Church, it matters not how many years it will be, our Heavenly Father will give him strength, power, wisdom, judgment, and inspiration to talk to Israel as they need to be talked to. We, in following his leadership,

"We . . . must be like Aaron and Hur of ancient times;
we must uphold [the prophet's] hands."

must be like Aaron and Hur of ancient times; we must uphold his hands, that through him the Lord will let the blessings of heaven descend on us and this people. [13]

I know that these men [the General Authorities] are servants of the Lord, and I know they are seeking to bless mankind. I hope that not any of you . . . will fail to sustain them, not only by your faith and prayers but if they are misrepresented and their attitude misrepresented, that you may be willing and anxious to defend them, if need be, because there is a time coming when they will need your defense. The Adversary has not forgotten them, and one of the evidences to me of the divinity of the calling of these men is that evil men speak evil of them, and good men and good women speak well of them. [14] [See suggestion 4 on page 66.]

When we criticize our leaders or disregard their counsel, we allow the adversary to lead us astray.

There are those among us . . . who have been blinded by the philosophies and foolishness of men. There are those who reject the advice and counsel of the man that God has placed at the head of this Church. . . .

People who haven't very much information suddenly come along with a bright idea, and they suggest "this is the way" or "that is the way," and although it is in conflict with the advice of the Lord some are persuaded to try it. The Lord has given safe advice and appointed the President of his Church to interpret that advice. If we ignore what he advises, as the President of the Church, we may discover that we have made a serious mistake.[15]

The Presidency of the Church . . . are the representatives of our Heavenly Father, not only to this people, but they represent him to all the people of the earth. We would do well if we would magnify and honor these men he has placed at our head. They are men with human frailties, they will make mistakes, but if we will be as charitable to the mistakes that they make as we are to our own failures and mistakes, we will see their virtues as we see our own.

I stand here to plead with you, my brethren and sisters, not to permit words of criticism or of unkindness to pass your lips about those whom the Lord has called to lead us. Do not be found in the companionship of those who would belittle them or weaken their influence among the children of men. If you do, I can say to you that you will find yourselves in the power of the adversary. You will be influenced by him to go as far as possible from the pathway of truth, and if you do not repent you may find when it is too late that you have lost the "pearl of great price." Because of your selfishness and your blindness you will have been led away, and your loved ones . . . will be sorrowing on the other side of the veil because of your weakness and your folly.[16] [See suggestion 5 on page 66.]

The adversary is not asleep. He is deceiving many and leading them to sin. . . . There are some who are teaching false doctrine; and some who are seeking to persuade men and women to violate the commandments of our Heavenly Father. . . . If the members of this

Church who find fault with the leaders of the Church and criticise those who are giving their very lives to bless and benefit us would only pause long enough to ask prayerfully, "Which of these teachers is it safe to follow?" they would have no difficulty in finding their right course and would sustain those whom the Lord sustains.[17]

When we sustain our leaders, we commit to follow their counsel and magnify our own callings.

It must be a source of strength to the President of this Church to look into the faces of thousands of honest men and women and observe them raise their hand in covenant with our Father in heaven, and sustain him in the office to which he has been called as president of this great Church. The obligation that we make when we raise our hands under such circumstances, is a most sacred one. It does not mean that we will go quietly on our way and be willing that the prophet of the Lord shall direct this work, but it means,—if I understand the obligation I assumed when I raised my hand—that we will stand behind him; we will pray for him; we will defend his good name, and we will strive to carry out his instructions as the Lord shall direct him to offer them to us while he remains in that position.[18]

When I think of the burdens that are carried by the President of this Church and his counselors, and realize the responsibilities that are placed upon their shoulders, with all my heart I desire to help them, that I may not be an encumbrance, but that in the position to which I have been called, with you, my brethren and my sisters, we may each take our place and carry our portion of the load and magnify our calling to the honor and glory of God.[19] [See suggestion 4 on page 66.]

God grant that we who have been so bountifully blessed may hold up the hands of the servant of the Lord who presides over us; that we may help him not only by our faith and prayers but by loving kindness as opportunity offers; that we may march under the banner that he shall hold aloft as God continues to sustain him as President of the Church, as the prophet of the Lord in these latter days.[20]

Let us sustain these men whom God has raised up to preside over us. Let us bless them, not only by our lips, but by assisting in

*We sustain our leaders when we "carry our portion of the load
and magnify our calling to the honor and glory of God."*

every possible way to carry this burden that rests so heavily upon
their shoulders. . . . Pray for and bless them and help them.²¹

Suggestions for Study and Teaching

Consider these ideas as you study the chapter or as you prepare to
teach. For additional help, see pages v–vii.

1. Read the last paragraph of "From the Life of George Albert
    Smith" (pages 57–58). What is "your part of the work"? As you
    study this chapter, consider ways you can show by your words
    and actions that you sustain the leaders of the Church.

2. Review the first section of teachings (pages 58–59), partic-
    ularly the second and fourth paragraphs. How is the Lord's
    way of choosing leaders different from the world's way? What

experiences have you had that strengthened your faith that our leaders are chosen by the Lord?

3. Study the section that begins on page 59 and read Doctrine and Covenants 21:4–7. What specific counsel has the Lord given through the current President of the Church? through your stake or district president? through your bishop or branch president? What blessings have you received as you have followed this counsel?

4. Review the section that begins on page 61 and read the first two full paragraphs on page 64. What does it mean to you to sustain Church leaders? How does sustaining Church leaders strengthen our families and homes?

5. Read the last full paragraph on page 63. Why is it dangerous to criticize the leaders of the Church? What would be an appropriate way to respond if someone were to point out a fault in one of your local leaders?

Related Scriptures: Amos 3:7; Ephesians 4:11–14; Hebrews 5:4; Doctrine and Covenants 84:109–10; 107:22; 112:20

Teaching help: One way to encourage diligent learning is to listen carefully when someone asks a question or makes a comment. "Listening is an expression of love. It often requires sacrifice. When we truly listen to others, we often give up what we want to say so they can express themselves" (*Teaching, No Greater Call,* 66).

Notes

1. In Conference Report, Oct. 1945, 174–75.
2. In Conference Report, Oct. 1946, 153–54.
3. In Conference Report, Apr. 1927, 86–87.
4. In Conference Report, Apr. 1931, 31.
5. "The Church with Divine Authority," *Deseret News,* Sept. 28, 1946, Church section, 6, 9.
6. In Conference Report, Apr. 1934, 29.
7. In Conference Report, Oct. 1917, 45.
8. In Conference Report, Oct. 1917, 40.
9. In Conference Report, Apr. 1945, 136.
10. In Conference Report, Apr. 1949, 192.
11. In Conference Report, Apr. 1937, 33.
12. In Conference Report, Apr. 1931, 32.
13. In Conference Report, Apr. 1942, 14.
14. In Conference Report, Oct. 1933, 29.
15. In Conference Report, Oct. 1936, 75.
16. In Conference Report, Apr. 1937, 34.
17. In Conference Report, Apr. 1937, 33.
18. In Conference Report, June 1919, 40.
19. In Conference Report, Oct. 1929, 24.
20. In Conference Report, Apr. 1930, 68–69.
21. In Conference Report, Oct. 1930, 69.

CHAPTER 7

The Immortality of the Soul

*Our life is eternal, and this knowledge helps us make
correct choices and comforts us in times of mourning.*

From the Life of George Albert Smith

George Albert Smith was blessed with a firm understanding of
the purpose of life, and this enabled him to encourage others as
they faced adversity. He frequently reminded the Saints that "we are
living eternal lives"—that eternity doesn't begin after this life but
that mortality is a crucial part of eternity. "I sometimes have said to
my friends when they seemed to be at the crossroads, uncertain as
to which way they wanted to go, 'Today is the beginning of eternal
happiness or eternal disappointment for you.'"[1]

President Smith testified of these truths at the funeral services of
Hyrum G. Smith, Patriarch to the Church, who had passed away at
a relatively young age, leaving behind his wife and eight children:

"I have felt, since I was asked to speak at this funeral, that perhaps I would not be able to do so. My emotions have been stirred,
and I have found myself incapable of controlling them, but since
I came into this building a beautiful, sweet influence of peace has
come into my soul. . . .

"Instead of mourning I feel to thank our Father in heaven for the
Gospel of His Beloved Son that has been revealed anew in our day.
. . . To know that life is eternal is a wonderful blessing,—to know
that throughout eternity the blessings that this good man has lived
for will be his. His mortal life has been terminated but this is only
part of eternal life. He has laid the foundation deep and secure
upon which he has built and will continue to build throughout
eternity. The joy that he has experienced here upon earth will be
added upon. . . .

"I am thankful that there has been revealed to us and made plain in this latter-day that this life is not the end, that this is but a part of eternity."

"As I think of the experiences of people in the world, on occasions of this kind, I marvel how we have been blessed. I have no more doubt about eternal life and the immortality of the soul than I have that the sun shines at midday. . . . It is a sad thing to part with our dear ones, even temporarily. We send them upon missions, or they go to other parts of the world to live and we miss them. When an occasion like this occurs it seems that they are more distant, but as a matter of fact they are not, if we but understood. . . . Instead of extending the condolence that sometimes might go to those who are bereaved, I feel more like rejoicing this day that I know that this is not the end. . . .

". . . So today, as I stand in your presence, when perhaps tears should be flowing, my soul is filled with comfort and satisfaction. I pray that that comfort may be in the lives of each of those who are bereaved."² [See suggestion 1 on page 77.]

Teachings of George Albert Smith

We lived as spirits before we came to earth, and our spirits will continue living after we die.

Our comprehension of this life is that it is eternal life—that we are living in eternity today as much as we ever will live in eternity. Our belief is that we lived before we came here; that which is intelligence, that which is spirit, did not have its beginning in this life. We believe that we received a spiritual tabernacle before we came into this world. That spiritual body was sent to this world, and here it received a physical tabernacle, the body which we see. The physical portion that we see is of earth, earthy [see 1 Corinthians 15:47], but that portion which leaves the body when our lives go out is that which is spiritual, and it never dies. The physical tabernacle lies in the tomb—it is a portion of the earth and goes back to mother earth—but the intelligence that God has placed within it, that which has power to reason and to think, that which has power to sing and to speak, knows no death; it simply passes from this sphere of eternal life, and awaits there the purification of the physical tabernacle, until the time it will be reunited with this tabernacle, which will

Isn't it a singular thing that what the world has struggled for from the beginning, wealth, power, all those things that make men comfortable, are to be had in abundance today—better and more clothing than ever before, more food than can be consumed, more wealth of all kinds than the world has ever had before. Our homes are more comfortable. The conveniences of life have been multiplied marvelously since the Gospel came upon the earth, and today everything that we have struggled for we have. Education has arrived at its highest point. More knowledge of the things of this earth is possessed by men than ever before. Everything mankind has struggled for from the beginning of time that is considered most desirable is upon the earth today; and notwithstanding that, there is doubt and dread of what the future has in store.

What is our trouble? It is that we have sought the creature comforts, we have sought the honors of men, we have sought those things that selfishness puts into our souls. We have sought to set ourselves up and have preferred ourselves to our Father's other children. [12]

Let us not be lulled to sleep, let us not be deceived by the abundance of good things of this world; for what doth it profit a man though he should gain the whole world and lose his own soul? [See Mark 8:36.] Let not the object of our creation be overlooked; but let us labor for the salvation of our souls. [13]

One of the sorrowful things in life is to see a man or a woman laid away in Mother earth with a realization of the fact that they have refused the greater blessings that our Father offered to them, and have continued grasping at the bubble that has itself disappeared. When I think of the millions of God's children in the world, and realize how little they are striving for the things that are really worth while, I feel sad. [14]

Remember that it is the intelligence that you acquire that is eternal, the truth which you learn here and apply in your lives, the knowledge and experience you gain and profit by—these you will take with you when you go home. [15]

"The thing . . . that is worth more than all the rest is the opportunity to obtain eternal life [with your] sons and daughters, husbands and wives."

The treasures that we will find when we go to the other side will be those that we have laid up there by ministering to our Father's other sons and daughters with whom we have associated here. He has made this possible for all of us, and during our stay here we will be happier serving our fellows than we could possibly be in any other way. [16]

It is not so important how many valuables you may have, how much property you may possess, and how many of the honors of men you may acquire, and all those things that are so desirable in the world. The thing that God has given to you that is worth more than all the rest is the opportunity to obtain eternal life in the celestial kingdom and have as your companions, throughout the ages of eternity, sons and daughters, husbands and wives with whom you have associated here on earth. [17] [See suggestion 4 on page 78.]

Because of Jesus Christ, we will be resurrected.

The Saviour's righteous life is a perfect example to all, and His resurrection was the first assurance to humanity that we, too, shall come forth from the tomb. [18]

When Jesus was raised from the dead He became the first fruits of the resurrection. The spirit begotten of the Father (the intelligent part of His soul) reinhabited His earthly tabernacle which had been purified, and He became a glorified celestial being, and took His place, on the right hand of the Father, as one of the Godhead. He had power to overcome death because He had complied with all the laws of His Father governing it; and having subdued death he turned the key whereby all mankind may be resurrected, and all may be glorified also by obeying His teachings, which are so simple that all may comply if they will. [19]

Jesus Christ was a man without sin. By reason of His purity, His uprightness and His virtue, He was able to unlock the doors of the prison, to overcome death and the grave, and pioneer the way . . . unto that heaven where we expect to go. [20]

We may turn to section 88 of the Doctrine and Covenants and see what the Lord has said about our resurrection, not only the resurrection of the Savior, but he tells us what may happen to us. . . . We are informed in this section that our bodies are to be raised from the tomb, not some other bodies, and that the spirits that possess these tabernacles now will inhabit the same tabernacles after they have been cleansed and purified and immortalized. [See D&C 88:14–17, 28–33.] [21]

Now a good many people in the world do not know what the resurrection is. Do you teach your children and your associates what it means? . . . [The Savior's] resurrection is plain to the Latter-day Saints who understand the gospel, but there are so many who do not understand what it means. . . . The purpose of the Gospel of Jesus Christ is to prepare every man, woman and child for the time when all those who have died will be brought forth from their graves, and when our Heavenly Father will establish his kingdom upon this earth and the righteous will dwell there and Jesus Christ will be our King and our Law-giver. [22] [See suggestion 5 on page 78.]

"The Saviour's . . . resurrection was the first assurance to humanity that we, too, shall come forth from the tomb."

Our knowledge of the immortality of the soul inspires, encourages, and comforts us.

We read in Job, "But there is a spirit in man; and the inspiration of the Almighty giveth them understanding." [Job 32:8.] Those who have not received that inspiration will not comprehend the meaning of the resurrection from the dead, and without that understanding it seems to me there would be little happiness for those who are living in mature years, waiting for the time when the spirit leaves the body to go they know not where. [23]

Oh, how sad we would be if we thought that death terminated our career. If, when our life's labor on earth was finished, we had no opportunity to go on developing, there would be little to inspire us to live as we should here. The knowledge that all the good we accomplish here, and all the development we make, will enhance our happiness eternally, encourages us to do our best. [24]

We are all of us passing rapidly to that time when we will be called hence. If we did not understand that there is a future life, if we did not realize that there is something more than the influence that we have received thus far, if there was not anything but the vanity and vexation of life for us to live for, there are many, it seems to me, who would grow weary in the struggle that is to be made for existence here. But in the mercy of our Heavenly Father he has bestowed upon us the most wonderful gifts that come to human kind. [25]

The Lord has blessed us with a knowledge that he lives, and has a body, and that we are created in his image. We do not believe that he is some kind of essence or that he is incomprehensible. If you have received the witness that has come to me and know as I know that our Heavenly Father has revealed himself to the children of men, that he is a personal God, that we are created in his image, that our spirits were begotten by him, that he has given us an opportunity to dwell upon the earth to receive a physical tabernacle, in order that we may be prepared to return into his presence and live eternally with him, I say, if you have received that assurance, then you have a foundation upon which you may build your faith. Take that from you, the knowledge that God really lives, the assurance that Jesus Christ was the manifestation of God in the flesh, take from you the assurance that there will be a literal resurrection from the dead, and you will find yourselves in the condition that our Father's children are in throughout the world, and I ask you, what comfort remains to you then? These are the truths that are fundamental. [26]

More of my dear ones are on the other side than are here, and it will not be long in the natural course of events before I, too, will receive my summons to pass on. I am not looking forward to that time with anxiety and distress, but with hope and with the assurance that the change, when it occurs, will be for increasing happiness and advantages that we cannot know in mortality. [27]

When we realize that death is only one of the steps that the children of God shall take throughout eternity, and that it is according to his plan, it robs death of its sting and brings us face to face with the reality of eternal life. Many families have been called upon to say good-bye temporarily to those they love. When such passings occur, they disturb us, if we will let them, and thus bring great sorrow into our lives. But if our spiritual eyes could be opened and we could see, we would be comforted, I am sure, with what our vision would behold. The Lord has not left us without hope. On the contrary he has given us every assurance of eternal happiness, if we will accept his advice and counsel while here in mortality.

This is not an idle dream. These are facts. To you who are members of the Church of Jesus Christ, this story is a simple one, but it is true. There are sacred volumes of scripture that our Heavenly Father has placed within our reach, teaching us that we live eternally. . . . The Lord has given us this information in great plainness, and from the depths of my heart I thank him for the knowledge that he has given us, that those who mourn may be comforted and that we ourselves may understand our purpose in being here. If those who have passed on could speak to us, they would say, "Press on, press on, for the goal that will bring us eternal happiness together." Do the things the Lord would have you do, and you will not miss anything that is worth while; but on the contrary you will be continually laying up treasures in heaven where moth and rust cannot corrupt or thieves break through and steal. [See Matthew 6:19–20.]

I leave my testimony with you that I know that we are living eternal life, and that the temporary separation of death . . . is but one of the steps along the pathway of eternal progress and will result eventually in happiness if we are faithful.[28] [See suggestion 6 on page 78.]

Suggestions for Study and Teaching

Consider these ideas as you study the chapter or as you prepare to teach. For additional help, see pages v–vii.

1. As you read "From the Life of George Albert Smith" (pages 67–69), think about a time when you have tried to comfort someone after the death of a loved one. What was it that brought President Smith comfort?

2. President Smith taught that "this [life] is but a part of eternity" (page 70). What does this mean to you? How does our understanding of this principle influence the choices we make?

3. Study the section that begins on page 70. How do the teachings in this section differ from what the world teaches about the purpose of life? What experiences do we have during mortality that can help us "partake of the attributes of deity"?

4. Review the section that begins on page 71, especially the last four paragraphs of the section. Why is striving for worldly things like "grasping at [a] bubble that has itself disappeared"?

5. On page 74, President Smith refers to information about the resurrection in Doctrine and Covenants 88. What do verses 14–17 and 28–33 of this section teach you about the resurrection? What are some effective ways to teach children about the resurrection?

6. Read the section that begins on page 75. What are some of the trials of life that are made more bearable because you have a testimony of the principles taught in this section?

Related Scriptures: 1 Corinthians 15:12–26, 35–42, 53–58; 2 Nephi 9:6–13; Alma 12:24; 28:12; Doctrine and Covenants 93:19–20, 29–34; 130:18–19; Abraham 3:24–26

Teaching help: "Ask participants to choose a section they are interested in and read it silently. Invite them to gather in groups of two or three people who chose the same section and discuss what they learned" (from page vii of this book).

Notes

1. In Conference Report, Oct. 1944, 94.

2. In *Deseret News*, Feb. 13, 1932, Church section, 5, 7.

3. "Mormon View of Life's Mission," *Deseret Evening News*, June 27, 1908, Church section, 2.

4. In Conference Report, Apr. 1905, 62.

5. In Conference Report, Oct. 1923, 70–71.

6. In Conference Report, Apr. 1905, 59.

7. In Conference Report, Oct. 1906, 48.

8. In Conference Report, Oct. 1926, 102.

9. "Mormon View of Life's Mission," 2.

10. In Conference Report, Apr. 1905, 63.

11. In Conference Report, Oct. 1909, 78.

12. In Conference Report, Apr. 1932, 44.

13. In Conference Report, Oct. 1906, 50.

14. In Conference Report, Oct. 1923, 70.

15. "Mormon View of Life's Mission," 2.

16. In *Deseret News,* May 26, 1945, Church section, 6.

17. In Conference Report, Apr. 1948, 163.

18. "President Smith Sends Greetings," *Deseret News,* Dec. 27, 1950, Church section, 3.

19. "Mormon View of Life's Mission," 2.

20. In Conference Report, Apr. 1905, 60.

21. In Conference Report, Apr. 1939, 122–23.

22. In Conference Report, Apr. 1950, 187–88.

23. In Conference Report, Apr. 1939, 121.

24. In Conference Report, Oct. 1921, 41.

25. In Conference Report, Oct. 1923, 71.

26. In Conference Report, Oct. 1921, 39.

27. In *Deseret News,* May 26, 1945, Church section, 4.

28. "Some Thoughts on War, and Sorrow, and Peace," *Improvement Era,* Sept. 1945, 501.

Interior of the Kirtland Temple, where the ancient prophet Elijah appeared to Joseph Smith and conferred on him the sealing power and the keys of the work for the dead.

CHAPTER 8

Temple Blessings for Ourselves and Our Ancestors

The purpose of temples is to provide a place
where holy ordinances are performed
for the living and for the dead.

From the Life of George Albert Smith

In 1905, as a new Apostle, George Albert Smith toured several important Church history sites with President Joseph F. Smith and other members of the Quorum of the Twelve. One place they visited was Kirtland, Ohio, where the early Saints had built the first temple in this dispensation. "Coming in sight of the town," Elder Smith recalled, "the first thing that greeted our vision was the beautiful temple of Kirtland. . . . It was there that the Prophet Joseph Smith and [Oliver Cowdery] saw the Savior upon the breastwork of the pulpit. It was there that Moses committed to them the keys of the gathering of Israel; and that Elias and Elijah came in the power and majesty of their great callings, and delivered the keys that had been committed to their care in the days of their ministry on the earth."

As the group walked through the temple, Elder Smith thought about the devoted Saints who built it. "When we realized that the building was constructed by people in extreme poverty, how courageous men worked during the day to lay the foundations and build the walls of that structure, and then at night stood and defended it with weapons against those who had sworn that the building should never be completed, we could not help but feel that it was no wonder the Lord received their offerings and blessed them as few people have been blest upon the earth."[1]

Years later, after being set apart as President of the Church, President Smith dedicated the Idaho Falls Idaho Temple. In the dedicatory prayer, he gave thanks for the saving work performed in the temple for the living and the dead:

"We thank thee, O God, for sending Elijah, the ancient prophet, to whom was '. . . committed the keys of the power of turning the hearts of the fathers to the children, and the hearts of the children to the fathers, that the whole earth may not be smitten with a curse.' [D&C 27:9.] We thank thee that he was sent to thy servant, Joseph Smith, to confer the keys and authority of the work for the dead, and to reveal that the plan of salvation embraces the whole of the human family, that the gospel is universal in scope, and that thou art no respecter of persons, having provided for the preaching of the gospel of salvation to both the living and the dead. We are most grateful unto thee that salvation is provided for all who desire to be saved in thy kingdom.

"May it be pleasing to thy people to search out the genealogy of their forebears that they may become saviors on Mt. Zion by officiating in thy temples for their kindred dead. We pray also that the spirit of Elijah may rest mightily upon all peoples everywhere that they may be moved upon to gather and make available the genealogy of their ancestors; and that thy faithful children may utilize thy holy temples in which to perform on behalf of the dead all ordinances pertaining to their eternal exaltation."

In his prayer President Smith also acknowledged that the temple is indeed the house of the Lord and a place where God's presence can be felt:

"Today we here and now dedicate the Temple unto thee with all that pertains unto it that it may be holy in thy sight; that it may be a house of prayer, a house of praise and worship, that thy glory may rest upon it and thy holy presence be continually in it; and that it may be an acceptable abode for thy Well-Beloved Son, Jesus Christ, our Savior; that it may be both sanctified and consecrated in all its parts sacred unto thee, and we pray that all those who may cross the threshold of this thine House may be impressed with the holiness of it. . . .

"Wilt thou, our Heavenly Father, let thy presence be felt here always, that all who assemble here may realize that they are thy guests and that this is thy House."[2] [See suggestion 1 on page 90.]

Teachings of George Albert Smith

In the temple we receive sacred ordinances, including ordinances that bind families for eternity.

In order that we might be prepared for [the celestial] kingdom, the Lord, in his mercy, in this latter day restored the Gospel of Jesus Christ, and placed in it divine authority, and then gave understanding to His children that certain ordinances may be received and performed. For this purpose temples were built and into those temples those who desire a place in the Celestial Kingdom have the opportunity to go and receive their blessings, to enrich their lives and prepare them for that kingdom.[3]

We are the only people in the world who know what temples are for.[4]

Each [temple] has been built to one great eternal purpose: to serve as a House of the Lord, to provide a place sacred and suitable for the performing of holy ordinances that bind on earth as in heaven—ordinances for the dead and for the living that assure those who receive them and who are faithful to their covenants, the possession and association of their families, worlds without end, and exaltation with them in the celestial kingdom of our Father.[5]

Grateful should we be for a knowledge of the eternity of the marriage covenant. If in this life only had we hope, we would indeed be of all men most miserable [see 1 Corinthians 15:19]. The assurance that our relationship here as parents and children, as husbands and wives will continue in heaven, and that this is but the beginning of a great and glorious kingdom that our Father has destined we shall inherit on the other side, fills us with hope and joy.[6]

If I were to think, as so many think, that now that my beloved wife and my beloved parents are gone, that they have passed out of my life forever and that I shall never see them again, it would deprive me of one of the greatest joys that I have in life: the contemplation of meeting them again, and receiving their welcome and their affection, and of thanking them from the depths of a grateful heart for all they have done for me.

But there are many, many millions of our Father's children who do not know that by partaking of certain ordinances prescribed by our Heavenly Father, husbands and wives may be united for time and eternity and enjoy the companionship of their children forever. How thankful we should be for that knowledge.[7]

There are only a few places in the world where we can be married for eternity, and that is in the temples of God. . . . There are also many of our brothers and sisters, all children of our Heavenly Father, who are denied this privilege because of . . . unavoidable reasons. But if they live worthily and if they would have availed themselves of the privilege if they had been able to do so, they will lose nothing by these temporarily unfavorable circumstances. But think then how much greater is the responsibility of those who live where men and women can be united for eternity, and where they can go and do the work for their dead! The people of the world do not have this blessing. I wonder if we appreciate it. . . .

Let us instruct our young people in these matters from their earliest youth, so that when they approach the time of marriage, there will be no question in their minds as to where or how or by whom that sacred ordinance should be performed—and the only place in which it may be performed for time and for eternity is in a temple.[8]

I thank [the Lord] for all the ordinances of the House of the Lord that I have received, each one of which has been intended not for me alone, but I have been permitted to receive a portion of that which has been intended for all his children, wherever they may be, if they are willing to receive what he offers to them, without money and without price.[9]

All of the . . . temples which have been built or yet will be dedicated, will prove to be a blessing beyond measure to all those who worthily avail themselves of the privilege of using it, both for themselves and for their kindred dead.[10] [See suggestion 2 on page 91.]

"There are only a few places in the world where we can be married for eternity, and that is in the temples of God."

Through temple work we make eternal blessings available to our deceased ancestors.

The genealogical society has spent years of time collecting [family history] information, and others spend years of time going into the House of the Lord to be baptized for those who are dead, to have husbands and wives and children sealed to one another, to unite the family as our Heavenly Father has instructed that we should do. It would be well if each of us would ask himself the question: What am I doing about it? Am I doing my part? Our Heavenly Father told the people through Joseph Smith that, unless we performed the work for our dead, we would lose our own blessings, and we would be cut off, and one of the very last things that the Prophet tried to do was to complete a temple in which the people could go and perform work for their dead. That is how important it is. It has to be done by someone.[11]

I am here reminded of a story of two brothers who lived in a northern Utah town: The older brother, Henry, was a banker and merchant, and had ample means. The other brother, George, was a farmer, and did not have very much beyond his needs, but he had a desire to do temple work for their dead. He searched out their genealogy and went to the temple and worked for those who had passed on.

One day George said to Henry, "I think you should go down to the temple and help."

But Henry said, "I haven't time to do anything like that. It takes me all my time to take care of my business." . . .

About a year after that, Henry called at George's home and said, "George, I have had a dream, and it worries me. I wonder if you can tell me what it means?"

George asked, "What did you dream, Henry?"

Henry said, "I dreamed that you and I had passed from this life and were on the other side of the veil. As we went along, we came to a beautiful city. People were gathered together in groups in many places, and every place we came they shook your hand and put their arms around you and blessed you and said how thankful they were to see you, but," he said, "they didn't pay a bit of attention to me; they were hardly friendly. What does that mean?"

George asked, "You thought we were on the other side of the veil?"

"Yes."

"Well, this is what I have been talking to you about. I have been trying to get you to do the work for those people who are over there. I have been doing work for many of them, but the work for many more is yet to be done. . . . You had better get busy, because you have had a taste of what you may expect when you get over there if you do not do your part in performing this work for them." [See suggestion 3 on page 91.]

I have thought of this story from the lives of two brothers a good many times. Many people do not understand the seriousness and the sacredness of life; they do not understand the sacredness of

"Think of the devotion and the faithfulness of those who day after day go into these temples and officiate for those who have passed to the other side."

eternal marriage. There are some of our people who have no interest in their genealogy. They care nothing about their forebears; at least you would think so by the way they behave. They do not go into the temple to do work for their dead. . . .

. . . After we have been to the House of the Lord for our own blessings, let us think of our responsibility to our forebears. What will be your reception when you go on the other side? Will you be the one they will reach out to and bless throughout the ages of eternity, or will you be like the brother who was selfishly working out his problems here and letting those who could not help themselves go on without his help?[12]

You know we are all tied together by the great work that is being done in the temples of our Father, where families that have not been united before are brought together by the power of the Holy Priesthood. The Lord intended that every one of his sons and daughters should have the opportunity to be blessed, not only here upon the earth, but to enjoy eternal blessings.

Think of the devotion and the faithfulness of those who day after day go into these temples and officiate for those who have passed to the other side, and know this that those who are on the other side are just as anxious about us. They are praying for us and for our success. They are pleading, in their own way, for their descendants, for their posterity who live upon the earth. [13]

The Lord will assist us in searching for our kindred dead.

In Chicago a number of years ago, during the Century of Progress Exposition, I went into our Church booth one day and inquired of the missionaries as to who had charge of the great cultural and scientific fair.

They told me the man's name was Dawes, and I asked, "Is he the brother of Charles G. Dawes, who was vice president of the United States and also ambassador to Great Britain?"

And they answered, "Yes."

"Well," I said, "I am delighted to know that. I happen to know him."

I said to myself, "I think I will go call on him. He will be Henry Dawes." I knew Henry Dawes, so I went to the telephone and called his office. His secretary . . . told Mr. Dawes that George Albert Smith of Salt Lake City was there and wanted to meet him, and he told her to have me come over. So, instead of running me behind a hundred people to wait my turn, she took me to a side door, and there stood before me a tall man whom I had never seen before in my life.

He said, "I am Mr. Dawes."

He was very pleasant, but you can imagine how embarrassed I was. He *was* Mr. Dawes, and he was Ambassador Dawes' brother, but he was Rufus Dawes. I did not know there was a Rufus Dawes in the world.

"Well," I said, "I have come to tell you that this is a wonderful fair, and to express to you my appreciation for what you have done in organizing and seeing it through. It is marvelous what has been accomplished, and what an education it is to so many people. Now, I understand that you are a busy man, and that is all I wanted to come and say, and to congratulate and thank you."

"That is very considerate," he said. "Come in."

"No, that is all I came to say," I replied.

He said, "Come right in."

I said, "No, there are a hundred people waiting to see you."

"None of them will say anything as nice as what you have said."

So I went in, out of ideas and out of breath, almost. He insisted on my sitting down, and the next thing I said was: "By the way, Mr. Dawes, where do your people come from?"

"Do you mean in America?" he asked.

"I mean anywhere."

He said, "Are you interested in genealogy?"

"I certainly am." I answered. "We have one of the finest genealogical libraries in Salt Lake City."

He said, "Excuse me just a moment," and walked out of his office and came back with a carton about the size of an old family Bible. He took his knife, opened the carton, and took out a package wrapped in white tissue paper. He took the tissue paper off and put on the table one of the most beautifully bound books I have ever seen. It was well printed and profusely illustrated, and the cover was elegantly embossed with gold.

As I looked it over, I said, "Mr. Dawes, that is a beautiful piece of work."

"It ought to be. It cost me twenty-five thousand dollars."

"Well," I said, "it is worth it."

He said, "Is it worth anything to you?"

I said, "It would be if I had it."

He said, "All right, you may have it!"—twenty-five thousand dollars worth of genealogy placed in my hand by a man whom I had met only five minutes before! Well, I was amazed. Our first visit continued but a short while longer. I told him how delighted I was to have it and that I would place it in the genealogical library in Salt Lake City.

Before I left the room, he said, "Mr. Smith, this is my mother's genealogy, the Gates' genealogy. We are also preparing my father's genealogy—the Dawes' family. It will be one just like this. When it is finished, I would like to send you a copy of that also."

Fifty thousand dollars of genealogy!—and just because I tried to be polite to someone. I do not think that was an accident. . . .

The Lord is helping us; it is marvelous how the way is opened and how other people frequently are prompted to prepare their genealogies. But sometimes we fail to take advantage of our opportunities to prepare our genealogies, notwithstanding the Lord has very pointedly said that unless we take care of our temple work we will be rejected with our dead [see D&C 124:32]. This is a very serious thing. This is something that we cannot change, if we have wasted our opportunities until life passes. . . . We cannot expect others to do this work for us.

So, the Lord, in one way or another, encourages, advises, and counsels us to do our work. Some families who can't do the work themselves have someone else working all the time on their temple genealogy, and records.

If we do our part, our genealogies will be unfolded to us—sometimes in one way, sometimes in another. So I want to suggest to you, my brethren and sisters: let us do our part.[14] [See suggestion 4 on page 91.]

Suggestions for Study and Teaching

Consider these ideas as you study the chapter or as you prepare to teach. For additional help, see pages v–vii.

1. Read the excerpts from the dedicatory prayer of the Idaho Falls Idaho Temple on pages 82–83, and read D&C 109:1–5, 10–13 (from the dedicatory prayer of the Kirtland Temple). Ponder the feelings you have when you attend the temple, and think about the experiences that have strengthened your testimony that the temple is the house of the Lord.

2. What reasons does President Smith give for building temples (see pages 83–84)? What can we do to encourage young people to prepare to be married in the temple?

3. Read the story on page 86. What are some simple ways for someone with many other responsibilities to participate in family history work? What can priesthood quorums and Relief Societies do to participate?

4. Review the section that begins on page 88. How has the Lord helped you as you've tried to find information about your ancestors? What other blessings have you received as you have participated in family history work?

Related Scriptures: Malachi 4:5–6; Doctrine and Covenants 97:15–16; 110; 124:39–41; 128:9, 15–24.

Teaching help: When one person reads aloud from President Smith's teachings, invite the other class members to "listen and look for specific principles or ideas. If a passage contains unusual or difficult words or phrases, explain these before the passage is read. If anyone in the group might have difficulty reading, ask for volunteers instead of having them take turns" (*Teaching, No Greater Call,* 56).

Notes

1. In Conference Report, Apr. 1906, 57.

2. "Dedicatory Prayer . . . Idaho Falls Temple," *Improvement Era,* Oct. 1945, 564–65.

3. In *Deseret News,* Feb. 13, 1932, Church section, 7.

4. In Conference Report, Oct. 1950, 159.

5. "The Tenth Temple," *Improvement Era,* Oct. 1945, 561.

6. In Conference Report, Oct. 1905, 29.

7. "Priceless Prospects," *Improvement Era,* June 1950, 469.

8. "The Tenth Temple," 561, 602.

9. In Conference Report, Oct. 1929, 25.

10. "The Tenth Temple," 602.

11. "The Tenth Temple," 602.

12. "The Tenth Temple," 561, 602.

13. In Conference Report, Apr. 1937, 34–35.

14. "On Searching for Family Records," *Improvement Era,* Aug. 1946, 491, 540.

"It is a wonderful blessing that we enjoy . . . to feel sure of divine guidance, to have absolute faith in a personal God who is interested in us and who hears and answers our prayers."

Open Your Soul to the Lord in Prayer

*Through personal and family prayer,
we can feel Heavenly Father's influence
in our lives and in our homes.*

From the Life of George Albert Smith

Prayer was an important part of the home where George Albert Smith grew up. "Secret and family prayers were attended to by each member of the household," he said. "I learned quite early in life that the Lord would answer prayer for He answered mine and in many ways He gave me evidence of His watchful care."[1]

Even late in his life, President Smith remembered with fondness how his mother, Sarah Farr Smith, taught him to pray:

"I was trained at the knee of a Latter-day Saint mother. One of the first things I remember was when she took me by the hand and led me upstairs. In the room there were two beds, the bed in which my parents slept, and a little trundle bed over on the other side. I can remember it as if it were yesterday. When we got upstairs, she sat down by my little trundle bed. She had me kneel in front of her. She folded my hands and took them in hers, and taught me my first prayer. I will never forget it. I do not want to forget it. It is one of the loveliest memories that I have in life, an angelic mother sitting down by my bedside and teaching me to pray.

"It was such a simple prayer, but . . . that prayer opened for me the windows of heaven. That prayer extended to me the hand of my Father in heaven, for she had explained to me what it all meant as far as a little child could understand. From that day until now, while I have covered approximately a million miles in the world among our Father's other children, every day and every night, wherever

I have been, when I have gone to my bed or arisen from it, I have felt I was close to my Heavenly Father. He is not far away."[2]

Throughout his life, President Smith relied on prayer not only as a means of drawing nearer to God but also to ask Him for help in times of need. One day while swimming in the Pacific Ocean, off the coast of California, he had the following experience:

"I was considered a very good swimmer and thoroughly enjoyed the sport. This particular day the tide was very high and very swift. As I left the shore and swam out into the ocean, I dived through the big breakers as they would crest and spray over me. My objective was the large swells beyond the breakers, where I could lie on my back and ride the big swells up and down.

"While engaging in this interesting sport, one very huge wave crested and broke before I could right myself following the dive through the previous one. The second one caught me and threw me to the floor of the ocean. I could feel myself being dragged out by the undertow. At this particular time many waves came in rapid succession and I was not able to right myself before I had to dive from one into another. I realized that my strength was rapidly leaving me, that it was going to be necessary for me to find some means of help. As I rode to the crest of one huge wave, I saw the underpilings of a pier close at hand, and I thought if with superhuman effort I could reach the security of the pilings that I would be able to save my life.

"I silently asked my Heavenly Father to give me the strength to reach my objective. As I was washed into arm's length of the pier, I reached out and put my arms around one of the posts. They were covered with sharp dark blue barnacles, and as I wound my arms and legs around its security, they cut my chest, legs and thighs. I hung on as long as I could stand the pain and watched for a big friendly swell to come my way that I might throw myself on it and travel to a piling closer to shore. Each time with a prayer in my heart I would make the effort of traveling from one pile to another with the aid of the rolling swell.

"Slowly but surely and with great difficulty, I made my way to the shore where the water was shallow enough for me to walk to the beach. When I reached the safety of the warm sand, I fell, exhausted. I was so weak, so nearly drowned I was unable to walk home until I had rested some time. Lying on the sand with its warmth and security, I thought of the harrowing experience that I had just endured and my heart was filled with gratitude and humility that the Lord had . . . spared my life."[3] [See suggestion 1 on page 100.]

Teachings of George Albert Smith

Prayer allows us to talk to our Heavenly Father as though He were present.

It is a wonderful blessing that we enjoy in these times of stress and uncertainty to feel sure of divine guidance, to have absolute faith in a personal God who is interested in us and who hears and answers our prayers.[4]

A number of years ago . . . I heard of [a] nine-year-old boy, an orphan, who was hurried off to the hospital, where examination indicated that he had to be operated upon without delay. He had been living with friends who had given him a home. His father and mother, (when they were alive) had taught him to pray; thus, when he came to the hospital, the thing he wanted was to have the Lord help him.

The doctors had decided to hold a consultation. When he was wheeled into the operating room, he looked around and saw the nurses and the doctors who had consulted on his case. He knew that it was serious, and he said to one of them, as they were preparing to give him the anesthetic: "Doctor, before you begin to operate, won't you please pray for me?"

The doctor, with seeming embarrassment, offered his excuses and said, "I can't pray for you." Then the boy asked the other doctors, with the same result.

Finally, something very remarkable happened; this little fellow said, "If you can't pray for me, will you please wait while I pray for myself?"

They removed the sheet, and he knelt on the operating table, bowed his head and said, "Heavenly Father, I am only an orphan boy. I am awful sick. Won't you please make me well? Bless these men who are going to operate that they will do it right. If you will make me well, I will try to grow up to be a good man. Thank you, Heavenly Father, for making me well."

When he got through praying, he lay down. The doctors' and the nurses' eyes were filled with tears. Then he said, "I am ready."

The operation was performed. The little fellow was taken back to his room, and in a few days they took him from the hospital, well on the way to complete recovery.

Some days after that, a man who had heard of the incident went to the office of one of the surgeons and said, "Tell me about the operation you performed a few days ago—the operation on a little boy."

The surgeon said, "I have operated on several little boys."

The man added, "This little boy wanted someone to pray for him."

The doctor said very seriously, "There was such a case, but I don't know but that it is too sacred a thing for me to talk about."

The man said, "Doctor, if you will tell me, I will treat it with respect; I would like to hear it."

Then the doctor told the story about as I have retold it here, and added: "I have operated on hundreds of people, men and women who thought they had faith to be healed; but never until I stood over that little boy have I felt the presence of God as I felt it then. That boy opened the windows of heaven and talked to his Heavenly Father as one would talk to another face to face. I want to say to you that I am a better man for having had this experience of standing and hearing a little boy talk to his Father in heaven as if he were present."[5] [See suggestion 2 on page 100.]

Let us so live that every night when we kneel to pray and every morning when we bow before the Lord in thanksgiving, there will be in us the power to open the heavens so that God will hear and answer our prayers that we will know that we are approved of Him.[6]

"We should live so near to our Heavenly Father that when we bow before him we may know that the thing we are asking will be pleasing unto him."

If we live near to our Heavenly Father, we will be inspired to know what to pray for.

My father as a young man came [near to] losing his life in the Provo River. . . . His father, who was at Salt Lake City, felt impressed to go into a room that had been set apart for prayer. He . . . knelt down . . . and said, "Heavenly Father, I feel that there is something seriously wrong with my family in Provo. Thou knowest I can not be with them there and be here. Heavenly Father, wilt thou preserve and safeguard them. . . ."

At the time when he was praying, just as near as it was possible to indicate by checking the time, my father had fallen into the river. It was at flood time. Timbers and rocks were pouring down from the canyon, and he was helpless. Those who were near saw his predicament, but they couldn't reach him. The turbulence of the water was such that nobody could live in it. They just stood there in horror. Father was doing everything he could to keep his head above water, but he was being thrown up and down and banged against the rocks and logs. All at once a wave lifted him bodily from the water and threw him upon the shore. It was a direct answer to . . . prayer.[7]

We should attend to our secret prayers. We should live so near to our Heavenly Father that when we bow before him we may know that the thing we are asking will be pleasing unto him, and if it isn't granted in the way that we ask it we may know that the blessing will come to us that we are entitled to and that will really be a blessing.[8] [See suggestion 3 on page 101.]

Prayer is a powerful influence in our personal lives, our homes, and our communities.

The Lord . . . has explained to us how we may receive blessings through prayer. There are many people in the world who do not realize the real benefits of prayer. Prayer is a power. It has an influence that comparatively few people seem to understand. . . .

. . . How many are there in this Church who do not know that they have the right, the absolute right, to pray to their Father in heaven, and ask Him to take from them their distress and lead them to contentment and happiness?[9]

It is strange that any member of the Church of Jesus Christ of Latter-day Saints should have to be urged to say his prayers, and yet there are some people who do not pray in secret or have their family prayers. Yet unless we pray we lose the protection that prayer offers.[10] [See suggestion 4 on page 101.]

I would like to emphasize this: I hope that the Latter-day Saints will not fail to hold their prayers, their secret prayers and their family prayers. Children who are reared in homes where they do not have family prayers and secret prayers lose a lot, and I fear that in the midst of the world's confusion, of hurry and bustle, many times homes are left without prayer and without the blessings of the Lord; these homes cannot continue to be happy. We live in an age when

*"Safeguard your families in every possible way.
Unite them under the influence of prayer."*

we need our Heavenly Father as much as they ever needed Him in any age.[11]

Do not put away from you the power of God. Retain in your homes the influences of prayer and of thanksgiving, and let gratitude flow to him who is the author of our beings and the giver of all good.[12]

Let our homes be the abiding place of prayer and thanksgiving and gratitude. . . . Let us pray for the great men and women of the world who need the Lord but do not understand his interest in them. Pray for . . . our governors, our mayors of cities, the men who have influence in politics in our various communities, that they may do the things that will be better for all of us and make us happier, and please our Heavenly Father. That is our privilege. I say to you that the power of prayer is something that cannot be measured.[13]

Family prayer brings unity to families.

We [as family members] will not always see alike; men will not always reason as their wives do and vice versa, but if you will pray together, with a real desire to be united, I can say to you, you will agree on all important matters.

I noticed . . . on a billboard: "The family that prays together stays together." I do not know who placed it there, but I want to say that if you will think about it for a moment you will know that it is true. I admonish you to pray together to the Lord, and I do not mean by that to just say prayers, I do not mean to . . . repeat something over and over again, but open your souls to the Lord as husbands and fathers in your home, and have your wives and your children join you. Have them participate. There then comes into the home an influence that you can feel when you go there.[14]

As one of those whom the Lord has asked to teach, I plead with you to set your houses in order. Don't take too many things for granted. Don't be led into the follies and foibles of the world. Safeguard your families in every possible way. Unite them under the influence of prayer. . . . What a power prayer is to keep us in the pathway to eternal life and lead us into the celestial kingdom![15] [See suggestion 5 on page 101.]

Suggestions for Study and Teaching

Consider these ideas as you study the chapter or as you prepare to teach. For additional help, see pages v–vii.

1. In "From the Life of George Albert Smith" (pages 93–95), notice how President Smith's early experiences with prayer influenced him throughout his life. What are some effective ways to teach children about the power of prayer?

2. Review the story about the nine-year-old boy (pages 95–96). Why is it that our prayers sometimes don't feel like a face-to-face conversation with Heavenly Father? Consider what you can do in your personal prayers to feel His presence more often.

3. As you ponder President Smith's teachings on pages 97–98, think of a time when you felt prompted to ask for something in prayer. What would you say to someone who feels that his or her prayers have gone unanswered?

4. Consider President Smith's statement, "Unless we pray we lose the protection that prayer offers" (page 98). In what ways have you felt the power and protection of prayer? Consider sharing your testimony of the power of prayer with those you visit as a home teacher or visiting teacher.

5. President Smith taught that prayer will "keep us in the pathway to eternal life" (page 100). Why do you think this is so? What can families do to make sure they pray together consistently? Consider what you can do to make personal prayer a more meaningful part of your life.

Related Scriptures: Matthew 6:7–13; 7:7–11; 2 Nephi 4:35; Alma 34:18–27; 37:37; 3 Nephi 18:20–21; Doctrine and Covenants 88:63–64

Teaching help: "It is the pupil who has to be put into action. When a teacher takes the spotlight, becomes the star of the show, does all the talking, and otherwise takes over all of the activity, it is almost certain that he is interfering with the learning of the class members" (Asahel D. Woodruff, in *Teaching, No Greater Call,* 61).

Notes

1. "Testimony of Elder George Albert Smith," *Liahona: The Elders' Journal,* Feb. 2, 1915, 501.
2. In Conference Report, Oct. 1946, 150–51.
3. "How My Life Was Preserved," George Albert Smith Family Papers, University of Utah, box 121, scrapbook 1, pages 45–46.
4. In Conference Report, Apr. 1931, 31.
5. "A Story of Two Boys," *Improvement Era,* June 1949, 365.
6. In Conference Report, Apr. 1942, 17.
7. "Pres. Smith's Leadership Address," *Deseret News*, Feb. 16, 1946, Church section, 1.
8. In Conference Report, Oct. 1934, 51.
9. "Saints Blessed," *Deseret News,* Nov. 12, 1932, Church section, 5.
10. In Conference Report, Apr. 1941, 25.
11. Priesthood meeting, Oct. 4, 1947, archives of The Church of Jesus Christ of Latter-day Saints.
12. "Pres. Smith's Leadership Address," 6.
13. In Conference Report, Apr. 1948, 163–64.
14. In Conference Report, Apr. 1949, 190.
15. In Conference Report, Apr. 1933, 72.

"[The scriptures contain] what your Father and mine has thought of enough importance to preserve and give to the children of men and make accessible in many languages of the World."

The Scriptures, the Most Valuable Library in the World

*God has given us the holy scriptures to help us
and our families prepare for eternal life.*

From the Life of George Albert Smith

Late in his life, President George Albert Smith recalled an experience from his youth when a passage of scripture had a long-lasting effect on him: "When I was about fourteen years of age, I read the fortieth chapter of Alma in the Book of Mormon in our Sunday School class. It made an impression on my mind that has been helpful when death has taken loved ones away. . . . It is one place in the scriptures that tells us where our spirits go when they leave this body [see verses 11–14], and I have wanted to go to that place called paradise ever since."[1] [See suggestion 1 on page 109.]

President Smith hoped others would have their own meaningful experiences reading the scriptures. In his public discourses and his personal interactions with others, he encouraged everyone to study the scriptures as a way to build their own testimonies of the gospel. Once, while traveling by train, he started a conversation with a man who was raised in a Latter-day Saint family but was no longer participating in the Church. "As we visited," he later said, "I talked to him about the gospel of Jesus Christ. . . . And he said as we discussed the principles of the gospel, 'These things interest me.' We visited quite a long time, and when we finished, that good man, I believe he was a good man, said to me, 'I would give all that I possess to have the assurance that you have. . . .'

"I said, 'My brother, you don't have to give all that you possess to have that assurance. All you have to do is to search the scriptures prayerfully. Go where they may be explained to you. Seek the truth, and the beauty of the truth will appeal to you, and . . . you can know as I know that God lives, that Jesus is the Christ, that Joseph Smith is a prophet of the Living God.'"[2]

Teachings of George Albert Smith

The truths contained in the scriptures are far more valuable than the philosophies of men.

The Bible, Book of Mormon, Doctrine and Covenants, and Pearl of Great Price, do not contain the wisdom of men alone, but of God. While they do not find their way into the homes of many people, they contain the word of the Lord. What mattereth it, though we understand Homer and Shakespeare and Milton, and I might enumerate all the great writers of the world; if we have failed to read the scriptures we have missed the better part of this world's literature.

My brethren and sisters, all the truth that is . . . necessary for our salvation, is contained within the lids of the books that I have already enumerated. We may not possess a library of two or three thousand volumes, but we may possess at small cost a priceless library that has cost the best blood that has ever been in this world.[3]

I am not concerned whether or not you have the books of the great libraries of the world in your home, provided you do have these books. Think of the millions of volumes that there are in [the] Congressional Library at Washington, in the British Library, and in the libraries of other countries, millions of volumes—and yet all that God has revealed and published to the children of men that is necessary to prepare them for a place in the celestial kingdom is contained within the covers of these sacred books. How many of us know what they contain? I frequently go into homes where I see all the latest magazines. I find the books that are advertised as best sellers on the bookshelves. If you were to throw them all away and retain only these sacred scriptures, you wouldn't lose what the Lord has caused to be written and made available for us all to enjoy. So, brethren and sisters, among our other blessings let us not forget that the Lord has made it possible for us to have, enjoy, and understand the scriptures and to have his word that has been given down through the ages for the salvation of his children.[4]

As I read the scriptures, . . . I marvel at the goodness of the Lord to bless those who accept his teachings, for we find more comfort in these sacred records than in all the philosophies of the ages, as given to us by the wisdom of men.[5]

We talk about the philosophies of men and hold them up sometimes as a pretty picture, but when they conflict with the teachings of our Heavenly Father as contained in Holy Writ, they are valueless. They will never lead anybody into eternal happiness, nor help him to find a place in the kingdom of our Heavenly Father.[6]

I sometimes feel that we do not appreciate the Holy Bible, and what it contains, and these other scriptures, the Book of Mormon, the Doctrine and Covenants, and the Pearl of Great Price that have been referred to . . . as letters from our Heavenly Father. They may be so received, at least they are his advice and his counsel to all the children of men given to them that they may know how to take advantage of their opportunities, that their lives may not be spent in vain.[7] [See suggestion 2 on page 109.]

The Lord gave us the scriptures to help us overcome our trials and prepare for exaltation.

This is a day of proving ourselves, a day of trial. This is a day when men's hearts are failing them with fear. When the multitudes in the world are asking themselves what the end will be. A few inspired men know what the end will be. The Lord has told us what would occur, in [the scriptures], this wonderful library that I hold in my hand. He has given us the information that we need to adjust our lives and to prepare ourselves that no matter what may transpire we will be on the Lord's side of the line.[8]

Let me read what the Lord says with reference to these latter days in the first section of the Doctrine and Covenants: . . .

"Wherefore, I the Lord, knowing the calamity which should come upon the inhabitants of the earth, called upon my servant Joseph Smith, Jun., and spake unto him from heaven, and gave him commandments. . . .

"Search these commandments, for they are true and faithful, and the prophecies and promises which are in them shall all be fulfilled.

"What I the Lord have spoken, I have spoken, and I excuse not myself; and though the heavens and the earth pass away, my word shall not pass away, but shall all be fulfilled, whether by mine own voice or by the voice of my servants, it is the same.

"For behold, and lo, the Lord is God, and the Spirit beareth record, and the record is true, and the truth abideth forever and ever. Amen." [D&C 1:17, 37–39.]

This preface is worthy [of] your earnest consideration. It is the admonition of the Father of us all. It is the loving advice of a tender parent who knows what we require, as he said in the chapter just read that knowing what was about to come upon the inhabitants of the earth he gave these commandments.[9]

Sometimes we forget that the Lord has spoken and we fail to inform ourselves of His decrees. . . .

Dozens of passages in the scriptures could be cited as evidence that our Heavenly Father in mercy and kindness has been talking to the children of men all down through the ages, not only telling them what would occur, but pleading with them to turn from the error of their ways lest destruction should overtake them. . . .

Our Heavenly Father, through His faithful representatives, has told us of the important things that should occur and we can read about them in His holy scriptures. If we really desire to be saved and exalted in His celestial kingdom He has told us how to proceed.[10]

[The scriptures are] the greatest library to be found in all the world. What does it contain? It contains what your Father and mine has thought of enough importance to preserve and give to the children of men and make accessible in many languages of the World. These scriptures are all important and should be understood by the Latter-day Saints. I am not going to ask you to hold up your hands to ascertain how many here assembled have ever read these books, but I desire to call your attention to the fact that these are precious truths, and they contain the revealed word of the Lord printed and published to the world for the purpose of preparing his children for a place in the celestial kingdom. That is why I say they are so valuable. . . . How thankful we ought to be that we live in a day and age when we can read his advice and counsel and have things explained that otherwise might be obscure and uncertain to us.[11] [See suggestion 3 on page 109.]

We inspire faith in our families by reading the scriptures with them.

I would like you to ask yourselves, how many of you have read anything to your families out of these books from time to time, called them together to teach them the things that they ought to know. I am afraid many of us would have to say we have been too busy.[12]

We have already heard of many of the blessings that the Lord has given to us in the sacred records that have been kept until our day, and that contain the advice and counsel of an all-wise Father. It seems strange that so many of our people, with the opportunities offered, lack familiarity with the contents of these sacred records.[13]

Will our Father hold us guiltless when we go home, if we have failed to teach our children the importance of these sacred records? I think not. . . . Do you suppose that after the Lord has . . . placed within our reach the excellent teachings contained in these holy records, that he will consider us appreciative if we fail to teach them to our families, and to impress them upon those with whom we come in contact?

Brethren and sisters, I desire to emphasize again the teaching of the Master: "search the scriptures;" read them prayerfully and faithfully, teach them in your homes; call your families around you and inspire in them a faith in the living God, by reading those things that have been revealed. They are the most precious of all the libraries in all the world.[14]

Keep this library where you can find it, and where your children will find it, and then have enough interest in the eternal salvation of those boys and girls that are in your home that you will find ways and means to interest them in what these books contain, that they may know how precious they are in the sight of their Heavenly Father.[15]

"Call your families around you and inspire in them a faith in the living God, by reading those things that have been revealed."

What a lovely thing it was to me when I was a child to have father and mother sit down by the fireplace and read the Bible while we children sat on the floor. . . .

Now, I want to say, my brothers and sisters, that the advice of Jesus Christ, is still in force with us wherein he said, "Search the scriptures, for in them ye think ye have eternal life, and they are they which testify of me." [John 5:39.] Do not neglect the old family Bible; do not put it away upon the shelf and forget it. Find out, if you do not already know, what it says, and if you have read it before, read it again often to your children and to your children's children. Read them not only the Bible, but other books of scripture that the Lord has given us for our exaltation, for our comfort and for our blessing. [16]

I admonish you, O Israel, search the scriptures; read them in your homes; teach your families what the Lord has said, and let us spend less of our time reading the unimportant and often harmful literature of the day, and go to the fountain of truth and read the word of the Lord.[17] [See suggestion 4 below.]

Suggestions for Study and Teaching

Consider these ideas as you study the chapter or as you prepare to teach. For additional help, see pages v–vii.

1. As you read the first paragraph on page 103, think of a time when a verse of scripture has inspired you in a similar way. How did you come to know that the scriptures are true? What experiences have you had with them recently that have strengthened that testimony?

2. Read the section that begins on page 104 and consider what place the scriptures have in your personal library (among the other things you read, watch, or listen to). What can you do to give the scriptures a more prominent place in your home and in your life?

3. Review the section that begins on page 105. How have the scriptures helped you face the calamities of the last days? Consider how you might use the scriptures to help someone you know who is facing a difficult trial.

4. Ponder President Smith's counsel to families on pages 107–9. What blessings come to families who study the scriptures together? What are some effective ways to inspire our children's (or grandchildren's) interest in the scriptures? Prayerfully consider what you can do to be more diligent in studying the scriptures with your family.

Related Scriptures: Deuteronomy 6:6–7; Joshua 1:8; Romans 15:4; 2 Timothy 3:15–17; 2 Nephi 4:15; Helaman 3:29–30; Doctrine and Covenants 33:16

Teaching help: "You can help those you teach feel more confident about their ability to participate in a discussion if you respond positively to every sincere comment. For example, you might say, 'Thank you for your answer. That was very thoughtful' . . . or 'That is a good example' or 'I appreciate all that you have said today'" (*Teaching, No Greater Call,* 64).

Notes

1. In Conference Report, Apr. 1949, 83–84.

2. In Conference Report, Oct. 1948, 165–66.

3. In Conference Report, Oct. 1917, 43.

4. In Conference Report, Oct. 1948, 164–65.

5. In Conference Report, Oct. 1931, 120.

6. In Conference Report, Apr. 1946, 125.

7. In Conference Report, Oct. 1923, 70.

8. In Conference Report, Apr. 1942, 14.

9. In Conference Report, Oct. 1917, 42–43.

10. In Conference Report, Oct. 1940, 107–9.

11. In Conference Report, Oct. 1948, 164.

12. In Conference Report, Oct. 1950, 179.

13. In Conference Report, Apr. 1929, 30.

14. In Conference Report, Oct. 1917, 43–44.

15. In Conference Report, Oct. 1948, 165.

16. "Pres. Smith's Leadership Address," *Deseret News,* Feb. 16, 1946, Church section, 6.

17. In Conference Report, Oct. 1917, 41.

CHAPTER 11

Revelation from God to His Children

Our Heavenly Father guides us individually
and as a Church through the Holy Ghost.

From the Life of George Albert Smith

To teach about the importance of revelation to guide the Church, George Albert Smith told of an experience he had on an airplane flight from Los Angeles, California, to Salt Lake City, Utah:

"Near Milford, Utah, we suddenly flew into one of the worst fogs I have ever seen. I tried to look out of the window of the plane but could not see anything through the fog. Not a thing could be seen in any direction outside the plane.

"I knew that we were approaching the mountains at the approximate rate of three miles a minute, that we were compelled to pass over them to get into the Salt Lake Valley. I was worried and asked myself, 'How can the pilot find the way when he cannot see a thing?' He had his compass but the plane might drift off its course. He had instruments indicating our distance above sea level but he had no way of knowing how far we were from the ground. I thought he might fly high enough to clear the mountains between us and the Salt Lake Valley and try to find the landing field by the flash of the beacons if we got close enough, but I chilled when I thought of the danger of losing our way and missing the beacons and the airport.

"In my anxiety I went up into the space that was occupied by the pilot and the co-pilot to see how they knew where we were going. I could not tell whether we were a hundred feet, a thousand feet or ten thousand feet above the ground and I did not know how they could tell, except approximately. I noticed that the pilot had a little

111

George Albert Smith and his wife, Lucy. President Smith used an experience he had on an airplane to teach about the importance of revelation.

device over his ear like operators in telephone offices use to receive with. I inquired of the co-pilot how they could tell whether we were flying in the right direction or know if we were off course. He replied, 'When we cannot see we are guided by the radio beam.'

" 'What is that?' I asked. He explained that the beam might be likened to an electric highway between two points, and in our case the points were Milford and Salt Lake City. He said that the device over the pilot's ear operated so that when the plane was in the beam a low, purring sound continued to be heard, but if the plane goes to the right or left the sound changes and the pilot is warned by clicking as of a telegraph key. If he . . . pulls back to the beam or highway, on to the path of safety, the clicking ceases and the purring resumes. If we continue on the beam we will arrive at our destination in safety.

"I returned to my seat greatly comforted to know that notwithstanding we were enveloped in fog and darkness and could neither see nor feel where we were, the pilot was receiving information constantly that we were on the highway and he knew that we would soon arrive at our destination. A few minutes later I felt the plane descending. We had passed over the mountain tops and were nearing the airport. When we were nearly down we could see the powerful lights of the field indicating where to land and the plane with its precious cargo touched the ground gently as a seagull lights on water, slowly came to a stop and we stepped from our conveyance to the ground, happy to be at home again. . . .

"I have thought many times of the lesson I learned on the plane and have applied it to experience in the Church of Jesus Christ of Latter-day Saints. . . .

"Not only has the Lord given us the advice already recorded in the scriptures to guide us but he has placed a leader in this Church, one of his sons who has been chosen and ordained and set apart to be the President. He is our pilot and he will be directed by a voice that will enable him to lead us where we should go. If we are wise we will not set up our judgment against him but will be happy to honor him in his place as long as the Lord sustains him."

President Smith also used his experience on the airplane to teach that each of us can receive revelation to guide our own lives if we are worthy:

"If we are living as we know that we should we are entitled to the whispering of a still small voice calling attention to danger, saying this is the pathway of safety, walk ye in it. . . . If we have erred in our conduct the voice will whisper to us 'turn back, you have made a mistake; you have disregarded the advice of your Heavenly Father.' Turn from the error of your way while there is yet time, for if you go too far from the right path you will not hear the voice and you may be hopelessly lost. . . .

"My advice to you is to get the Spirit of God and keep it and the only way we will retain it is by living near him, by keeping his commandments. . . . Listen to the still small voice that will always direct you if you are worthy of it in a path that means eternal happiness."[1] [See suggestion 1 on page 120.]

Teachings of George Albert Smith

God manifests Himself to His children in our day just as He has done in ages past.

What a privilege it is to live in an age of the world when we know that God lives, when we know that Jesus Christ is the Savior of the world and our Redeemer, and when we know that the Lord continues to manifest himself to his children who have prepared themselves to receive his blessings! I am looking into the faces of a great audience this morning [at a session of general conference], most of whom enjoy the inspiration of the Almighty, and when they pray, they pray to their Father in heaven knowing that their prayers will be answered in blessings upon their heads. . . . We know there is a God in heaven, that he is our Father, that he does interest himself in our affairs, and he has done that ever since the world began, when his first children were placed upon the earth.[2]

The distinction between this great Church and that of all other churches from the beginning has been that we believe in divine revelation; we believe that our Father speaks to man today as he has done from the time of Adam. We believe and we know—which is more than mere belief—that our Father has set his hand in this world for the salvation of the children of men.[3]

It is not only because we have faith in these books [the Book of Mormon, the Doctrine and Covenants, and the Pearl of Great Price] that we are considered a peculiar people but also because we confidently believe that our Father in heaven has spoken in this day and age. In fact, we know that there is communication with the heavens. We believe that Jehovah has the same feeling towards us, the same influence over us that he had for and over his children who lived in this world in times that are past.

By the unbeliever, the members of the Church of Jesus Christ in all ages of the world have been considered a peculiar people. When the Lord has spoken through his servants, there have been at different periods of time many people in the earth who have said, "I do not believe in revelation." This age is no exception to the rule. The thousands, yes, the millions, of our Father's children who live in the earth are but repeating the history of the past when they deny that God has revealed again his will to the children of men, and say that they have no need of any further revelation.[4]

We do not believe that the heavens are sealed over our heads, but that the same Father who loved and cherished the children of Israel loves and cherishes us. We believe that we are as much in need of the assistance of our Heavenly Father in the directing of our lives as they were. We know that in the day and age in which we live the seal has been broken, and God has again spoken from the heavens.[5] [See suggestion 2 on page 120.]

The Lord guides His people through revelation to the President of the Church.

The Church of Jesus Christ of Latter-day Saints was organized by direct commandment from our Heavenly Father. Upon the rock of revelation this Church was founded and by revelation it has been guided.[6]

It is unique these days to belong to a church, wherein those who are members believe that the Lord speaks through their leaders. When we are instructed by the President of this Church, we believe he tells us what the Lord would have us do. To us it is something more than just the advice of man. We believe that, and it searches our souls, and we are prompted to renew our determination to be what God would have us be.[7]

We have had misguided souls in the Church who have, in their ignorance, opposed the advice of the [President of the Church], not sensing the fact that they were opposing the Lord and they have fallen into darkness and sorrow, and unless they repent they will not find a place in the celestial kingdom.

Let us remember that the President of this Church has been officially designated as the pilot of the Church here in mortality to represent the Master of heaven and earth.[8]

When men, as they have sometimes done in order to win their success along some line or another, have come to an individual or individuals and said, "I have had this dream and this is what the Lord wants us to do," you may know that they are not on the Lord's side of the line. The dreams and visions and revelations of God to the children of men have always come through his regularly appointed servant. You may have dreams and manifestations for your own comfort or for your own satisfaction, but you will not have them for the Church. . . . We need not be deceived.[9]

My soul is filled with gratitude this day to know that as we continue our membership in the Church we do have a pilot who knows the way, and if we will follow his direction . . . we will not meet the spiritual disasters that the world is meeting but we will go about doing good, blessing mankind, and rejoicing in the companionship of those we love.[10] [See suggestion 3 on page 120.]

We are each entitled to personal inspiration from the Holy Ghost if we obey the commandments.

I believe in you, my brethren and sisters. . . . You are entitled to the same knowledge that he is who presides over the Church. You are entitled to the same inspiration that flows to those whom God has caused to be ordained as His leaders. You are entitled to the inspiration of the Spirit, and the knowledge that He is your

"Each of us is entitled to the inspiration of the Lord in proportion to the manner in which we live a godly life."

Father, and when I say "you" I speak of all those who have obeyed the commandments of our Father, and have partaken of the sweet influence of the Spirit of the Lord in the Church of Christ. . . . Each of us is entitled to the inspiration of the Lord in proportion to the manner in which we live a godly life.[11]

Go where you will, you will find no other group assembled, each of whom has faith in God; and if we were to ask all of you how many have a testimony, not a belief because somebody else has said so, but how many of you have an assurance that this is God's work, that Jesus is the Christ, that we are living eternal lives, that Joseph Smith was a prophet of the Living God, you would answer that you have this testimony that buoys you up and strengthens you and gives you satisfaction as you go forward in the world. . . .

. . . I learned when I was a boy that this is the work of the Lord. I learned that there were prophets living upon the earth. I learned that the inspiration of the Almighty would influence those who lived to enjoy it, so we are not dependent upon one or two or a half dozen individuals. There are thousands of members of this Church who know—it is not a question of imagination at all—they know that God lives and that Jesus is the Christ and that we are the children of God.[12]

You are not dependent alone upon history, nor upon the teachings of any man, to know that this is the work of the Lord, because you have had it burned into your souls by the gift of the Holy Ghost. There is no doubt in your mind as to your origin, nor as to the place you will go to when this life is over, if you are faithful to the trust reposed in you.[13]

A testimony cannot be given to us by somebody else. The conviction comes from our Heavenly Father.[14]

I stand here today profoundly grateful for the knowledge that has come to me. I am thankful that I am not dependent upon any individual for the testimony that I possess. Of course, I am grateful for the encouragement I received from others who possess light and truth, and who give encouragement by lives of righteousness, but I do not depend on any of them for a knowledge that God lives, that Jesus Christ is the Redeemer of mankind and Joseph Smith is a prophet of the Lord. These things I know for myself.

. . . I rejoice to testify that I know the gospel is true, and with all my soul I thank my Heavenly Father that he has revealed it to me.[15]

Of all the blessings that have come to me in life the most precious is the knowledge that God lives and that this is his work, because that comprehends all other blessings that I may hope to enjoy in this life or in the life that is to come.[16] [See suggestion 4 on page 120.]

The Holy Ghost is a safe guide along the pathway of mortal life.

The companionship of [God's] Spirit . . . is a safe guide along the pathway of mortal life and a sure preparation for a home in his celestial kingdom.[17]

We read in Job that there is a spirit in man, and the inspiration of the Almighty giveth him understanding [see Job 32:8]. If we keep the commandments of God we are entitled to that inspiration, and if we live as the sons of God ought to live, we will have that inspiration, and nobody can prevent it, and the result will be our own physical and mental and moral development in mortality, and continued development throughout the ages of eternity. [18]

The companionship of the spirit of the Lord is an antidote for weariness, . . . for fear and all those things that sometimes overtake us in life. [19]

When the disciples of the Savior were with him they admired him not knowing how great he really was, but not until the power of the Holy Ghost came upon them, not until they had the baptism of fire were they able to face the problems and endure the persecutions that almost made life unendurable. When the inspiration of the Almighty gave them understanding they knew they were living [an] eternal life, and if they proved faithful they knew that when they laid their bodies down in death they would be raised from the tomb to glory and immortality.

That was the result of the inspiration of the Spirit of God that came upon them, the inspiration of the Almighty that gave them understanding. . . .

I pray that that Spirit which keeps us in the pathway of truth and righteousness may abide with us, and I pray that that desire that comes from the inspiration of our Heavenly Father may direct us on that pathway of life. [20]

When life's labor is complete may we find that we have listened to the whispering of that still, small voice that always guides us in the path of righteousness, and know that it has meant for us the opening of the door to the Celestial kingdom, for ourselves and those we love, to go forward throughout the ages, . . . happy eternally. [21] [See suggestion 5 on page 120.]

Suggestions for Study and Teaching

Consider these ideas as you study the chapter or as you prepare to teach. For additional help, see pages v–vii.

1. As you read "From the Life of George Albert Smith" (pages 111–14), consider how President Smith's analogy applies to our journey through mortality. What could the fog, the radio beam, and the clicking sound represent? How has the Lord warned you of danger and helped you stay on the path to eternal life?

2. On pages 114–15, President Smith declares that revelation is as necessary today as it was in biblical times. How would you respond to someone who says the revelations in the scriptures are sufficient for our day? What experiences have taught you that Heavenly Father "does interest himself in our affairs"?

3. Review the section that begins on page 115. How have you come to know that the counsel of the prophet comes from the Lord and is "more than just the advice of man"? (page 116). How can personal revelation help you accept and apply revelation given through the prophet?

4. As you study the section that begins on page 116, think about how you gained a testimony of the gospel. How did the testimonies of others help you? What did you do to come to know the truth for yourself?

5. In the last section of teachings (pages 118–19), look for words and phrases that describe ways the Holy Ghost can help us. Consider what you can do to be worthy of the companionship of the Holy Ghost more often in your life.

Related Scriptures: John 15:26; 1 Nephi 10:17–19; 2 Nephi 32:5; Moroni 10:3–5; Doctrine and Covenants 1:38; 42:61; 76:5–10; Articles of Faith 1:9

Teaching help: "Do not be concerned if learners are silent for a few seconds after you have asked a question. Do not answer your own question; allow time for learners to think of responses. However, prolonged silence may indicate that they do not understand the question and that you need to rephrase it" (*Teaching, No Greater Call,* 69).

Notes

1. In Conference Report, Oct. 1937, 50–53.
2. In Conference Report, Apr. 1946, 4.
3. In Conference Report, Apr. 1917, 37.
4. "Some Points of 'Peculiarity,'" *Improvement Era,* Mar. 1949, 137.
5. In *Proceedings at the Dedication of the Joseph Smith Memorial Monument,* 55.
6. "Message to Sunday School Teachers," *Instructor,* Nov. 1946, 501.
7. In Conference Report, Oct. 1930, 66.
8. In Conference Report, Oct. 1937, 52–53.
9. In Conference Report, Oct. 1945, 118–19.
10. In Conference Report, Oct. 1937, 53.
11. In Conference Report, Oct. 1911, 44.
12. In Conference Report, Apr. 1946, 124–25.
13. In Conference Report, Apr. 1905, 62.
14. "Opportunities for Leadership," *Improvement Era,* Sept. 1949, 557.
15. In Conference Report, Oct. 1921, 42.
16. In Conference Report, Apr. 1927, 82.
17. "To the Latter-day Saints Everywhere," *Improvement Era,* Dec. 1947, 797.
18. In Conference Report, Apr. 1944, 31.
19. In Conference Report, Oct. 1945, 115–16.
20. In Conference Report, Apr. 1939, 124–25.
21. In Conference Report, Apr. 1941, 28.

"It is the Gospel of Jesus Christ that we bear. It is the desire to save the souls of the children of men that burns in our hearts."

An Enthusiastic Desire to Share the Gospel

*Our brothers and sisters throughout the world
need the message of the restored gospel, and
it is our privilege to share it with them.*

From the Life of George Albert Smith

A close friend of George Albert Smith wrote: "President George Albert Smith is a natural missionary. From his youth he has had an ardent desire to share the teachings of the gospel with his fellow men, to make known to 'the sons and daughters of God,' all of whom he considers to be his brothers and sisters, the truths that were revealed to the Prophet Joseph Smith.

"On several occasions I have had the privilege of traveling on the train with President Smith. Each time I observed that as soon as the journey was well underway, he would take a few gospel tracts from his bag, put them into his pocket, and then move about among the passengers. In his friendly, agreeable manner he would soon make the acquaintance of a fellow traveler, and in a short time I would hear him relating the story of the founding of the Church by the Prophet Joseph Smith or telling of the exodus of the Saints from Nauvoo and their trials and difficulties in crossing the plains to Utah or explaining some of the gospel principles to his new-found friend. Conversation after conversation would follow with one passenger after another until the journey was ended. In my entire acquaintance with President Smith, which has extended more than forty years, I have learned that wherever he is, he is first and foremost a missionary for the Church of Jesus Christ of Latter-day Saints."[1]

It was also written of President Smith: "He would talk religion with a chimneysweep who was working at his home. Seldom did he miss an opportunity to explain the 'eternal truths of the restored gospel' to either friend or stranger. From his point of view, this was the ultimate kindness, for the message of Christ was the most significant gift he had to give."[2] [See suggestion 1 on page 132.]

Because sharing the gospel was a topic that President Smith addressed often in his teachings, this is the first of three chapters on the subject in this book. This chapter focuses on the reasons we share the gospel; chapter 13 presents several ways in which we can participate in this important work; and chapter 14 describes how we can be most effective in our efforts.

Teachings of George Albert Smith

The world needs what we have—the gospel of Jesus Christ, restored in its fulness.

The world is in distress, in travail, from one end of it to the other. Men and women are looking here and there, seeking where they shall go to do the things that will bring them peace. . . . The gospel of Jesus Christ has been restored. The truth revealed from heaven is here and it is that truth, that gospel, which, if the world only knew it, will be a panacea for all their ills. It is the only thing that will bring them peace while they remain upon the earth.[3]

There is need for the people of this world to retrace their steps and get back to the foundation that was laid by the Master of heaven and earth, the foundation of faith, repentance and baptism by immersion for the remission of sins, and the reception of the Holy Ghost under the hands of those possessing divine authority. That is what the world needs. I am grateful indeed that many are looking that way. They have been going blindly along a pathway that has led to sorrow and distress, but there has been placed within reach a remedy for all ills—the gospel of Jesus Christ. There has been mapped out for all a path that, while it is narrow, and difficult to follow, leads back to the Father of us all; and there is no other path that leads there.[4]

The churches of the world are trying, in their way, to bring peace into the hearts of men. They are possessed of many virtues and many truths, and accomplish much good, but they are not divinely authorized. Neither have their priests been divinely commissioned.[5]

The Latter-day Saints are the only ones who bear the authority of our Heavenly Father to administer in the ordinances of the Gospel. The world has need of us.[6]

There is a real famine in the world for the words of the Lord, and many honest souls are earnestly seeking to know what our Heavenly Father desires of them. I have met a number of the leaders of the churches of the world, and have found among them noble characters devoted to doing good, but I have rarely found among those who have been called to the ministry in the various church organizations, men who have an understanding of the purposes of their being, or who realize why we are here in the world. Men cannot teach what they do not themselves know. These good men, not understanding the gospel and the necessity for the ordinances of the same, confine their teachings very largely to moral lessons and to reading the psalms to their congregations. Isolated passages of scripture are chosen as texts for addresses on virtue, honesty, etc., all of which are helpful and uplifting, but few sermons are preached explaining the requirements made of every soul before we can enter the kingdom of heaven. It is this information of which the world is most in need. Few ministers have a message for their congregations that inspires in them the belief in the divinity of Jesus Christ and the necessity of partaking of the ordinances of the gospel prescribed by him.[7] [See suggestion 2 on page 132.]

There are many people who would embrace the truth if given the opportunity.

Our Father's children everywhere are anxious to know what they should do, but, by reason of the evil influences that have pervaded the earth, they have been deceived; honorable men of the earth are blinded to the truth. . . . The adversary is at work, and the only power that can neutralize his influence is the gospel of Jesus Christ.[8]

People have been suspicious of one another. They have not believed what they have heard, and they have not been willing to do as Philip, one of the disciples of the Savior, recommended to Nathanael who was visiting with him. Philip said, "The Lord has come."

And he described him and Nathanael asked, "Where did he come from?"

And Philip answered, "Why, he came from Nazareth." And then the good man said, "Can any good thing come out of Nazareth?" Philip said, "Come and see." (See John 1:43–46.)

Nathanael had been taught to believe that no good could come from Nazareth, and yet he was the man whom the Savior later referred to as an Israelite without guile—a good man, but deceived because of the stories that he had heard.

But when he once learned, when he had accepted the invitation of the disciples to "Come and see," he came to see.

We have had great joy under the influence of His Spirit. We would like everybody to enjoy that blessing, and so when they have asked, "What kind of people are these here?" our answer has been, "Come and see."[9]

My Heavenly Father . . . has called me to go to many parts of the earth, and more than a million miles have been traversed since I was called into the ministry. I have traveled in many lands and climes, and wherever I have gone I have found good people, sons and daughters of the living God who are waiting for the gospel of Jesus Christ, and there are thousands, hundreds of thousands, millions of them, who would be accepting the truth if they only knew what we know.[10]

There are many great church organizations in the world, many devout men and women living according to the will of our Heavenly Father as they understand it. . . .

All men who will live up to the light that the Lord has offered to them and seek him in earnest prayer will have their hearts touched, their minds will be influenced, and opportunity will be offered to them to know that God has spoken again.[11] [See suggestion 3 on page 132.]

"It is the Gospel of Jesus Christ that we bear. . . . And those who believe will follow the pattern given by the Savior when He said to His disciples, 'He that believeth and is baptized shall be saved.'"

We are enthusiastic about sharing the gospel because we love our neighbors.

Perhaps it might appear to the outside observer that there is among the Latter-day Saints an unusual enthusiasm. As one man recently said: "It is strange to me how joyfully you people carry your work forward. It matters not whether I speak to a youth or to a mature man, to a gardener or a policeman among your people, they are all happy and satisfied and confident that they possess the gospel of Jesus Christ." . . .

. . . Is it any wonder that there is enthusiasm in our worship, that we have a disposition to be anxious to divide these glorious truths with our neighbors? Is it to be wondered at, that when the time comes that our sons are called into the mission field, or we are asked to lay aside our duties and go out as servants of the living God, endued with power from on high, possessing authority that has been conferred in this latter-day, in order that we may divide with all people this wonderful truth that has made our lives so rich, . . . that we respond willingly and gladly?[12]

It is the Gospel of Jesus Christ that we bear. It is the desire to save the souls of the children of men that burns in our hearts. It is not that we may build ourselves up and become a mighty people financially; it is not that we may have our names glorified in the earth for our accomplishments; but it is that the sons and daughters of God, wherever they may be, may hear this Gospel, which is the power of God unto salvation to all those who believe and obey its precepts. And those who believe will follow the pattern given by the Savior when He said to His disciples, "He that believeth and is baptized shall be saved; but he that believeth not shall be damned." [Mark 16:16.][13]

Think of the responsibility that is upon us, if in carelessness or indifference we live our lives, not seeking to divide the truth with those whom the Lord loves as much as he loves us, and who are precious in his sight. I feel that there should be an awakening among some of the members of this Church. I think a greater effort should be made to divide with our Father's children all the truth that is deposited with this Church.[14]

When a man is sick, if he is our neighbor, we minister to him gladly; if there is a death in his family, we try to comfort him. But year in and year out we allow him to walk in paths that will destroy his opportunity for eternal life, we pass him by, as if he were a thing of naught.[15]

Do we realize that every man is in the image of God and is a son of God, and every woman his daughter? No matter where they may be, they are his children, and he loves them and desires their salvation. Surely as members of this Church we cannot sit idly by. We cannot receive the beneficent favor of our Heavenly Father that is bestowed upon us, the knowledge of eternal life, and selfishly retain it, thinking that we may be blessed thereby. It is not what we receive that enriches our lives, it is what we give.[16]

Let us be sufficiently interested in the salvation of men to exercise a holy zeal for their conversion: that we may enjoy their eternal gratitude and love, and the appreciation of our Heavenly Father, because of our unselfish interest in His children. [17]

Our mission to our Father's children . . . is a mission of peace, of good will towards all men. It is an intense and enthusiastic desire to divide with all our Father's children the good things that he has so generously bestowed upon us; and it is with the hope that they may understand, that we go upon our bended knees, day after day, and pray that their hearts may be touched, that the spirit of God may come into their souls, that they may understand the truth as it is given unto them. [18]

O that this great Church, with the power that has been given to it of God, might be able to more rapidly disseminate the truth, and save the nations from destruction. We are growing rapidly, as an organization, but I rejoice not so much in the increase numerically as I do in the belief that the influence that we radiate is being felt for good and that our Father's children, from the north to the south, and from the east to the west, are hearing the message of life and salvation, without which they cannot dwell in the presence of the Redeemer of mankind. [19] [See suggestion 4 on page 133.]

The Lord will hold us accountable for our efforts to share the gift of the gospel.

We have received a wonderful gift, but with that gift comes a great responsibility. We have been blessed of the Lord with a knowledge beyond our fellows, and with that knowledge comes the requirement that we divide it with His children wherever they may be. [20]

Now, I do not understand that we are serving God with all our might if we forsake his children, or if we spend so much of our time selfishly building up ourselves, accumulating things of this life, and leave his children in darkness, when we could bring them into the light. My understanding is that the most important mission that I have in this life is: first, to keep the commandments of God, as they have been taught to me; and next, to teach them to my Father's children who do not understand them. [21]

There is no other Gospel of salvation, and we, my brethren who bear the holy priesthood, have the responsibility of carrying that message, not only to the nations of the earth, but of exemplifying it in our lives and teaching it to those who are our neighbors, not of our faith. I warn you this day that the Lord holds us responsible to call His children to repentance and for the promulgation of His truth. If we fail to take advantage of our opportunities to teach the sons and daughters of God, who are not of our faith, who dwell in our midst, this Gospel of our Lord, He will require at our hands on the other side of the veil what we have failed to do.[22]

After awhile we will have to meet our record, and if we have been faithful, I am sure the Father of us all in the world will thank us and bless us for bringing so many of his sons and daughters to an understanding of the purpose of life and how to enjoy it under the influence of his spirit.[23]

When we have the spirit of the gospel our desire is that we may be able to teach just as many of our Father's children as it is possible for us to reach, the glorious truths that are necessary for their exaltation; that when the time comes that we shall stand in the presence of the Redeemer of mankind, that we may be able to say to him: "With such power as thou gavest me, with such wisdom and knowledge as thou has given unto me, I have sought in tenderness and with love unfeigned, and with determination and with kindness to bring as many of thy children unto a knowledge of the gospel as it has been possible for me to do."[24] [See suggestion 5 on page 133.]

If we share the gospel with God's children, our reward will be great joy with them in the celestial kingdom.

We spend most of our time, many of us, seeking the things of this life that we will be compelled to leave when we go from here, yet there are the immortal souls all around us whom, if we would, we could teach and inspire to investigate the truth, and implant in their hearts a knowledge that God lives. What treasure in all the world could be so precious to us, for we would have their gratitude here and their everlasting and eternal appreciation in the world to come. It is a most important mission.[25]

Think what it will mean if, instead of having been selfish trying to save only our own little family, we can count by the dozens and

"When we have the spirit of the gospel our desire is that we may be able to teach just as many of our Father's children as it is possible for us to reach."

by the hundreds men and women that we have influenced to accept the Gospel of our Lord. Then will we feel blessed indeed and enjoy their love and appreciation forever. [26]

What a joy it will be on the other side of the veil, to find these good men and women who are living up to such light as they have, trying to do their duty to God, and by reason of our contact, by reason of our anxiety and willingness to share with them, they will receive other information about the gospel of our Lord and accept the ordinances of His Holy House and be prepared for membership in the Celestial Kingdom. How happy it will make you, if when that time comes, when you stand in the presence of the great Judge to give an account of the few years of life that have been spent in mortality, if these our Father's children that He loves as much as He loves us, standing by us, say, "Heavenly Father, it was this man, it was this woman who first brought to me the information of Thy glorious truth that provoked in me a desire to seek after Thee more fervently than I had done before. It was this man or this woman who did this blessed thing for me." And that is not all.

When that time comes, when you go down through the ages of eternity, that is a long time, you will have the love and the gratitude of every man, woman and child to whom you have been instrumental in bringing eternal happiness. Isn't that worth while? We may spend our lives here and acquire a few hundreds or thousands of dollars, we may have flocks, herds, houses and lands, but we cannot take these with us to the other side. They are not necessary to eternal life, they are only necessary for us here, but if we have earned the gratitude and the love of God's other children, that will flow to us forever. Think what that will mean! When the time comes that this world shall be cleansed and purified by fire and becomes the celestial kingdom, all impurity, and everything that is not desirable having been swept away how gratifying it will be to find that we have companionship with those we have served in mortality, have inheritance with, and be directed by Jesus Christ our Lord forever—is not that worth while? Isn't it a joyful opportunity?[27] [See suggestion 6 on page 133.]

Suggestions for Study and Teaching

Consider these ideas as you study the chapter or as you prepare to teach. For additional help, see pages v–vii.

1. Review "From the Life of George Albert Smith" (pages 123–24). Why do you think President Smith was so enthusiastic about missionary work? What does it mean to you to be "first and foremost a missionary for the Church"?

2. What does the restored gospel offer the world in addition to the "moral lessons" offered in most religions? (For some examples, see pages 124–25.)

3. Read the section that begins on page 125 (see also D&C 123:12). What examples have you seen of people overcoming misconceptions about the Church by accepting the invitation to "come and see"? What are some effective ways to extend such an invitation?

4. Read the last two full paragraphs on page 128. Why do you think we are sometimes reluctant to share the gospel with our neighbors? As you study pages 127–29, think about what we can do to overcome that reluctance.

5. As you read the section that begins on page 129, ponder whether you are doing what the Lord expects you to do to share the gospel. Prayerfully consider how you might keep this commandment more fully.

6. Review the last section of teachings (pages 130–32) and think about the person who first introduced you or your family to the restored gospel of Jesus Christ. What can you do to show or express your gratitude to that person?

Related Scriptures: Amos 8:11–12; Mosiah 28:1–3; Alma 26:28–30; Doctrine and Covenants 4:4; 18:10–16

Teaching help: "It's better to take just a few good ideas and get good discussion—and good learning—than to be frenzied, trying to teach every word in the manual. . . . An unrushed atmosphere is absolutely essential if you are to have the Spirit of the Lord present in your class" (Jeffrey R. Holland, "Teaching and Learning in the Church," *Ensign,* June 2007, 91).

Notes

1. Preston Nibley, "Sharing the Gospel with Others," *Improvement Era,* Apr. 1950, 270.
2. Merlo J. Pusey, *Builders of the Kingdom* (1981), 240.
3. In Conference Report, June 1919, 43.
4. In Conference Report, Apr. 1922, 54–55.
5. In Conference Report, Apr. 1922, 53.
6. In Conference Report, Apr. 1916, 47.
7. In Conference Report, Oct. 1921, 38.
8. In Conference Report, Apr. 1922, 53.
9. In Conference Report, Oct. 1949, 5.
10. In Conference Report, Oct. 1945, 120.
11. In Conference Report, Apr. 1935, 43–44.
12. In Conference Report, Oct. 1927, 46–47.
13. In *Proceedings at the Dedication of the Joseph Smith Memorial Monument,* 55.
14. In Conference Report, Apr. 1934, 28.
15. In Conference Report, Oct. 1916, 50.
16. In Conference Report, Apr. 1935, 46.
17. "Greeting," *Millennial Star,* July 10, 1919, 441.
18. In Conference Report, Oct. 1927, 49.
19. In Conference Report, Oct. 1922, 98.
20. In Conference Report, Apr. 1922, 53.
21. In Conference Report, Oct. 1916, 50.
22. In Conference Report, Apr. 1916, 48.
23. In Conference Report, Oct. 1948, 7–8.
24. In *Deseret News,* Aug. 20, 1921, Church section, 7.
25. In Conference Report, Oct. 1916, 50.
26. In Conference Report, Oct. 1941, 102.
27. *Sharing the Gospel with Others,* sel. Preston Nibley (1948), 214–16; address given Nov. 4, 1945, in Washington, D.C.

*George Albert Smith served as president of the European Mission
from 1919 to 1921.*

CHAPTER 13

Doing Our Part to Share the Gospel

There are many ways we can participate in the great work of sharing the restored gospel of Jesus Christ.

From the Life of George Albert Smith

In addition to serving nearly 48 years as a General Authority, George Albert Smith served three full-time missions for the Church, including two years as president of the European Mission. He encouraged Church members to prepare spiritually for full-time missionary service and to accept such calls when they come. But he also taught them that they need not receive a formal mission call in order to preach the gospel. George Albert Smith was a missionary throughout his life, and he often reminded Church members of their many opportunities to share the gospel with their neighbors and friends and encouraged them to be good examples of disciples of Christ.

President Smith's service in the European Mission began shortly after the end of World War I. Because of the war, the number of missionaries in the mission had been drastically reduced, and efforts to increase that number were hindered because missionaries were being denied visas. In addition, enemies of the Church were spreading false stories about Latter-day Saints, creating prejudices that were difficult to overcome. Notwithstanding these limitations, President Smith was confident that the work would move forward because of the examples set by faithful Latter-day Saints. He noted that as the Church becomes more well known, "its members are esteemed for their virtues," and critics "are quickly divested of their unjustified prejudices, by coming in direct contact with the Latter-day Saints in their daily lives. . . . They then judge us by our fruits, from personal observation, and such information, as they impart it, can have but one effect, and that most favorable to us."[1]

Shortly after beginning his service as president of the mission, he wrote to the members of the Church in Europe, reminding them of their responsibilities to share the gospel and help the work progress:

"With full confidence that the Lord will incline the hearts of all worthy people to the gospel when they understand it, let us unitedly avail ourselves of the opportunity to labor while there is yet time. Let us disseminate the teachings of the Master for the salvation, both temporal and spiritual, of the good people of Great Britain and the other countries of the European mission."[2]

A few months later he wrote: "Every member of the Church should delight in teaching the truth. We should each do something every day to bring the light to our fellow beings. All are precious in our Heavenly Father's sight, and he will adequately reward us for enlightening them. Our responsibility cannot be shifted to other shoulders."[3]

After returning from Europe in 1921, George Albert Smith reported in general conference, "The prejudice that has existed against us in the past has in large measure been dissipated and hundreds and thousands of men and women have been made aware of the labor we are performing." He then admonished the Saints to constantly seek for ways to share the gospel with others: "Our problem is to find a way whereby we may present to all the people the gospel of our Lord. It is our problem, and with divine assistance we will find a way to solve it. It is incumbent upon us to ascertain if there is not some means whereby we may be able to do more than we have already done, if we would satisfy the requirements of our Heavenly Father."[4] [See suggestion 1 on page 145.]

Teachings of George Albert Smith

Every member of the Church has the responsibility to share the gospel.

I feel so grateful for my privileges in the Church of Jesus Christ, for my companionship with the men and women of this Church and of other churches. I am grateful to have a host of friends in the various churches of the world, scattered in different places.

I am grateful for those friendships, but I will not be satisfied until I can share with them some of the things which they have not yet received.[5]

We send missionaries to the nations of the earth to proclaim the Gospel as revealed in this latter day. But that is not all our duty. Right at our doors, by the hundreds and thousands, are choice sons and daughters of our Heavenly Father. They live among us, we become friends, but we fail to teach them to the extent we should, concerning the Gospel that we know is the power of God unto salvation. The Presidency of the Church are doing all that lies in their power; they devote their time during the day, and often into the late hours of the night, in the interest of the Church. The brethren who are associated with them give liberally of their time, traveling and teaching the Latter-day Saints and carrying the Gospel to our Father's children. The presidents of stakes, high councilors, bishops of wards, and their assistants, labor unceasingly to bless the people, and their reward is sure. But are we doing all we ought, so that when we stand before the bar of our Heavenly Father He will say we have done our full duty by our fellows, His children?[6]

One of the very first revelations . . . in the Doctrine and Covenants, reads as follows:

"Now behold, a marvelous work is about to come forth among the children of men; . . .

"Therefore, if ye have desires to serve God, ye are called to the work." [D&C 4:1, 3.]

It is not necessary for you to be called to go into the mission field in order to proclaim the truth. Begin on the man who lives next door by inspiring confidence in him, by inspiring love in him for you because of your righteousness, and your missionary work has already begun,

"For behold the field is white already to harvest." [D&C 4:4.][7]

Disseminating the truth is not the responsibility of someone else, but it is your responsibility and mine to see that the gospel of Jesus Christ in its purity is taught to the children of men. Doesn't it make you feel grateful?[8]

There is great opportunity for every one of us. I would like to emphasize individual missionary work by each of us among our neighbors. We will be surprised, if we do our best, how many will be interested, and not only will they be grateful to us because of our bringing to them the truth, and opening their eyes to the glories and the blessings that our Heavenly Father has prepared, but they will love us and be grateful to us throughout the ages of eternity.

There are so many things that the Lord has bestowed upon us that other people have not yet received. Surely we are not going to be selfish. There should be in our hearts a desire to share with every other soul as far as possible the joyous truths of the gospel of Jesus Christ.[9]

So, as we go forward, each of us, each having an influence with our neighbors and our friends, let us not be too timid. We do not need to annoy people, but let us make them feel and understand that we are interested, not in making them members of the Church for membership, but in bringing them into the Church that they may enjoy the same blessings that we enjoy.[10] [See suggestion 2 on page 145.]

If we are living exemplary lives, our influence may encourage others to learn about the gospel.

Remember, we all have responsibilities. We may not be called to some definite duty, but in every neighborhood there is opportunity for each of us to radiate a spirit of peace and love and happiness to the end that people may understand the gospel and be gathered into the fold.[11]

Only a few days ago, one of our sisters, visiting in the east, in a conversation with an educated man, was told by him, "I cannot believe as you do but I wish that I could. It is beautiful." And so it is with many of our Father's children, who, observing the character of this work, watching the actions of the men and women who have embraced the truth, they are filled with amazement at what has been accomplished, and the peace and happiness that follows the sincere believer, and wish that they too might have part in it; and they could if they had faith.[12]

*"In every neighborhood there is opportunity for each of us to radiate
a spirit of peace and love and happiness."*

I have often observed, and I think most of you who have had
missionary experience will bear me out, that no good man or
woman can come under the influence of the faithful members of
the Church of Jesus Christ of Latter-day Saints, and withhold their
commendations of what they observe while with us. When they
leave us, sometimes it is different, but while they are under that
influence that comes from the Lord, possessed by His servants, who
are serving him, they are usually pleased to commend what they
have seen and felt.[13]

The adversary has used his strongest efforts to prevent the spread
of the truths of the gospel. And it is your duty and mine, by tact and
brotherly love and faith, to overcome the prejudice that the adversary has sown in the hearts of our Father's children, to break down
the false impressions that exist in some cases even in the minds of
good men and good women, and to teach them the gospel of our

Lord, that it is the power of God unto salvation unto all those who believe and obey it. [14]

I think this great organization we belong to ought to be able to set such an example that people in our neighborhoods, not members of the Church, seeing our good works, would be constrained to glorify the name of our Heavenly Father. That is the way I feel with regard to that. All that we need to do is to set an example, be good men and good women, and they will observe it. Then perhaps they will afford us the opportunity to teach them the things that they do not know. [15]

If we, as members of the Church, were keeping the commandments of God, if we put upon the truth the value that we ought, if our lives conformed to the beauties of its teachings, so that our neighbors, observing our conduct, would be constrained to seek after the truth, we would be doing splendid missionary work. [16] [See suggestion 3 on page 145.]

We participate in missionary work by helping prepare future missionaries and by supporting them on their missions.

It is not only our mission to teach the Gospel of Jesus Christ and live it, but it is our mission to send into the world our sons and daughters as they are called upon from time to time to labor in the ministry of the Church. As they go they should have been so trained that they would be adamant against the temptations of the adversary; they should be as pure and virtuous and righteous in their lives as it is possible to be, and then the influence of their very presence will be felt by those whom they contact. The Spirit of God will not dwell in unclean tabernacles, but his Spirit will dwell with those who keep themselves clean and sweet.

Therefore, let us [rear] our boys and girls under the influence of the Spirit of God. [17]

Don't let your children grow up without teaching them the principles of the gospel of Jesus Christ. Don't wait to send them into the mission field to learn what the gospel means. I remember when I was in the South [as a missionary] fifty-five or sixty years ago, a man who came from a large family said, "I don't know what to say. I don't know what to tell these people."

"Why," one of the brethren said, "teach them the Bible. Go and get your Bible and read Genesis." He said, "I don't know where Genesis is in the Bible," and yet he had gone from a . . . Latter-day Saint home to carry the message of life and salvation to those people in the South. However, it was not very long after that until his mind was changed. He had received a testimony of the truth through study and prayer, and he knew that the gospel was here, and he was able to stand on his feet and freely bear testimony that the gospel of Jesus Christ is the truth.[18]

I am impressed with the importance of preparing for the work. It is not sufficient merely that a boy signify his desire, because of his confidence in his parents, to do what they would have him do, go into the world and preach the gospel; it is not sufficient that he answer the calls that our Heavenly Father makes from time to time through his servants for mission service; but it is also necessary that he qualify for the work, search the scriptures, and learn what the Lord would have him know. It is important that our sons and daughters become established in their faith and know as their parents know, that this is our Father's work. . . .

A dozen men qualified for the work are worth more in the mission field than a hundred who are ignorant of the truth and who themselves have to be taught before they are capable of explaining it to others.

This is our Father's work and is not to be trifled with. It is of the utmost importance to us. Let us . . . endeavor to establish faith in our children, that they may be willing to respond to every call, and feel in the depths of their souls to say, "I am ready to go wherever my Heavenly Father desires me to go."[19] [See suggestion 4 on page 145.]

A plea has been made . . . that we send our sons and daughters into the mission field. . . . It has been a joy to me to see men and women economize and plan in order that their children may go into the world. Within the last few weeks a young man . . . left to go into the mission field, and his two sisters . . . are sending him part of their small salaries that he may enjoy the blessing of a mission. He is the first of a large family of children to go into the mission field to disseminate the truth. . . . I know the joy that will come into the hearts of those two fine women who have faith to give their means to their brother in order that he may serve the Lord in the field. They will receive the blessing that comes from teaching the Gospel, as far as it is possible to receive it without personal service. [20]

I am thinking . . . of our representatives in the missionary field, scattered throughout the different sections of this country and in some foreign lands. Pray for them, brethren and sisters. They need the help of the Lord and they need our faith and prayers. Write to them and encourage them, that when they get a letter from home they will know that they are remembered all the time. [21]

We participate in missionary work by preparing to serve missions ourselves.

It will not be long until there will be a demand for capable men and women in this Church to teach the truth in portions of the earth where heretofore we have been excluded; and if we would have eternal joy in the kingdom of our Father with those he has blessed us with here, let us be unselfish in our lives; let us prepare for the work, and go out into the world and proclaim the truth, when the opportunity comes, and be the means in the hands of our Father of drawing his children back to him by teaching them the beauties of his gospel. [22]

Only a few years ago many of my friends were well-to-do, they had the necessities of life, and many of the luxuries, and when it was intimated that they might go into the mission field some of them would say: "I can not leave my business, I can not get along if I go off and leave what I have." But their business has gone off and left them. The things that they thought they could not get along without have disappeared from their control, and many of these very men today would be happy if they could go back ten years, and if they were then called to go into the service of the Lord, they could say: "I will adjust my affairs, I am happy at the opportunity that is offered me to be a minister of life and salvation."

"There are in this Church thousands of men and women who are capable of teaching the gospel and who can become more capable by doing their duty in the mission field."

. . . Think of our opportunities and privileges, to be able to sit down in homes of the honorable men of the world and teach them the Gospel of Jesus Christ; think what it might mean to sit down with men who do not possess divine authority, and teach them the plan of salvation and explain to them the manner by which they too may enjoy the blessings of divine authority which you enjoy.

I feel that some of us are selfish. We are so glad to enjoy our blessings, we are so happy to be surrounded by the comforts of life and to have the association of the best men and women that can be found in the world, that we forget our duty to others. How happy we could be if we would strive to be more potent for good in the world by ministering to those who have not yet understood the Gospel of our Lord.

Many of us have passed middle life, many of us are completing our work. The Church needs missionaries in the field. Men who understand the Gospel and who are willing to give their lives for it if need be, and when I say we need missionaries I mean that the world needs them. [23]

Our missionary field is before us. Our Father's sons and daughters need us. . . . There are in this Church thousands of men and women who are capable of teaching the gospel and who can become more capable by doing their duty in the mission field. They will be blessed with means, sufficient to take them to perform the work that the Lord wants us to perform. [24]

Now that the time is near at hand when the bars will be let down and the barriers overthrown that have been raised to the spread of the gospel, when the sound of the voice of the Lord shall come to you, through his servants, "Prepare to go into the world and preach the gospel," do not do as Jonah did, do not try to hide or run away from your duty; do not make excuses that you do not have the necessary means to go; do not set up foolish things in the way of your vision that will prevent your seeing eternal life in the presence of our Heavenly Father, which can come only by reason of faith and devotion in his cause. Let every man set his house in order; let every man who bears the priesthood, set himself in order, and when the call comes from the servants of the Lord, telling him to go into the world to teach the truth, to warn the children of men, as our Father requires they shall be warned, let no man hide behind some foolish thing, to be swallowed up, if not by a great fish, by the foolish things of the world. [See Jonah 1:1–17.] [25]

It is not an easy task; it is not a pleasant thing, perhaps, to be called out into the world, to leave our dear ones, but I say to you it will purchase for those who are faithful, for those who discharge that obligation as they may be required, peace and happiness beyond all understanding, and will prepare them that, in due time, when life's labor is complete, they will stand in the presence of their Maker, accepted of Him because of what they have done. [26]

I pray that his Spirit may be throughout [the Church], that the love of our Father's children may be in our hearts, that we may sense the importance of our mission in the world, while we are grasping for the things that are not ours, that are only loaned to us as stewards, that we may not forget the priceless gift, the priceless privilege, within our reach, of teaching the gospel and saving the souls of the children of men.[27] [See suggestion 5 below.]

Suggestions for Study and Teaching

Consider these ideas as you study the chapter or as you prepare to teach. For additional help, see pages v–vii.

1. Ponder President Smith's words in "From the Life of George Albert Smith" (pages 135–36). Why do you think he was so optimistic about missionary work in Europe despite the opposition he faced? How can his example help you if your family members or friends decline your invitation to learn about the gospel?

2. Review the first section of teachings (pages 136–38). What methods have you found most effective in your efforts to share the gospel with neighbors and friends?

3. As you read the section that begins on page 138, think about an instance you know of when the example of a Church member has led someone to learn more about the Church. What are some other reasons that living the Church's standards is so important in missionary work?

4. On pages 140–41, look for things prospective missionaries need to do to prepare spiritually for their missions (see also D&C 4). What can parents do to help their sons and daughters prepare? How can priesthood quorums and Relief Society sisters help?

5. Review the last section of teachings (pages 142–45). What are some of the "foolish things" that might keep us from serving a mission? What are some of the blessings that come through the service of senior missionaries? Ponder what you need to do to prepare yourself for missionary service.

Related Scriptures: Matthew 5:14–16; Mark 16:15–16; 1 Timothy 4:12; Alma 17:2–3; Doctrine and Covenants 31:1–8; 38:40–41

Teaching help: "When you use a variety of learning activities, learners tend to understand gospel principles better and retain more. A carefully selected method can make a principle clearer, more interesting, and more memorable" (*Teaching, No Greater Call,* 89).

Notes

1. "New Year's Greeting," *Millennial Star,* Jan. 6, 1921, 2.
2. "Greeting," *Millennial Star,* July 10, 1919, 441.
3. "New Year's Greeting," *Millennial Star,* Jan. 1, 1920, 2.
4. In Conference Report, Oct. 1921, 37–38.
5. In Conference Report, Oct. 1950, 159.
6. In Conference Report, Apr. 1916, 46.
7. In Conference Report, Oct. 1916, 50–51.
8. In Conference Report, Oct. 1929, 23.
9. In *Deseret News,* June 25, 1950, Church section, 2.
10. In Conference Report, Apr. 1948, 162.
11. In Conference Report, Apr. 1950, 170.
12. In Conference Report, Oct. 1913, 103.
13. In Conference Report, Apr. 1922, 49.
14. "The Importance of Preparing," *Improvement Era,* Mar. 1948, 139.
15. In Conference Report, Apr. 1941, 26.
16. In Conference Report, Oct. 1916, 49.
17. In Conference Report, Oct. 1932, 25.
18. In Conference Report, Oct. 1948, 166.
19. "The Importance of Preparing," 139.
20. In Conference Report, Apr. 1935, 45.
21. In Conference Report, Oct. 1941, 98.
22. In Conference Report, Oct. 1916, 51.
23. In Conference Report, Oct. 1933, 27–28.
24. In Conference Report, Apr. 1946, 125.
25. In Conference Report, June 1919, 44.
26. In Conference Report, Apr. 1922, 53.
27. In Conference Report, Oct. 1916, 51.

How to Share the Gospel Effectively

*Our efforts to share the gospel are most effective
if we love our brothers and sisters and have the
companionship of the Holy Ghost.*

From the Life of George Albert Smith

In his tireless efforts to share the gospel with others, George Albert Smith followed this statement from his personal creed: "I would not seek to force people to live up to my ideals but rather love them into doing the thing that is right."[1] He felt that the most effective way to share the gospel was to look for the good virtues in people of other faiths and then, with boldness but kindness, offer to share the additional truths of the restored gospel of Jesus Christ. He related the following experience he had while presiding over the European Mission:

"I was riding on the train one day. My companion in the compartment was a Presbyterian minister, a very pleasant, fine gentleman, and when he gave me the opportunity to do so, I told him I was a member of the Church of Jesus Christ of Latter-day Saints. He was amazed and he looked at me with astonishment. He said, 'Aren't you ashamed of yourself to belong to such a group?'

"I smiled at him and said, 'My brother, I would be ashamed of myself not to belong to that group, knowing what I know.' Then that gave me the opportunity I desired to talk to him and explain to him some of the things we believe. . . .

"There was a good man who had no conception of what we were trying to do. We were not there to give him sorrow nor distress; we were trying to help him. And as we talked the situation through I said to him: 'You have a misconception of the purpose of the Church

147

"We desire to do good to all, and to assist all to understand the plan of life and salvation that the Lord revealed in this latter day."

of Jesus Christ of Latter-day Saints in this land. I am here as one of its representatives, and if you will just let me tell you a few things, I think you will feel better towards us.' I said, 'First of all, we are asking all you fine people over here to keep all the glorious truths that you have acquired in your churches, that you have absorbed from your scriptures, keep all that, keep all the fine training that you have received in your educational institutions, all the knowledge and truth that you have gained from every source, keep . . . everything that is good in your character that has come to you as a result of your lovely home; keep all the love and the beauty that is in your heart from having lived in so beautiful and wonderful a land. . . . That is all a part of the gospel of Jesus Christ. Then let us sit down and share with you some of the things that have not yet come into your lives that have enriched our lives and made us happy. We offer it to you without money and without price. All we ask you to do is hear what we have to say, and if it appeals to you, accept it freely. . . .'

"That is the attitude of the Church of Jesus Christ of Latter-day Saints."[2] [See suggestion 1 on page 155.]

Teachings of George Albert Smith

Missionary work is most effective when we do it with love and kindness, not coercion or criticism.

Our Heavenly Father . . . has sent us, his representatives, into the world, not to drive or coerce, but to invite. "Come follow me," is what the Savior said, "And I will give you peace." That is what the Gospel teaches, and that is our ministry.[3]

It is not the purpose of this Church to make statements that would hurt the feelings of those who do not understand things. This Church is not one that goes about criticising and finding fault with others, but in the spirit of loving kindness and the desire to be helpful, its representatives carry the Gospel message to the nations of the earth.[4]

In all . . . churches there are good men and good women. It is the good that is in these various denominations that holds them together. It has been my privilege to be with people in many parts of the world and to be in the homes of many people of the various denominations of the world, both Christian and Jew. I have been with the [Muslims]; I have been with those who believe in Confucius; and I might mention a good many others. I have found wonderful people in all these organizations, and I have the tremendous responsibility wherever I go among them, that I shall not offend them, not hurt their feelings, not criticize them, because they do not understand the truth.

As representatives of the Church we have the responsibility to go among them with love, as servants of the Lord, as representatives of the Master of heaven and earth. They may not altogether appreciate that; they may resent that as being egotistical and unfair, but that would not change my attitude. I am not going to make them unhappy if I can help it. I would like to make them happy, especially when I think of the marvelous opportunities that have come to me because of membership in this blessed Church.[5]

Our ministry is one of love and forbearance, and we desire to do good to all, and to assist all to understand the plan of life and salvation that the Lord revealed in this latter day.[6]

We cannot drive these young people, and our neighbors and friends into the kingdom of heaven by scolding them and finding fault with them, but I want to tell you that we can love them into the direction of our Father in heaven, and by and by, perhaps, lead them there too.

That is our privilege. Love is the great power to influence this world.[7]

Let us who know, those of us who have a testimony, go forth day by day and with love and kindness unfeigned go among these men and women, whether they be in the Church or out of the Church, and find a way to touch their hearts and lead them into that pathway that will insure them a knowledge of the truth.[8]

How I pray that we as the servants of the Lord may have charity for mankind, may have patience with those who err, and in kindness and love go forward teaching the simple principles of the gospel of our Lord to the blessing of every soul with whom we come in contact.[9] [See suggestion 2 on page 155.]

We need not be ashamed in sharing what we know to be true.

I feel sometimes that we do not sufficiently sense the importance of [the gospel], that we do not teach it with the earnestness it demands.[10]

This gospel of Jesus Christ is the power of God unto salvation, as the Apostle Paul declared [see Romans 1:16]. It is the Redeemer's work. It is the only way whereby we may attain the highest exaltation that the Savior of mankind intended that those who followed him should enjoy. I do not say that egotistically, I say it with charity for our Father's children who belong to other churches. I say it with love for his sons and daughters who do not understand, but he has commanded that we should say this thing. It is his will that people should know.[11]

I know that God lives. I know that Jesus is the Christ. I know that Joseph Smith was a prophet of the Lord. I have never been anywhere that I have been ashamed to testify to these truths. I do not know why a man should be ashamed of knowing the truth because somebody else does not know it, especially when it pertains to the gospel which is the power of God unto salvation.[12]

It should not be considered boastful if we know the truth for us so to express ourselves. It should not be considered egotistical so far as we are concerned if we can say to our Father's other children: "This I know, and you too may know it if you desire."

That is the beauty of the gospel of Jesus Christ. It is not for a few individuals, but it is for every soul that is born into the world to know. . . . Today there are those who know that God lives, and there are thousands of others who could know it if they would. . . . These people are not dependent upon us to know, but they are dependent upon us to teach them how they may know.[13]

I know that our Heavenly Father has spoken in this day and age of the world, that his Gospel is upon the earth, and while I would not compel any soul to accept it, I pray that we may have power and wisdom and strength to reach out after these neighbors of ours who do not understand the truth. Let us do our duty, and draw them into the fold of the Master, that they, with us, may know that he lives.[14] [See suggestion 3 on page 155.]

We seek to add to the happiness and goodness that God's children already possess.

When [people] have asked me, "What is there about this organization that you belong to? What is it that you are so concerned about, that you send your missionaries all over the world?" I have replied sometimes, "We want you all to be happy. We want you all to rejoice as we rejoice."[15]

Thousands upon thousands of missionaries . . . have gone out into the world, and in love and kindness they have gone from door to door saying to our Father's other children:

"Let us reason with you; let us explain to you something that we are sure will make you happy as it has made us happy!"

That is the history of the missionary work of the Church with which we are identified.[16]

I remember, upon one occasion, a man said to me, after we had talked some time, "Well, from all I can learn, your church is just as good as any other church." I presume he thought he was paying us a great compliment; but I said to him: "If the Church I represent here is not of more importance to the children of men than any other church, then I am mistaken in my duty here. We have come not to take away from you the truth and virtue you possess. We have not come to find fault with you or to criticize you. . . . Keep all the good that you have, and let us bring to you more good, in order that you may be happier and in order that you may be prepared to enter into the presence of our Heavenly Father." [See suggestion 4 on page 155.]

. . . In the time that the Savior was on earth, in the meridian of time, there were other churches; there were numerous denominations and sects, and they believed that they were serving the Lord. The great synagogues of Judea were filled with men who believed they had the authority of the priesthood. They had been following the teachings, as they thought, of Abraham and Moses. They continued to proclaim the coming of the Savior of the world. They had encouraged men and women to works of righteousness. They had builded a temple, and houses of worship. They had erected monuments to the prophets who had borne testimony of the existence of God, and some of whom had been slain and had sealed their testimony with their life's blood. These were the people to whom the Savior came. . . . There was much good in them. There were many good men and women among them. There was much righteousness among that people. The Savior did not come to take away any of those good things from them. When he appeared among them it was not to condemn them, but it was to call them to repentance, it was to call them from their error and to encourage them to retain all the truth that they possessed.

. . . When we proclaim to the human family, as we do, that man has apostatized from the gospel, we are not proclaiming something that has not occurred in the world before. When we say good men and women have been led to do and believe things that are not correct, we do not say that in condemnation, we do not speak with a desire to wound, but we speak with a desire that men may pause sufficiently long to examine themselves, to see where they are going and what will be their final destiny.[17]

Oh! that we might be able to give mankind an understanding of our feelings, that they might realize that we do not desire to curtail their opportunities, but that they might feel that our hearts reach out to them in love and kindness, not with any desire to hurt. Our mission in the world is to save souls, to bless them, and to place them in a condition that they may go back into the presence of our Father, crowned with glory, immortality, and eternal life.[18]

If we teach with the Holy Ghost, He will bear witness of the truth to those we teach.

Missionaries have been sent to the four corners of the earth by this Church and they have proclaimed the Gospel of Jesus Christ. Many have not had training in the great universities of the world. Their education has been largely limited to the practical experiences of life, but they have had what is more potent in inspiring the human family, the companionship of the Holy Ghost.[19]

As I go to and fro in the mission field I see the development of these fine young men and women who are unselfishly serving, and realize that not only do they learn the language of the countries in which they labor, but they know that they have a gift from the Lord to disseminate a truth that the people may not obtain in any other way.[20]

Many of you or your forebears have heard the gospel as it has been taught by the Church of Jesus Christ of Latter-day Saints. . . . Sometimes you have heard it on the street where there was a humble missionary, teaching what the Lord had called him to teach.

There was something that touched the hearts of those who heard. I have had experiences in the mission field. I have seen groups of people stand and listen to a humble missionary explain the purpose of life and talk to the people and encourage them to repent of their sins, and I have sometimes heard people say, "I have never before felt an influence like I feel while I hear that man talk."[21]

"Let us labor day by day that our Father may bless us. If we have His Holy Spirit, the people with whom we come in contact will feel it."

No matter how gifted we may be, or how choice our language, it is the Spirit of our Father that reaches the heart and brings conviction of the divinity of this work. [22]

This is the Lord's work. Men could not have carried it forward successfully as it has been done by the simple means employed by us. Ordinary man could not have brought into your souls the knowledge that you possess. Neither can we as men inspire those in the world with the assurance that God lives and that this is his Church, but if we will do our part, our Heavenly Father will bless our effort. [23]

Let us labor day by day that our Father may bless us. If we have His Holy Spirit, the people with whom we come in contact will feel it, because it will permeate the atmosphere in which we live, and they will partake of it and drink it in. [24]

There are only a few comparatively who have accepted the gospel as it has been revealed in the latter day; but there are millions of our Father's children who are desirous of knowing His will; and when the truth shall be brought to them, and the convincing influence of the Spirit shall bear witness of the truth to them, they will rejoice in accepting it.[25] [See suggestion 5 below.]

Suggestions for Study and Teaching

Consider these ideas as you study the chapter or as you prepare to teach. For additional help, see pages v–vii.

1. Study the last two paragraphs of "From the Life of George Albert Smith" (pages 147–49). Think of someone you know who is not a member of the Church. What qualities do you admire in this person? What truths of the gospel does he or she already believe? What additional gospel truths would be especially helpful to him or her? How does thinking about people in this way affect the way we share the gospel with them?

2. As you read the first section of teachings (pages 149–50), think about a time when you were influenced for good by the love someone showed for you. Why is it so important to avoid being critical of those whose beliefs differ from ours?

3. Read the section that begins on page 150. What does it mean to share the gospel with "earnestness"? How can we share our testimonies of the restored gospel without sounding boastful or egotistical?

4. What do you think President Smith meant when he said, "If the Church I represent here is not of more importance to the children of men than any other church, then I am mistaken in my duty here"? (page 152). What does the Church of Jesus Christ offer that can add to the happiness in a person's life?

5. As you read the last section of teachings (pages 153–55), think about an experience you have had in which you shared the gospel with someone. What made the experience successful? What can you do to improve in your efforts to share the gospel?

Related Scriptures: John 13:34–35; 2 Timothy 1:7–8; 2 Nephi 33:1; Alma 20:26–27; Doctrine and Covenants 50:13–22

Teaching help: Consider dividing class members into small groups of three to five individuals. Designate a leader in each group. Assign each group a different section. Ask them to read as a group their section and discuss the corresponding questions at the end of the chapter. Then have class members share with the entire class what they learned in their groups. (See *Teaching, No Greater Call,* 161.)

Notes

1. "President George Albert Smith's Creed," *Improvement Era,* Apr. 1950, 262.

2. *Sharing the Gospel with Others,* sel. Preston Nibley (1948), 199–201; address given Nov. 4, 1945, in Washington, D.C.

3. In Conference Report, Oct. 1930, 67–68.

4. In Conference Report, Oct. 1931, 120.

5. In Conference Report, Oct. 1945, 168.

6. In Conference Report, Oct. 1927, 47.

7. In Conference Report, Apr. 1950, 187.

8. In Conference Report, Apr. 1934, 30.

9. In Conference Report, Oct. 1928, 94.

10. In Conference Report, Apr. 1916, 47.

11. In Conference Report, Oct. 1927, 48.

12. "'At This Season,'" *Improvement Era,* Dec. 1949, 801, 831.

13. "Opportunities for Leadership," *Improvement Era,* Sept. 1949, 557, 603–4.

14. In Conference Report, Oct. 1930, 69.

15. In Conference Report, Oct. 1948, 7.

16. In Conference Report, Oct. 1946, 5.

17. In *Deseret News,* Aug. 20, 1921, Church section, 7.

18. In Conference Report, Oct. 1904, 66.

19. In Conference Report, Apr. 1940, 85.

20. In Conference Report, Apr. 1935, 45.

21. In Conference Report, Oct. 1949, 7.

22. In Conference Report, Oct. 1904, 66.

23. In Conference Report, Oct. 1929, 25.

24. In Conference Report, Oct. 1906, 50–51.

25. In *Deseret News,* Jan. 12, 1907, 31.

Advancing the Work of the Lord

God directs His work, and He calls upon every member
of the Church to participate in moving it forward.

From the Life of George Albert Smith

When George Albert Smith was called to the Quorum of the Twelve Apostles in 1903, Church membership stood at just over 300,000. By the end of his service as President of the Church, it had surpassed 1 million. President Smith rejoiced in such growth because it meant that the message of salvation was reaching more and more people. "How happy we should be," he said to a general conference audience in 1950, "not that we have increased in numbers in the organization that we belong to, but that more of our Father's children, more of his sons and daughters, have been brought to an understanding of the truth, and are coming into his organization that he prepared to teach us the way of life and lead us along the pathway of eternal happiness."[1]

Between 1903 and President Smith's death in 1951, the Church faced many challenges to its progress worldwide. Events such as World War I, World War II, and the Great Depression (a widespread economic crisis) severely limited the number of missionaries that could be sent abroad. Despite these difficulties, George Albert Smith remained confident that the Church would continue to grow and realize its destiny to "fill the whole earth" (Daniel 2:35). In 1917, at the height of World War I, he told the Saints: "I do not become discouraged because this truth does not find its way more rapidly. On the contrary I see in the events of today the hand-dealing of an all-wise Father to prepare the way for the spread of the gospel that he has restored to the earth in our day."[2]

President Smith believed that advances in technology "can indeed become blessings if we utilize them in righteousness for the dissemination of truth and the furtherance of the work of the Lord among men."

While the first half of the 20th century saw significant challenges, it also brought new technologies that President Smith believed would further the Lord's work. He was a strong proponent of the aviation industry and saw it as a way to fulfill his travel assignments as a General Authority more efficiently. He also supported the Church's use of radio and television to take the word of the Lord to a broader audience. "We ought to regard these [inventions] as blessings from the Lord," he said. "They greatly enlarge our abilities. They can indeed become blessings if we utilize them in righteousness for the dissemination of truth and the furtherance of the work of the Lord among men. The great challenge facing the world today lies in the use we make of many of these inventions. We can use them to destroy, as we have sometimes done in the past, or we can utilize them to enlighten and bless mankind, as our Heavenly Father would have us do."[3]

In a general conference address in 1946, President Smith prophesied about the use of such technologies: "It will not be long until, from this pulpit and other places that will be provided, the servants of the Lord will be able to deliver messages to isolated groups who are so far away they cannot be reached. In that way and other ways, the gospel of Jesus Christ our Lord, the only power of God unto salvation in preparation for the celestial kingdom, will be heard in all parts of the world, and many of you who are here will live to see that day."[4] [See suggestions 1 and 4 on page 166.]

President Smith understood that the work of the Church is successful because it is the Lord's work, and he taught the Saints that the opportunity to participate in that work is a blessing the Lord offers each member of His Church. During the first general conference after he was set apart as President of the Church, he said: "I realize the great responsibility that is upon my shoulders. I know that without the help of our Heavenly Father, the organization with which we are identified cannot be successful. No man or group of men can make it successful, but if the members of this Church will continue to keep the commandments of God, live their religion, set an example to the world, [and] love their neighbor as themselves, we will go forward, and increasing happiness will flow to us."[5]

Teachings of George Albert Smith

**There is ample opportunity for every member
to participate in the work of the Lord.**

The responsibility for the conduct of this work does not devolve alone upon [the President of the Church], nor upon his counselors, nor upon the quorum of the Apostles; but it devolves also upon every man and woman who has been baptized by the servants of God and become a member of the Church of Jesus Christ of Latter-day Saints. . . . We cannot shift the responsibility if we would; our Father has placed it upon our shoulders, and we must round them up and help to carry it off triumphant.[6]

I believe in you, my brethren and sisters. I have confidence in your faith and in your integrity. . . . Each of you also [is] responsible to [the Lord] for the promotion of this work, as are those who preside over you. I cannot say, "Am I my brother's keeper?" I cannot shift the responsibility . . . , but standing in the ranks of the children of our Father I must bear my portion, I must carry that part of the load that the Lord places upon me, and if I shirk, then I realize that I forfeit the blessing that would come to me by obedience to the commandments of our Father.[7]

How anxious we should be to go about doing good. It is a slothful servant who waits until he is commanded in all things. [See D&C 58:26–27.] Our Heavenly Father expects us to magnify our calling, no matter where it may be, no matter how humble our lot in life may be.[8]

It is not necessary that a man should be a member of the Quorum of the Twelve, or the Presidency of the Church, in order to obtain the greatest blessings in the kingdom of our Heavenly Father. These are but offices required in the Church, and there are many faithful and devoted men worthy to fill these offices whose time and talents are needed throughout the Church. . . . Remember that in the ranks and throughout the Church there is ample opportunity for every man and for every woman to do something for the blessing of their fellows and for the advancement of the work of the Lord.[9]

There is a disposition on the part of some who hold the priesthood and of some who hold positions in the Church, to neglect sacrament meetings and other important duties, and to confine their labors to some special calling. They may be officers and teachers in the Sunday School, and when they perform their Sabbath school labor, consider that sufficient; or, they may be [Young Men or Young Women], or Primary, or genealogical, or welfare workers, or have some other such assignment, and if they discharge their obligations in that regard they consider their whole duty done.

Much as we love and bless all such for the great service they render, we are obliged to remind ourselves that it is required of all of us to live by every word that proceedeth from the mouth of our Father in heaven [see D&C 84:44]. Generally speaking, special assignments do not relieve us of our other obligations; and special meetings do not usually replace or supersede the general meetings of the Church. And quite beyond our special obligations and assignments, we are expected to conduct ourselves day by day as Latter-day Saints in the broadest meaning of the term, so that if we see distress or want, or need of advice and counsel on any occasion, we should forthwith act as servants of the Lord in very deed.

And then there are those who accept nominal membership in the Church but who seem to feel themselves exempt from rendering any kind of service. But sooner or later they find themselves uneasy in their hearts, and doubtful in their thoughts, as we all do when we fail to do what we know to be our full duty. A man who is living in accordance with the gospel of Jesus Christ is never in doubt about its success; but the man who neglects his duty, who fails to keep his covenants, loses the Spirit of the Lord, and then he begins to wonder what will become of Zion. . . .

Whenever you are doing your full duty, you will know, as you know that you live, that it is our Father's work, and that he will bring it off triumphant.[10]

Can you not see how a marvelous work and a wonder has been going forward? Can you not see how we as individuals have only contributed our mite, but the multitude has united, and the word of the Lord has been disseminated among the children of men; not

"Throughout the Church there is ample opportunity for every man and for every woman to do something for the blessing of their fellows and for the advancement of the work of the Lord."

in a militant way, but in kindness and in love, with a desire to bless all mankind?[11] [See suggestion 2 on page 166.]

Opposition will not stop the progress of the Church, because it is the work of God, not of man.

The Church began with only six members. It has grown day by day in spite of the opposition of the adversary. But for the powerful arm of righteousness, but for the watchcare of our Heavenly Father, this Church would have been crushed like a shell long ago. However, the Lord has said that he would safeguard us, and has promised us protection if we will honor him and keep his commandments.[12]

The growth of this Church has not come because it was popular. It has been in spite of the opposition of the wise men of the world; it has been in spite of the opposition of religious teachers, and it has continued to gather here and there choice spirits who have lived in such a way that they could comprehend the truth. [13]

I have been reading a journal of my grandfather, George A. Smith. . . . I have read his personal experiences, some most painful and others miraculous. In his youth he was sent out to preach the Gospel of our Lord. His was the experience of other men who have been called to the ministry. Those of evil minds made false accusations against him and his associates but he continued faithful and the Lord vindicated them and magnified them in the eyes of the people and gave them a testimony of the divinity of this work that was so positive that no task was too difficult for them to undertake for the dissemination of truth.

Grandfather was among the group sent to England to preach the Gospel in 1839. There the adversary sought to discourage them in every way. Their journals written at the time disclose the fact that they were misrepresented by evil men and attacked by evil spirits, but the Lord preserved them and they performed a great labor. Eight of the Quorum of the Twelve were there at that time. Among those called to go to England were men without means to pay their way but they started from their homes on foot. Due to prolonged illness one of these men was too weak to walk two miles to take a stage coach but was helped that distance by a friend. They had faith in God; they knew that this was his Church and so they went their way and friends not of the Church were raised up to give them money and pay their passage across the ocean, where they delivered their message and many faithful people accepted the truth as a result of their ministry. [14]

This is God's work. It is not the work of any man. No man or set of men could have carried it forward and made it successful in the face of the opposition of the world. Many times they [who oppose the work] have felt that the end of the Church had come, and each time by the majesty of his power, the Lord has lifted it up, and it has gone forward from city to city, from village to village, from nation to nation. [15]

I know that there are many problems and there will be greater problems as the days come and go, but the same Father in heaven that led the Children of Israel, that saved Daniel and the three

Hebrew children from destruction, the same Heavenly Father that preserved our forebears that came into [the Salt Lake Valley] and established them here, and blessed them and made it possible in the poverty of the people to have this great [Salt Lake] temple and other great temples, . . . that same Father, your Father and mine, is ready to pour out his blessings upon us today.[16]

There is no occasion for discouragement. The gospel of Jesus Christ continues to roll forth. We have the promise from our Heavenly Father that it will continue to roll forth. No other dispensation has had the assurance that we have. In the dispensations of the past the Gospel has been taken from the earth. When it was restored in our day it was with the promise that it will never again be taken from the earth or given to another people. So I beg of you who have put your hand to the plow, do not turn back. Serve God and keep his commandments.[17]

We need not feel anxious about the progress of Zion, for the good old ship will sail proudly on, and those who are faithful and true will land with her safely in the harbor of God, crowned with glory, immortality and eternal life. I have no fear for these aged men and women that have kept the faith. I have no fear for the boys and girls who are walking in obedience to the commandments of the Lord. . . . But the Latter-day Saints who knowing the will of our Father have not done it, those who hear the teachings of the Lord from time to time and turn their backs upon them, I fear they will not reach the goal unless they turn and repent with all their hearts.[18]

His work is progressive, we must be active if we would keep pace with it. Every passing year, since the organization of the Church, has seen it grow stronger than the year before. Today the prospect of continual success is better than ever before. More people are learning the truth about us, and our attitude towards them. The prejudice due to ignorance is being overcome, as the light is disseminated among the masses. . . .

It should be evident to all, and it will be some day, that the opposition to this work would have overcome it long ago if it had not been divine. Let all the world know that it cannot be overthrown, for "it is the power of God unto salvation unto all those who believe." [See Romans 1:16.][19] [See suggestion 3 on page 166.]

God adjusts conditions in the world so that His work can spread throughout the earth.

[God] has determined that the message that was proclaimed by his servants in ages past, renewed and promulgated by his servants in the latter days, shall be heard, and by the power of his might he will level the conditions of this world and humble the children of men until they are repentant and willing to listen. The truths that we are teaching, that is, the truths that God required us to teach in the world, are finding their way. [20]

The Lord revealed to one of his prophets that at the coming forth of the Book of Mormon he would commence his work among the nations for the restoration of his people. [See 2 Nephi 30:3–8; 3 Nephi 21:1–14; 29:1–2.] When we realize with what speed the gospel of Jesus Christ may be disseminated now as compared with the year 1830, we can see that the Lord has set his hand and the opportunity to know is offered to men. It will not be long now, until in every part of this world the gospel may be heard through the servants of the Lord proclaiming it in power. Our Heavenly Father will adjust conditions in the world so that the gospel may be preached. [21]

The Savior said this gospel of the kingdom shall be preached in all the world for a witness unto all nations, and then shall the end come! [See Joseph Smith—Matthew 1:31.] The Lord would not require an impossibility. He is removing the obstructions, and the gospel "shall be preached." [22]

Zion will be redeemed, and the world, which now misunderstands the work of "Mormonism," will live to know that it is the power of God unto salvation to those who will keep the commandments of our Father. My testimony is that the work grows apace, and that the children of men are receiving "Mormonism" in their souls; that it is the work of our Father. We may be puny and weak of ourselves, but if we will be virtuous and pure in our lives, if we will do what we know to be right, men and women will be raised to continue the work of the Lord, until our Father's work will have been done in the way that He desires. Those who misunderstand us now will know us better. Those who believe we have selfish motives will be undeceived, and our brothers and sisters of the world, who desire the truth and wish to know what the Lord wants of them, will be pricked in their hearts and accept the Gospel. Zion will rise and shine, and will become the glory of the whole earth, the Lord God of Israel has so decreed.[23] [See suggestion 4 below.]

Suggestions for Study and Teaching

Consider these ideas as you study the chapter or as you prepare to teach. For additional help, see pages v–vii.

1. President Smith prophesied that "the gospel of Jesus Christ our Lord . . . will be heard in all parts of the world" (page 159). What technologies are helping to make this possible? In what other ways are new technologies or scientific advancements contributing to the Lord's work?

2. As you read the first section of teachings (pages 160–62), think about your current calling or assignment in the Church. How does fulfilling your calling allow you to participate in "the advancement of the work of the Lord"? How do your efforts as a home teacher or visiting teacher contribute to this work? In what ways can we all participate beyond our formal callings and assignments?

3. On pages 162–64, President Smith bears his testimony that the Lord directs the work of His Church. What experiences have you had to show you that this is true? How does teaching and living the gospel in our homes demonstrate our faith in the Lord's work?

4. On pages 159 and 165–66, look for things that President Smith said the Lord will do to prepare the way for His gospel to be preached. What evidence do you see that these things have happened or are happening in the world today?

Related Scriptures: Daniel 2:44–45; Joel 2:27–28; Mosiah 27:13; Doctrine and Covenants 64:33–34; 65:1–6; 107:99–100; Moses 1:39

Teaching help: "There may . . . be times when you do not know the answer to a question. If this happens, simply say that you do not know. You may want to say that you will try to find the answer. Or you may want to invite learners to find the answer, giving them time in another lesson to report on what they have learned" (*Teaching, No Greater Call,* 64).

Notes

1. In Conference Report, Apr. 1950, 6.
2. In Conference Report, Apr. 1917, 37.
3. In *Deseret News,* May 10, 1947, Church section, 10.
4. In Conference Report, Oct. 1946, 6.
5. In Conference Report, Oct. 1945, 173.
6. In Conference Report, Apr. 1904, 64.
7. In Conference Report, Oct. 1911, 44.
8. In Conference Report, Apr. 1934, 30.
9. In Conference Report, June 1919, 42–43.
10. "Our Full Duty," *Improvement Era,* Mar. 1946, 141.
11. In Conference Report, Apr. 1930, 68.
12. In Conference Report, Oct. 1945, 170–71.
13. In Conference Report, Oct. 1916, 47.
14. In Conference Report, Apr. 1931, 32–33.
15. In Conference Report, Oct. 1931, 122–23.
16. In Conference Report, Oct. 1945, 174.
17. In *Deseret News,* Aug. 20, 1921, Church section, 7.
18. In Conference Report, Oct. 1906, 49.
19. "New Year's Greeting," *Millennial Star,* Jan. 1, 1920, 3.
20. In Conference Report, Apr. 1917, 37.
21. In Conference Report, Apr. 1927, 82–83.
22. "New Year's Greeting," 2.
23. In Conference Report, Apr. 1906, 58.

*"Honor the Sabbath day and keep it holy, Latter-day Saints,
and it will bring to you great joy."*

"Offer Up Thy Sacraments upon My Holy Day"

Keeping the Sabbath day holy and worthily partaking of the sacrament bring us increased spiritual strength.

From the Life of George Albert Smith

As a child, George Albert Smith learned the importance of honoring the Sabbath day. Often on Sundays a group of neighborhood boys would come to his house after Sunday School to invite him to play ball. "I was like the boys," he said. "I thought it would be lots of fun to play ball and to play other games. But I had a wonderful mother. She did not say, 'You cannot do it,' but she did say: 'Son, you will be happier if you do not do that. . . .' I want to tell you I am grateful for that kind of training in the home."[1] The impact of his mother's teachings can be seen in President Smith's frequently reminding the Saints that keeping the Sabbath day holy brings great blessings.

As a General Authority, George Albert Smith had the opportunity to attend Sunday services of the Church in numerous locations. As he observed the Saints worshipping together on the Sabbath, he was pleased with their reverent attitude toward the sacrament: "I feel that a comprehension of the sacredness of the sacrament of the Lord's Supper is important to the members of the Church. . . . I rejoice when I find our brethren and sisters coming to the sanctuary and partaking of these emblems . . . worthily."[2] [See suggestion 1 on page 177.]

Teachings of George Albert Smith

God's commandment that we keep the Sabbath day holy is not a burden but a blessing.

[The Lord] has taught us that we must observe the Sabbath Day to keep it holy. One day of the seven he has set apart as his day, and in consideration of all his blessings bestowed upon us on the other days it would appear to me that we ought to find joy in doing the things that he asks us to do on his holy day, and I believe that unless we do we will find no happiness. . . . He wants us to be happy and has told us how we may earn that happiness.[3]

We should think of the purpose of the [Lord's] day and partake of the influence of worship. What would it accomplish for the world if all the children of our Heavenly Father—and we are all his children—would respect his desire that the Sabbath should be a day of worship. There is no way of estimating what a beneficial change might be wrought, not only in our own nation, but in all nations of the world if we honored the Sabbath Day and kept it holy.[4]

The Sabbath has become the play-day . . . —the day set apart by thousands to violate the commandment that God gave long, long ago, and I am persuaded that much of the sorrow and distress that is afflicting and will continue to afflict mankind is traceable to the fact that they have ignored his admonition to keep the Sabbath day holy.[5] [See suggestion 2 on page 177.]

One of the first sermons that were preached in this [the Salt Lake] valley was by President Brigham Young, and he warned the people to honor the Sabbath day and to keep it holy, and no matter how difficult their circumstances they were not to go out and do manual labor on the Sabbath day. . . . The Church of Jesus Christ of Latter-day Saints has encouraged its people to remember the Sabbath day to keep it holy because it is pleasing to our Heavenly Father that we do so.[6]

Let us teach these boys and girls [of the Church] as they grow up to do the things that the Lord would like to have them do on the Sabbath day, and it will be surprising the influence they can have in the communities that they live in. Unless the world repents of its carelessness and indifference, unless we the Latter-Day Saints, in many cases, repent of our attitude of indifference toward the holy day of our Heavenly Father, there will not come to us all the joy and happiness we desire to enjoy here, and it will not be with us in eternity.[7]

Some people appear to think that if they have attended religious meetings or performed some portion of the service required of them on Sunday, they are then at liberty to pursue pleasures and engage in activities incompatible with the spirit of the Sabbath and still continue to enjoy the favor of our Father. I say to you that if the members of the Church, knowing better, persist in desecrating the Sabbath day in the pursuit of worldly pleasures, they will lose their faith; and the Spirit of our Heavenly Father will withdraw from them.[8]

It is not an insignificant thing to violate the Sabbath day. I want to say that you lose every time you violate the Sabbath day, you lose more than you can gain, no matter what you may think you are going to gain.[9]

To forget that it [the Sabbath day] is the Lord's day, as some of us appear to do, is ungrateful. He has set apart one day in seven, not to make it a burden, but to bring joy into our lives and cause that our homes may be the gathering place of the family, that parents and children may assemble around the family hearth increasing our love for one another. . . .

Honor the Sabbath day and keep it holy, Latter-day Saints, and it will bring to you great joy and our Heavenly Father will bestow upon you the blessings that result from obedience to his advice and counsel.[10]

Attending church is an important part of keeping the Sabbath day holy.

If we do what our Heavenly Father would have us do we will go to his holy house upon the Sabbath day and there partake of the sacrament in remembrance of the sacrifice that was made for us by the Redeemer of mankind.[11]

This [the Sabbath day] is the Lord's holy day; this is the day that he has set apart in which we are to worship him, and in this latter day he has given an additional commandment that we shall go to the house of prayer and fasting upon his holy day, and there acknowledge our faults and bear our testimonies in the presence of one another [see D&C 59:9–12]. . . .

In this marvelous age when people can sit comfortably at home and hear the music of the world and listen to public addresses, and sermons, they will remain at their own fireside and perhaps feel that they are receiving all that they could receive were they to go to the place appointed for religious services.

The Latter-day Saints need not be deceived in this matter. It is not only the word that we hear that is profitable, but it is the influence that pervades our houses of worship that comes from our Heavenly Father that is essential. We may have a radio receiving set in our home, but we will not benefit by it spiritually, as much as if we go to the house of the Lord upon his holy day, where we are permitted to partake of the Sacrament and where we pray and invoke the blessings of our Heavenly Father and receive [a] witness of the truth calculated to save mankind.[12] [See suggestion 3 on page 177.]

It is a sacred privilege to partake of the sacrament on the Sabbath day.

I think perhaps most of us realize what a gift has come to us on those occasions when we are permitted to assemble in peace and in quiet, to meet together and partake of the emblems of the broken body and the shed blood of the Master. It should be, and I presume [it] is, in the minds of every one of us a most sacred and solemn occasion to realize that we are renewing our covenants with him who gave his life that we might be resurrected and exalted. When we partake of these emblems, I am sure we all realize that the sacrament, established by him before he passed away, is to be to us an uplift and inspiration and a blessing throughout eternity.[13]

The sacrament is of great importance. The Lord Himself ordained that we partake of these emblems. There are many people who believe it is necessary to be baptized, and to have other ordinances of

"The sacrament, established by [the Master] before he passed away, is to be to us an uplift and inspiration and a blessing throughout eternity."

the Gospel performed in their behalf, and yet they become indifferent and careless regarding the sacrament of the Lord's Supper. It was regarded of such importance by our Father in Heaven that, through His beloved Son, and the apostles and prophets, as recorded in the scriptures, the Saints were admonished to partake of it regularly. Three of the evangelists [Gospel writers] refer to it [see Matthew 26:26–28; Mark 14:22–24; Luke 22:19–20], and we find that the scripture, in many places, teaches the importance of it, as it was taught by the Lord Himself when He dwelt in the flesh. Our Father in Heaven does not give us commandments or advice that are not of importance. He teaches us for our uplifting, for our growth and development, and if we will follow His counsel it will prepare us to go back into His presence. . . . Each Sabbath day we are expected to meet together and partake of the emblems of the body and blood of our risen Redeemer. . . .

We also find reference to this in the 18th chapter of Third Nephi, where the Savior is instructing the people on this [the American] continent, just as He had taught His disciples in the old world to observe the sacrament. It reads as follows:

"And when the multitude had eaten and were filled, He said unto the disciples, behold there shall one be ordained among you, and to him will I give power that he shall break bread, and bless it, and give it unto the people of my Church, unto all those who shall believe and be baptized in my name.

"And this shall ye always observe to do, even as I have done, even as I have broken bread, and blessed it, and given it unto you."

. . . The next verse reads as follows:

"And this shall ye do in remembrance of my body, which I have shown unto you. And it shall be a testimony unto the Father, that ye do always remember me. And if ye do always remember me, ye shall have my Spirit to be with you." [3 Nephi 18:5–7.]

. . . In addition to that, we find that in our own day the Lord has given us revelation upon that subject. In section 20 of the Doctrine and Covenants, the Lord gives unto us instructions upon the matter. In that revelation, beginning with the 75th verse, He says:

"It is expedient that the church meet together often to partake of bread and wine in the remembrance of the Lord Jesus;

"And the elder or priest shall administer it; and after this manner shall he administer it—he shall kneel, with the church . . . and call upon the Father in solemn prayer, saying—"

Note the beautiful prayer that follows . . . :

"O God, the Eternal Father, we ask Thee, in the name of Thy Son, Jesus Christ, to bless and sanctify this bread to the souls of all those who partake of it, that they may eat in remembrance of the body of thy Son, and witness unto Thee, O God, the eternal Father, that they are willing to take upon them the name of Thy Son, and always remember Him and keep His commandments which He has given them, that they may always have His Spirit to be with them. Amen." [D&C 20:75–77.]

The prayer and the blessing upon the water is somewhat similar [see D&C 20:78–79].

How sacred, how profoundly sacred, are the thoughts expressed in the sacrament prayer. I admonish you, my brethren, that when we officiate in administering the sacrament, we repeat . . . the exact words given by revelation, and that we do so with the Spirit of the Lord. When we repeat these prayers, we should feel the sentiments expressed by the words that we speak.[14]

I fear sometimes that as the sacrament is administered in some of our meetings there is not the solemn atmosphere that there should be. It is such a sacred privilege. . . . Those who [partake] of the sacrament should have in their minds the obligation that is indicated in the prayer.[15] [See suggestion 4 on page 177.]

Worthily partaking of the sacrament renews our spiritual strength.

We partake of physical food—that is, we partake of bread and water etc., to nourish the physical body. It is just as necessary that we partake of the emblems of the body and blood of our risen Lord to increase our spiritual strength. It is observed that men and women who go from year to year without partaking of the Lord's Supper, gradually lose the Spirit of our Heavenly Father; they forfeit its companionship where they have had opportunity to participate in that blessing, but have failed to take advantage of it. . . .

I have turned to a passage of scripture in the 11th chapter of First Corinthians, beginning with the 23rd verse, which reads as follows:

"For I have received of the Lord that which also I delivered unto you, That the Lord Jesus, the same night in which he was betrayed, took bread:

"And when He had given thanks, He brake it, and said, Take, eat; this is my body, which is broken for you; this do in remembrance of me.

"After the same manner also he took the cup, when he had supped, saying, This cup is the new testament in my blood: this do ye, as oft as ye drink it, in remembrance of me.

"For as often as ye eat this bread, and drink this cup, ye do show the Lord's death till He come.

"Wherefore, whosoever shall eat this bread, and drink this cup of the Lord, unworthily, shall be guilty of the body and blood of the Lord.

"But let a man examine himself, and so let him eat of that bread, and drink of that cup.

"For he that eateth and drinketh unworthily, eateth and drinketh damnation to himself, not discerning the Lord's body.

"For this cause many are weak and sickly among you, and many sleep." [1 Corinthians 11:23–30.]

. . . I desire to call your attention to the fact that there is danger if we do it [partake of the sacrament] unworthily. Before partaking of this sacrament, our hearts should be pure; our hands should be clean; we should be divested of all enmity toward our associates; we should be at peace with our fellow men; and we should have in our hearts a desire to do the will of our Father and to keep all of His commandments. If we do this, partaking of the sacrament will be a blessing to us and will renew our spiritual strength. . . .

. . . We should consider seriously the covenants we make with our Father. Let us pay strict attention to those covenants, and let us see to it that we eat and drink worthily, for the blessings of our souls and for the increase of our spiritual strength. These blessings are for you, my brethren and sisters, who are of the household of faith. Let us appreciate them, and live worthy of them, that by our lives we may exemplify our belief. Let none of us be under condemnation by partaking of the sacrament unworthily, thereby being deprived of the companionship of the Spirit of our Father.[16]

We should partake of it [the sacrament] in humility, with preparation of clean hands and pure hearts, and with a desire to be acceptable to our Father; then we will receive it worthily, and rejoice in the blessing that comes to us.[17]

May the Lord bless us; may His Spirit continue to be poured out upon us. May we love each other, as our Father commanded that we should do. If we can partake of the sacrament worthily, we can love each other, even as our Father has ordained; remembering that He has said unto us: "If ye are not one, ye are not mine." [D&C 38:27.][18] [See suggestion 5 on page 177.]

Suggestions for Study and Teaching

Consider these ideas as you study the chapter or as you prepare to teach. For additional help, see pages v–vii.

1. Read the last paragraph on page 169. If the President of the Church were to attend your sacrament meeting, what do you think his impressions would be? What can you do personally to show greater reverence for the Lord and the sacrament?

2. Ponder President Smith's words in the second and third paragraphs on page 170. How would society in general benefit if more people honored the Sabbath day? What are some appropriate ways to help our families and others see Sabbath-day observance as a blessing rather than a burden?

3. What are some of the benefits of worshipping together on Sunday that we don't receive by simply studying the gospel in our homes? (See page 172 for some examples; see also D&C 59:9–12.)

4. As you read the section that begins on page 172, ponder what you can do to make the ordinance of the sacrament a more meaningful part of your life. What are some effective ways to help children prepare for the sacrament and treat it with reverence?

5. As you read the last four paragraphs of teachings (page 176), look for what President Smith says qualifies us to worthily partake of the sacrament. Why do you think worthily partaking of the sacrament increases our spiritual strength?

Related Scriptures: Exodus 20:8–11; Isaiah 58:13–14; Matthew 18:20; 3 Nephi 18:1–12; 20:8–9; Moroni 6:5–6

Teaching help: "A skilled teacher doesn't think, 'What shall I do in class today?' but asks, 'What will my students do in class today?'; not, 'What will I teach today?' but rather, 'How will I help my students discover what they need to know?'" (Virginia H. Pearce, in *Teaching, No Greater Call,* 61).

Notes

1. In Conference Report, Oct. 1948, 188.

2. In Conference Report, Apr. 1908, 34–35.

3. In Conference Report, Oct. 1937, 50.

4. "A Faith Founded upon Truth," *Deseret News,* June 17, 1944, Church section, 4.

5. In Conference Report, Oct. 1935, 120.

6. In Conference Report, Apr. 1948, 13–14.

7. "Tribute to Richard Ballantyne," *Instructor,* Nov. 1946, 505.

8. "Faith—and Life," *Improvement Era,* Apr. 1949, 252.

9. In Conference Report, Oct. 1948, 188.

10. In Conference Report, Oct. 1932, 23.

11. In Conference Report, Oct. 1932, 23.

12. In *Deseret News,* Jan. 31, 1925, section 3, page 4.

13. "The Sacredness of the Sacrament," *Improvement Era,* Apr. 1946, 206.

14. In Conference Report, Apr. 1908, 35–37.

15. "The Sacredness of the Sacrament," 206.

16. In Conference Report, Apr. 1908, 34–35, 37.

17. In Conference Report, Apr. 1908, 36.

18. In Conference Report, Apr. 1908, 37.

The Strengthening Power of Faith

Faith is a gift from the Lord through which the righteous are empowered to do remarkable things.

From the Life of George Albert Smith

In 1919 George Albert Smith, then a member of the Quorum of the Twelve Apostles, was called as president of the European Mission. In a message to the local Saints shortly after his arrival, President Smith noted the difficult conditions in Europe, which was still recovering from the devastations of World War I: "I realize that we are living in an important period in the world's history. With new, strained conditions confronting the nations, and a spirit of unrest rife almost everywhere, among the children of men, I, therefore, sense the great responsibility assumed in meeting them, and most earnestly desire divine guidance in the discharge of my duties." President Smith had faith that despite the trying times they faced, the efforts of the members and the missionaries would be rewarded with success: "Assisted by good, capable associates at [mission] headquarters, and faithful men and women in the field, I look with pleasant anticipation for a fruitful harvest of honest souls."[1]

One of President Smith's most pressing duties as mission president was to increase the number of missionaries in Europe. The Church had sent very few missionaries to Europe during the war, and now food shortages and other economic problems made European government officials unwilling to grant visas to foreigners. President Smith's difficult task was to persuade these officials to allow missionaries into their countries. In a letter to his daughter Emily, President Smith told of a trip to London for this purpose.

"Scripture is replete with evidences of the power of faith. . . . By faith, the Prophet Elijah called down fire from heaven to consume his offering."

"Our American Ambassador has been very kind and succeeded in securing an interview for us with Sir Robert Horne, the Minister of Labour for Great Britain. When we presented ourselves at his office, we handed our letter from the Ambassador to Sir Robert's secretary, who asked us if our business would hold over as his chief was leaving in a few minutes for Scotland to be gone three weeks. I assured him that we would greatly appreciate five minutes of his time now as we did not live in London and our business was urgent. The secretary went in to Sir Robert and soon returned with the information that he would postpone his trip and meet us at four o'clock that day. I had prayed most fervently that morning that our way might be opened and when we were invited to return I felt most grateful to our Heavenly Father."

At the appointed hour, President Smith and his companions were invited into Sir Robert Horne's private office. "We tried to tell him what we needed and assured him that Great Britain needed what we were asking. For an hour and nearly a half he was a most interested listener to part of the history of the Church and our belief, etc.

"When I had finished he again asked what we wanted of him and when we told him we wanted the privilege of recruiting our missionary forces up to two hundred and fifty, the same as before the war, he said it would afford him pleasure to issue instructions to his department to allow that number to land as fast as they should arrive. Of course we were much pleased and left him with the assurance that he had lifted quite a burden from our minds.

"I feel sure we made a friend of one of England's most influential men and I would not hesitate to go to him at any time if necessity required." [2]

James Gunn McKay, one of President Smith's missionaries who was present at the meeting with Sir Robert Horne, later said: "Look at the wonderful work he accomplished. There were only a few elders there [in the mission]. The way seemed to be hedged up, and yet he came imbued with the inspiration of the Lord, and was able to knock at the doors of the officials, to gain their confidence; and eventually we obtained the privileges we wanted, that elders might come to take up their work and fulfil their missions in furthering the cause of God and accomplishing his work, and in that way he secured to us a testimony that God directs that work."³ Elder McKay attributed President Smith's success to his "faith and devotion and charity toward all those with whom he associated." "I labored with him," he said. "I counseled with him; I prayed with him, and I know that his faith and loyalty are as deep as life itself."⁴ [See suggestion 1 on page 188.]

Teachings of George Albert Smith

The power of faith is evident in the scriptures.

We are informed that without faith we cannot please God [see Hebrews 11:6]. It is the moving cause of all action, and Scripture is replete with evidences of the power of faith. It was Noah's faith that enabled him to build an ark, and as a result of obedience to the commandments of God he and his household were saved, while those who lacked faith were buried in the great flood [see Genesis 6:13–22; 7:1–24].

It was through faith that Lot and the members of his family were preserved when fire from heaven consumed the cities of Sodom and Gomorrah, and destroyed the inhabitants who had not faith [see Genesis 19:12–25].⁵

By faith Moses led the children of Israel from bondage, passing through the Red sea as by dry land, which, the pursuing hosts of the Egyptians essaying to do, were drowned. The multitude were fed with bread from heaven. When Moses smote the rock in Horeb, water gushed forth to slake [satisfy] their thirst; and, passing through the wilderness, they were led to the promised land. [See Exodus 14:21–31; 16:14–15; 17:5–6.]⁶

When Daniel continued to pray openly to the God of Israel, contrary to a decree which had been prepared by his enemies purposely to destroy him, he was cast into a den of lions and left there all night. He knew his Heavenly Father could preserve him and his confidence was unshaken. The next morning the king went early to the pit and found Daniel alive. His faith had rendered the wild

*"By faith Moses led the children of Israel from bondage,
passing through the Red sea as by dry land."*

beasts harmless and earned for him the devotion of the king. [See Daniel 6:4–28.]

Three Hebrews, Shadrach, Meshach, and Abednego, who refused to worship a golden image set up by Nebuchadnezzar, were cast into a fiery furnace heated seven times hotter than usual. They trusted in the living God and their faith was rewarded by the preservation of their lives. [See Daniel 3:8–28.]

By faith, the Prophet Elijah called down fire from heaven to consume his offering, and the king and the people were convinced that the God of Israel was God and that Baal was not [see 1 Kings 18:36–40].

It was by faith that the brother of Jared and his followers retained the language of their fathers during the confusion of tongues at the Tower of Babel, and were brought to this Western Hemisphere [see Ether 1:33–43]. . . . It was a similar faith that enabled Lehi to bring his family across the sea and plant their feet on this land, choice above all other lands.

It was faith that enabled the disciples of Jesus to endure the persecution that overtook them, and in spite of the opposition of the Jews, to establish the gospel which the Savior had delivered to them.[7]

It was by faith that all the miracles were wrought by the Redeemer of the world, and by those who were associated with Him. From the beginning of time until now it has been the faithful man who has had power with God.[8] [See suggestion 2 on pages 188–89.]

The power of faith is evident in the lives of righteous Saints in this dispensation.

In this latter dispensation it was because of his implicit faith in God that the boy prophet [Joseph Smith] went into the woods and knelt down and prayed, and received the first great heavenly manifestation that came to him, by which the personality of the Godhead was again made known to mankind. It was by faith that he was able to go to the hill Cumorah and receive from the hands of the angel those sacred records that he later translated by the gift and power of God. It was by faith he led his people from Kirtland to the land of Missouri and back to Illinois, and though repeatedly plundered and driven from their homes, the faith that had been planted in their hearts remained with them, and they knew that God was mindful of them. It was by faith that the great city of Nauvoo was founded, under the direction of the Prophet Joseph Smith; and by faith the glorious truths contained in the Doctrine and Covenants were received by him.

It was by faith that Brigham Young led the people into this western land [the Salt Lake Valley]; and, when he arrived upon the summit of the mountain and looked over the valley, God gave to him a witness that this was the place where Israel should be planted. . . . It was by faith that the people laid the corner stone of this great Temple [the Salt Lake Temple], in their weakness and in their poverty, believing that God would prepare the way and provide the means whereby the structure might be completed. It was by faith

"It was by faith that Brigham Young led the people into [the Salt Lake Valley]."

that the mercy of our Heavenly Father was extended to the people, when, in their distress, they saw their crops being consumed by the crickets, with no means of preventing it, and, in the providence of God, their prayers were answered, and they received a witness of it in the coming of the gulls to preserve their harvest and deliver them from starvation. . . .

. . . It has been by faith that the men who have stood at the head of this work have been inspired, from time to time, to give the instructions that we have needed. It is by faith that we are edified . . . by those who minister in the name of the Lord, and the Comforter quickens their understanding, bringing things past to their remembrance and showing them things to come; thus evidencing the spirit of revelation.[9]

It has been by faith that the elders of Israel have gone forth, leaving home and loved ones, and enduring the reproach of the world, to bear witness that God lives and that Jesus is the Christ, and that Joseph Smith was a prophet of the Lord. By faith your sick have been healed, your dead have been raised to life. Were the records available of the miracles wrought among this people . . . , it would be a testimony of the power of God, through faith, unsurpassed in any age of the world.

It is this principle, my brethren and sisters, that points us heavenward, that gives us hope in the battle of life. When we become confused, and find ourselves confronted by obstacles we, seemingly, cannot overcome, having faith in the Redeemer of the world, we can go to Him and know that our prayers will be answered for our good.[10] [See suggestion 3 on page 189.]

The question has often been asked: Is it possible that the boys and girls, the young men and women who have been reared in this generation of the Church would be willing to suffer the hardships, privations and trials that their fathers and mothers endured for the gospel's sake? Would they leave their homes of comfort to people a new country in the interest of their faith?

I say to you that if there has been planted in their hearts a knowledge of the divinity of this work as we know it, if faith has been given them by reason of our keeping the commandments of the Lord, if they have been taught to know that Jesus is the Christ and that Joseph Smith was a prophet of the Lord, then I say unto you, Yes! they would do what their fathers and mothers have done, take their place in the ranks of latter-day Israel.

If it meant privation, if it meant sickness and distress, or even expatriation from home, there are hundreds and thousands of our sons and daughters who, knowing that this is the gospel of Christ, would, if need be, seal their testimony with their lives.[11] [See suggestion 2 on pages 188–89.]

The Lord will open the way for us to do what He asks if we exercise faith.

I remember one day I was impressed to say to a missionary who was going to a certain town where they would not let us hold street meetings:

"Now remember, give the Lord a chance. You are going to ask a favor. Give the Lord a chance. Ask him to open the way."

The young man went to that city, went into the office of the mayor, and asked if he could see him. He was going to ask if they might change the rule.

When he got there, he found that the mayor was out of town. The young man came out of the office, looked down the hall and saw on a door at the end of the hall, "Chief Constable's Office." He hesitated a moment, and something said to him: "Give the Lord a chance." He walked into the chief constable's office and told him what he had come for. When he finished the man said:

"Well, what street corner would you like?"

He said: "I don't know this city as well as you do. I would not ask for a corner that would be undesirable, or where we would block the traffic. Would you mind going with me to select a corner?"

Just think of a missionary asking the chief constable to pick a corner on which to preach the gospel!

The constable said:

"Surely, I will go with you."

In fifteen minutes they had one of the best corners in town, with permission to preach the gospel of Jesus Christ where it had not been preached on the streets since before the war [World War I]. . . .

The Lord has a way of accomplishing things that we are unable to do, and never asks us to do anything that he does not make the way possible. That is what he told us through Nephi. He will not require anything without preparing the way.

"And it came to pass that I, Nephi, said unto my father: I will go and do the things which the Lord hath commanded, for I know that the Lord giveth no commandments unto the children of men, save he shall prepare a way for them that they may accomplish the thing which he commandeth them." [1 Nephi 3:7.]

If you have something that the Lord asks or expects you to do and you don't know just how to proceed, do your best. Move in the direction that you ought to go; trust the Lord, give him a chance, and he will never fail you.[12]

What a wonderful thing it is to know that we can, if we will, hold our Heavenly Father's hand and be guided by him. No other people in the world have the assurance that this group of people has.[13] [See suggestion 4 on page 189.]

God grants faith as a gift to the righteous.

Our faith is conditioned upon our righteous lives. We cannot live improperly and have faith as we should, but if we keep the commandments of the Lord, we can have faith, and it will grow and increase as our righteousness increases.[14]

If there are any of us who lack faith in this work it is because we have not kept the commandments of God. If there are any who do not know that this is the work of our Father, it is because they have not done their duty. I know as I know that I live that this is the Lord's work, and that knowledge comes as a result of keeping His commandments.[15]

We know that faith is a gift of God; it is the fruitage of righteous living. It does not come to us by our command, but is the result of doing the will of our Heavenly Father. If we lack faith let us examine ourselves to see if we have been keeping His commandments, and repent without delay if we have not. . . . May the Lord increase our faith, and may we live to be worthy of it.[16]

I hope that those who have received this wonderful gift of faith are living to retain it.[17] [See suggestion 5 on page 189.]

Suggestions for Study and Teaching

Consider these ideas as you study the chapter or as you prepare to teach. For additional help, see pages v–vii.

1. Look for evidences of George Albert Smith's faith in the story on pages 179–81. One of President Smith's missionaries said that his accomplishments "secured to us a testimony that God directs that work" (page 182). How have you been influenced by the faith of others, such as a family member or a close friend?

2. Review the examples of faith on pages 182–86. What other examples of faith are particularly meaningful to you? How could

you use these examples to help someone who is exercising faith but has not yet received the blessings he or she desires?

3. How has your faith given you "hope in the battle of life"? How can faith help us overcome fear or other "obstacles we, seemingly, cannot overcome"? (page 186).

4. Read the story that begins on page 186, and compare it with the story in "From the Life of George Albert Smith." What experiences have you had that are similar to these? What do you think it means to "give the Lord a chance"?

5. President Smith taught that "faith is a gift of God" that "does not come to us by our command" (page 188). How does this principle influence the way you try to increase your faith and inspire faith in others? What are some specific things we can do to "retain" the gift of faith? (see Alma 32:35–43).

Related Scriptures: Hebrews 11:1–11, 17–34; James 2:17–24; Alma 32:26–43; Ether 12:6–22; Moroni 7:27–39; Doctrine and Covenants 136:42

Teaching help: "To help learners prepare to answer questions, you may want to tell them before something is read or presented that you will be asking for their responses. . . . For example, you could say, 'Listen as I read this passage so that you can share what most interests you about it' or 'As this scripture is read, see if you can understand what the Lord is telling us about faith'" (*Teaching, No Greater Call,* 69).

Notes

1. "Greeting," *Millennial Star,* July 10, 1919, 440–41.

2. In Glenn R. Stubbs, "A Biography of George Albert Smith, 1870 to 1951" (PhD diss., Brigham Young University, 1974), 142–43.

3. James Gunn McKay, in Conference Report, Oct. 1921, 156.

4. James Gunn McKay, in "A Biography of George Albert Smith," 160.

5. In Conference Report, Apr. 1923, 75–76.

6. In Conference Report, Oct. 1913, 102.

7. In Conference Report, Apr. 1923, 75–76.

8. In Conference Report, Oct. 1913, 102.

9. In Conference Report, Oct. 1913, 102–3.

10. In Conference Report, Oct. 1913, 102–3.

11. "As to This Generation," *Improvement Era,* Feb. 1949, 73.

12. "Give the Lord a Chance," *Improvement Era,* July 1946, 427.

13. In Conference Report, Apr. 1947, 164.

14. In Conference Report, Oct. 1950, 6.

15. In Conference Report, Oct. 1915, 27–28.

16. In Conference Report, Oct. 1913, 103.

17. In Conference Report, Apr. 1923, 77.

*"If we will follow the advice and counsel that the Lord has given,
our pathway will be one of happiness."*

Stay on the Lord's Side
of the Line

*The Lord has given us commandments so that
we can resist evil and find happiness.*

From the Life of George Albert Smith

George Albert Smith's grandfather George A. Smith served for many years in the Quorum of the Twelve Apostles and in the First Presidency as a counselor to Brigham Young. George Albert Smith often repeated the counsel his grandfather used to give to his family: "There is a line of demarcation well defined between the Lord's territory and the devil's territory. If you will stay on the Lord's side of the line you will be under his influence and will have no desire to do wrong; but if you cross to the devil's side of that line one inch you are in the tempter's power and if he is successful, you will not be able to think or even reason properly because you will have lost the Spirit of the Lord."

George Albert Smith said that he used this counsel throughout his life to guide his choices: "When I have been tempted sometimes to do a certain thing, I have asked myself, 'Which side of the line am I on?' If I determined to be on the safe side, the Lord's side, I would do the right thing every time. So when temptation comes think prayerfully about your problem and the influence of the Lord will aid you to decide wisely. There is safety for us only on the Lord's side of the line."[1] [See suggestion 1 on page 199.]

Teachings of George Albert Smith

Staying on the Lord's side of the line requires strict obedience to the commandments.

All safety, all righteousness, all happiness are on the Lord's side of the line. If you are keeping the commandments of God by observing the Sabbath day, you are on the Lord's side of the line. If you attend to your secret prayers and your family prayers, you are on the Lord's side of the line. If you are grateful for food and express that gratitude to God, you are on the Lord's side of the line. If you love your neighbor as yourself, you are on the Lord's side of the line. If you are honest in your dealing with your fellow men, you are on the Lord's side of the line. If you observe the Word of Wisdom, you are on the Lord's side of the line. And so I might go on through the Ten Commandments and the other commandments that God has given for our guidance and say again, all that enriches our lives and makes us happy and prepares us for eternal joy is on the Lord's side of the line. Finding fault with the things that God has given to us for our guidance is not on the Lord's side of the line. [2] [See suggestion 2 on page 199.]

[The Lord has said]: "I cannot look upon sin with the least degree of allowance;" not with the least degree of allowance [D&C 1:31]. Why? Because He knows that if we partake of sin we lose a blessing that we would enjoy if we did not forsake the pathway that leads to that blessing. [3]

Every once in a while we hear somebody say, "Oh, I wouldn't be so particular. The Lord is not going to be very severe with us if we just go part way." The one who is talking that way is already on the devil's side of the line, and you do not want to listen to him because if you do, you may be misled. Nobody talks that way who has the Spirit of the Lord. The Lord himself has said that we must keep his commandments: "There is a law, irrevocably decreed in heaven before the foundations of this world, upon which all blessings are predicated." (D&C 130:20.) The gospel of Jesus Christ is to teach us how to earn that blessing. [4]

"The revelations of the Lord to us in this day and age of the world, are but the sweet music of the voice of our Father in heaven in His mercy to us."

Our loving Father in Heaven gives us commandments to help us find happiness.

The Lord, in His kindness, seeing the attitude of His children, and knowing that they would need guidance, gave to us the Ten Commandments, and other commandments that have been given from time to time, to help us to find happiness. You observe people running to and fro in the world, seeking happiness but not finding it. If they would only pause long enough to accept the Lord's advice happiness would follow, but they will find it in no other way.[5]

When I was a child I recognized, or thought I did, that the commandments of the Lord were His laws and regulations for my guidance. I thought I recognized in the disobedience to those laws that punishment would follow, and as a child I presume I may have felt that the Lord had so arranged affairs and so ordained matters in this life that I must obey certain laws or swift retribution would follow. But as I grew older I have learned the lesson from another viewpoint, and now to me the laws of the Lord, so-called, the counsels contained in the Holy Scriptures, the revelations of the Lord to us in this day and age of the world, are but the sweet music of the voice of our Father in heaven in His mercy to us. They are but the advice and counsel of a loving parent, who is more concerned in our welfare than earthly parents can be, and consequently that which at one time seemed to bear the harsh name of law to me is now the loving and tender advice of an all-wise Heavenly Father. And so I say it is not hard for me to believe that it is best for me to keep the commandments of God.[6]

All the happiness that has come to me and mine has been the result of trying to keep the commandments of God and of living to be worthy of the blessings that he has promised those who honor him and keep his commandments.[7]

If we will follow the advice and counsel that the Lord has given, our pathway will be one of happiness. It will be a pathway, perhaps not of ease and comfort always, but in the end it will terminate in the presence of our Heavenly Father, and glory, immortality and eternal lives will be our portion.[8] [See suggestion 3 on page 199.]

The adversary tries to lead us astray with his deceptions and subtleties.

There are two influences in the world today and have been from the beginning. One is an influence that is constructive, that radiates happiness and that builds character. The other influence is one that destroys, turns men into demons, tears down and discourages. We are all susceptible to both. The one comes from our Heavenly Father and the other comes from the source of evil that has been in the world from the beginning seeking to bring about the destruction of the human family.[9]

We will all be tempted; no man is free from temptation. The adversary will use every means possible to deceive us; he tried to do that with the Savior of the world without success. He has tried it on many other men who have possessed divine authority, and sometimes he finds a weak spot and the individual loses what might have been a great blessing if he had been faithful.[10]

A man once said to me—or remarked in a place where I happened to be—"Why, these people here seem to think I am full of the devil, but I am not." And I said to him, "My brother, did you ever know anybody that was full of the devil and knew it?" That is one of the tricks of the devil: To get possession of you and keep you from knowing it. And that is one of our difficulties.[11]

The Prophet Nephi, hundreds of years ago, saw what would occur, that the people were to contend with one another and deny the power of the Holy Ghost and the Holy One of Israel, and were to teach for doctrine the commandments of men. An influence is in the world today trying to make people believe that by their own intelligence and by their own power they can gain eternal life. Let me . . . read from Nephi:

"And there shall also be many which shall say, Eat, drink and be merry, nevertheless fear God, he will justify in committing a little sin."

I want you to note that: "He will justify in committing a little sin." That cunning adversary knowing that if he could only get a man or woman to do a little wrong, that far they had gone into his territory, that far they were in his power.

"Nevertheless, fear God, he will justify in committing a little sin, yea, lie a little, take the advantage of one because of his words, dig a pit for thy neighbor; there is no harm in this. And do all these things, for tomorrow we die; and if it so be that we are guilty, God will beat us with a few stripes, and at last we shall be saved in the Kingdom of God." [2 Nephi 28:8.]

Isn't that just exactly what the devil says to the children of men today as plainly as it is written here? Oh, commit a little sin, that won't do any harm, lie a little, that won't do any particular damage, the Lord will forgive that and you will only be beaten with a few stripes and at last you shall be saved in the kingdom of God. That is what he says to the man or the woman who has been taught the Word of Wisdom when he says, oh, drink a little tea, that won't hurt you; use a little tobacco, that won't make any difference; a little liquor won't do any harm. These are little things; he always does it a little at a time, not all at once. That is what I would like us to remember. . . . It is these insignificant insidious whisperings that betray mankind and that place us in the power of the devil. . . .

And Nephi says further:

"And others will he pacify and lull them away into carnal security, that they will say, All is well in Zion; yea Zion prospereth, all is well; and thus the devil cheateth their souls."

Now, I want you to note that: "And thus the devil cheateth their souls and leadeth them away carefully down to hell." [2 Nephi 28:21.] And that is the way he does it, that's exactly the way he does it. He does not come and grab you bodily and take you into his territory, but he whispers, "Do this little evil," and when he succeeds in that, another little evil and another, and, to use the expression quoted, "He cheateth their souls." That's what he does. He makes you believe that you are gaining something when you are losing. So it is every time we fail to observe a law of God or keep a commandment, we are being cheated, because there is no gain in this world or in the world to come but by obedience to the law of our Heavenly Father.

. . . That peculiar suggestion, "And he leadeth them *carefully* away down to hell" is significant, that is his method. Men and women in the world today are subject to that influence, and they are being drawn here and there, and that whispering is going on and they do not understand what the Lord desires them to do, but they continue in the territory of the evil one, subject to his power where the Spirit of the Lord will not go.

He says further: . . .

"And behold, others he flattereth away, and telleth them there is no hell; and he saith unto them, I am no devil, for there is none; and thus he whispereth in their ears, until he grasps them with his awful chains, from whence there is no deliverance." [2 Nephi 28:22.]

Now, my brethren and sisters, that is the condition of the world today. Nephi could not have stated it plainer if he had been right here in the world now. And the adversary is at work, and because our Heavenly Father desired to preserve his children from the evil of that teaching and of that belief he sent the boy prophet, Joseph Smith, into the world, commissioned him with divine authority, organized His Church, and began again to teach the truth to the children of men, that they might be led from the error of their ways.[12]

We must learn to overcome our passions, our evil tendencies. We must learn to resist temptations. That is why we are here, and in order that we may more perfectly do that, the gospel has been restored to the earth, and we have been made partakers of it, and we have the strength that comes to us as a result of the power of the Holy Ghost. We not only have the resistance of an ordinary individual, with the limitations that such an individual has who has not the knowledge of the truth—we have equal resistance with him, and in addition the resistance which comes from knowing the truth and knowing the purpose of our being.[13] [See suggestion 4 on pages 199–200.]

We can resist evil by choosing to subject ourselves to the influence of the Lord.

I remember a number of years ago a good man who was at that time chairman of the board of control of the Universalist Church of America. He came here to visit [Salt Lake City] and attended two of our Sunday schools. In one of the [children's] classes he became much interested. Eventually, when the [class] was about to close, the superintendent said, "Wouldn't you like to say a few words to the [class]?" . . . He said, "I would like to say a few words." He said, "If I could only live in the atmosphere that I found in that little . . . class in this Sabbath school this morning, I couldn't help but be a good man." [See suggestion 5 on page 200.]

I have thought of that a good many times. We choose carefully the atmosphere that we breathe, that we may live in health. But sometimes, in our carelessness, we place ourselves in subjection to immoral influences that destroy our resistance of evil, and we are led to do things that we ought not to do and would not do if under the influence of the Lord. If we would only be humble, if we would only be prayerful, if we would only live in such a way that each hour of our lives we could truthfully say, "Father in heaven, I am willing and anxious to do what thou wouldst have me do,"

"How careful we as Latter-day Saints ought to be to live every day of our lives that we may be influenced by the power of the Lord."

our lives every day would be enriched as we go through this earth experience.[14]

We choose where we will be. God has given us our agency. He will not take it from us, and if I do that which is wrong and get into the devil's territory, I do it because I have the will and power to do it. I cannot blame anybody else, and if I determine to keep the commandments of God and live as I ought to live and stay on the Lord's side of the line I do it because I ought to do it, and I will receive my blessing for it. It will not be the result of what somebody else may do.[15]

How careful we as Latter-day Saints ought to be to live every day of our lives that we may be influenced by the power of the Lord, and that we may be able to turn aside from those things that have a tendency to break down our power to earn the celestial kingdom.[16]

See that your feet are planted upon the rock. See that you learn the desires of the Master toward you, and, knowing those desires, see to it that you keep His laws and commands. See to it that the purity of your lives shall entitle you to the companionship of the Holy Spirit, because if you are pure and virtuous and upright, the evil one will have no power to destroy you.[17]

I pray that we examine ourselves and find out which side of the line we are on; and if we are on the Lord's side, stay there, because that means eternal happiness in the companionship of the best men and women that have lived upon the earth.

If we have slipped in any way, if we have been careless; if we have listened to the tempter and gone across the line to partake of those things that the world thinks are so desirable and the Lord has said are not good for us, let us as quickly as possible get back on the other side, ask the Lord to forgive us our foolishness, and then with his help go on living the life that means eternal happiness.[18]

Suggestions for Study and Teaching

Consider these ideas as you study the chapter or as you prepare to teach. For additional help, see pages v–vii.

1. Read "From the Life of George Albert Smith" (page 191) and Moroni 7:10–19. How do you know when you are "on the Lord's side of the line"? What can we do to help each other stay on the Lord's side of the line?

2. In the first paragraph on page 192, President Smith names several commandments that we should obey to stay on the Lord's side of the line. What other standards has the Lord given us to help us stay on His side of the line?

3. As you read the section that begins on page 193, consider how you might use President Smith's teachings to help someone who feels that the commandments are too restrictive.

4. As you review pages 194–97, look for the tactics of Satan that President Smith describes, and think about times when you have seen evidence of these tactics. How can we help young

people recognize and overcome them? How does "knowing the purpose of our being" (page 197) help us resist temptation?

5. Think about how the story on page 197 might apply to you. What are some of the places or circumstances in which you feel no desire to do evil? What can we do to create such an atmosphere in our homes? in our workplaces? in our communities? in our personal lives?

Related Scriptures: Matthew 4:1–11 (including excerpts from the Joseph Smith Translation in the footnotes); James 4:7; 1 John 5:3–4; Alma 13:27–28; Helaman 5:12; Doctrine and Covenants 82:8–10

Teaching help: "Questions written on the chalkboard before class will help learners begin to think about topics even before the lesson begins" (*Teaching, No Greater Call,* 93).

Notes

1. "A Faith Founded upon Truth," *Deseret News,* June 17, 1944, Church section, 9.
2. In Conference Report, Oct. 1945, 118.
3. *Sharing the Gospel with Others,* sel. Preston Nibley (1948), 198; address given Nov. 4, 1945, in Washington, D.C.
4. "'Seek Ye First the Kingdom of God,'" *Improvement Era,* Oct. 1947, 690.
5. In Conference Report, Apr. 1941, 25.
6. In Conference Report, Oct. 1911, 43–44.
7. In Conference Report, Apr. 1949, 87.
8. In Conference Report, Apr. 1937, 36.
9. "A Faith Founded upon Truth," 9.
10. In Conference Report, Oct. 1945, 117.
11. In Conference Report, Apr. 1948, 179.
12. In Conference Report, Apr. 1918, 39–41.
13. In Conference Report, Oct. 1926, 102.
14. In Conference Report, Oct. 1929, 23.
15. In Conference Report, Oct. 1932, 27.
16. In Conference Report, Oct. 1926, 103.
17. In Conference Report, Oct. 1906, 48.
18. "'Seek Ye First the Kingdom of God,'" 691.

Temporal and Spiritual Blessings from the Word of Wisdom

Our Heavenly Father gave us the
Word of Wisdom to bless us with physical health
and prepare us for eternal life.

From the Life of George Albert Smith

When George Albert Smith was a child, he was afflicted with typhoid fever. The doctor who diagnosed him told his mother that he should stay in bed for three weeks, eat no solid food, and drink some coffee. President Smith later recalled:

"When he went away, I told mother that I didn't want any coffee. I had been taught that the Word of Wisdom, given by the Lord to Joseph Smith, advised us not to use coffee.

"Mother had brought three children into the world and two had died. She was unusually anxious about me."

Young George Albert Smith asked instead for a priesthood blessing, which he received from his home teacher.

"When the doctor came the next morning I was playing outside with the other children. He was surprised. He examined me and discovered that my fever was gone and that I seemed to be well.

"I was grateful to the Lord for my recovery. I was sure that he had healed me."[1]

President Smith wanted the Saints to understand that obedience to the Word of Wisdom brings not only physical health but spiritual blessings as well. In a priesthood session of general conference, he told the story of the Old Testament prophet Daniel, who was taken

President Smith taught that because Daniel observed the Lord's law of health in his day, he was worthy of "the inspiration of the Almighty."

captive into Babylon and was expected to eat the king's meat and drink the king's wine:

"Daniel was a prophet of God, and he was a prophet because he kept the commandments of God. I would like you . . . to take this message with you. Daniel observed the teachings of God with his companions, with reference to the kind of food and drink they should have, and refused to accept the food that was served upon the king's table. [See Daniel 1:3–16.]"

President Smith went on to explain that because of Daniel's obedience to the Lord's law of health in his day, not only was his life preserved, but Daniel also received a great spiritual blessing: "the inspiration of the Almighty."[2] [See suggestion 1 on page 209.]

Teachings of George Albert Smith

The Word of Wisdom is loving counsel from our Father, who knows all things.

I am going to read you a portion of what the Lord said to the Church on February 27th, 1833.

"A Word of Wisdom, for the benefit of the council of high priests, assembled in Kirtland, and the Church and also the Saints of Zion—

"To be sent greeting; not by commandment or constraint, but by revelation and the word of wisdom, showing forth the order and will of God in the temporal salvation of all saints in the last days."

Now just think of that for a moment—"in the temporal salvation of all saints in the last days."

"Given for a principle with promise, adapted to the capacity of the weak and the weakest of all saints, who are or can be called saints." [See D&C 89:1–3.]

Then the Lord continues to tell us the things that are good for us, explains the kind of food that it is desirable for us to use, and then warns us against some of the things that have been most deleterious and harmful [see D&C 89:5–17].

It seems to me that as a people we have been marvelously blessed. . . . The Lord has been merciful to us, to caution us, advise us and warn us with regard to many things.[3]

I look upon the Word of Wisdom as kind advice of our Father in heaven, who desires to see His children become more like Him. . . . I take it as the fatherly counsel of one who, knowing what I needed, said to me: "My son, these things are not good for you, and if you will avoid them I will give you the companionship of my Holy Spirit and joy while you live in the world and in the end eternal life." How foolish I would be then to partake of these forbidden things, having the assurance that it is the counsel of the Lord I should abstain therefrom. I would feel under condemnation if I should partake of them, when He who knows better than anybody else says that they are harmful, and has warned me against them. . . .

. . . He thought it of enough importance to give it unto us, and to warn us, and if He who knows all things thought it necessary to give advice and counsel upon these temporal matters, how carefully we, who know not what the morrow has in store for us, should observe that divine counsel. I feel that the Latter-day Saints have in the Word of Wisdom a law that will exalt them and lift them above those who fail to keep it.[4]

The gospel of Jesus Christ is to preserve souls, of which the body is the tabernacle, for eternal happiness. How foolish we are if we give way to the habits and customs of the world! . . . Our Heavenly Father in his kindness and love [warned]: "In consequence of the evils and designs which do and will exist in the hearts of conspiring men in the last days, I have warned you and forewarn you by giving unto you this word of wisdom by revelation." (D&C 89:4.) . . . The purpose of the gospel of Jesus Christ is to prepare us to understand the beauty of life as the Lord has indicated it should be lived, by telling us how we may avoid the things that are destroying the world.[5]

Do you believe that the Lord gave to us the Word of Wisdom? Do you really think that he knows what is good for us? Do you think it would please him if we would observe that law? He says it would. Do you think he meant it?[6]

Brethren and sisters, we cannot with impunity look slightingly upon the Word of Wisdom. It was given as counsel and advice, not by commandment or constraint, but as a word of wisdom, from our Father, for the temporal salvation of our bodies and the preparation of our souls for eternal life.[7] [See suggestion 2 on page 210.]

The Lord promises mental and physical health to those who obey the Word of Wisdom.

I am grateful for that wonderful Word of Wisdom, simple as it is, and as the Lord says, "adapted to the capacity of the weak or the weakest of all who are or can be called Saints." I pause to ask . . . , are we worthy to be called Saints? All who hope to be called Saints should certainly be observers of the Word of Wisdom. And what does it mean to us? It gives us sweetness of life, it takes from us the poisonous vapors that many people breathe as the result of smoking tobacco. It avoids for us that nauseating condition that is the result of chewing tobacco. It preserves us, if we observe it, from the infirmities due to taking into our systems the [drugs] contained in tea and coffee, and from the disastrous effects of liquor. . . .

Our Heavenly Father not only tells us what we should avoid, but tells us what we may use with profit. He has said to us that all grain, all wholesome herbs, the fruit of the vine etc., are good for man. Flesh of beast and fowls of the air; and these things he refers to we may use with prudence and thanksgiving; and I want to emphasize with thanksgiving.[8]

We observe that compliance with the laws of health produces mental and physical strength, and we discover that through disobedience thereto, mental and physical deterioration follows. It is our Creator, the Father of our spirits, who gave us opportunity to dwell upon this earth, who has said that certain things referred to in that revelation are not good for us. He has made us valuable promises, if we will obey this law,—promises of wisdom, of health and strength, and that the destroying angel shall pass us by and not hurt us, as he did the children of Israel [see D&C 89:18–21].[9] [See suggestion 3 on page 210.]

*"Our Heavenly Father not only tells us what we should avoid,
but tells us what we may use with profit."*

Obeying the Word of Wisdom strengthens our faith and spirituality.

I am fully convinced that the Lord in His mercy, when He gave us the Word of Wisdom, gave it to us, not alone that we might have health while we live in the world, but that our faith might be strengthened, that our testimony of the divinity of the mission of our Lord and Master might be increased, that thereby we might be better prepared to return to his presence when our labor here is complete. I fear that as sons and daughters of Zion we sometimes fail to realize the importance of this great message to the world. [10]

I want to say to you, in my judgment, that the use of tobacco, a little thing as it seems to some men, has been the means of destroying their spiritual life, has been the means of driving from them the companionship of the Spirit of our Father, has alienated them from the society of good men and women, and has brought upon them the disregard and reproach of the children that have been born to them, and yet the devil will say to a man, Oh, it's only a little thing![11]

We are living in a day when the Lord has spoken again to His people. We, who are members of the Church, who have complied with the requirements of our Father in Heaven, understand perfectly that God lives and that He is a rewarder of those who diligently serve Him. We understand that He has given certain rules and regulations to govern us in this life, and obedience to His requirements insures us His pleasure, and the blessings promised will follow our obedience; but, if we fail to obey His teachings, if we ignore His wise counsels, then we have no promise from Him, and we are wasting opportunities that will not come to us again. I feel the importance of the Latter-day Saints observing this particular law [the Word of Wisdom]. I believe that by obedience to it, much more faith may be enjoyed by the Latter-day Saints. We read in the teachings of Mormon that if there were not miracles wrought among that people it was because they did not have faith; and he told them, further, that without faith, "awful was the state of man." [See Moroni 7:37–38.] If we violate the known will of the Lord it is natural that our faith will wane, for the Spirit will not always strive with us. . . .

. . . I firmly believe that by reason of neglect of this simple requirement, faith has diminished in the hearts of some of our people—that, by a more general observance of the Word of Wisdom, faith will be increased among the Latter-day Saints, and greater knowledge will flow to us as a result; for by obedience to it, there will come a disposition to obey other laws of our Father, and compliance with each insures a blessing.[12] [See suggestions 3 and 4 on page 210.]

**By obeying the Word of Wisdom,
we prepare for eternal life.**

I sometimes wonder if Latter-day Saints realize that [the Word of Wisdom] has been given to us for our exaltation; not only for our temporal blessing, but to prepare us for spiritual life. . . .

We are told that the glory of God is intelligence [see D&C 93:36], and we all admire intelligent men and women, therefore it should be our desire to lay the foundation for increased mental power and not do anything to weaken it. It is evident in the lives of some that they deprive themselves of the brain power they might enjoy, by the continued use of things our Heavenly Father has said are not good; they become less intelligent as a result, and fail to make the preparation for Eternal life that should be their ambition.[13]

If we believe as we claim, that Jesus is the Christ, and that we are the children of our Heavenly Father, then how careful we should be to conduct ourselves that we may be worthy of the temples we occupy, which were created in the image of God. How many of us realize that by taking into our systems things that our Father has forbidden, we defile the temple of the spirit? How many of us stop to consider that when we give way to weakness of the flesh, we deprive ourselves of opportunities that await us in the future, and cut ourselves off from the blessings that the Lord hath in store for the faithful?[14]

If this law, that is adapted to the capacity of the weakest of us, is obeyed, it will be a foundation upon which may be added many great blessings that our Father will be pleased to bestow, that otherwise we would not be entitled to and could not receive. How can any of us feel justified in ignoring a simple law of God that He, by His own voice, has said any of us can obey? Can we expect to be able to keep a higher law, and be able to attain great exaltation, if we fail to keep this simple requirement?[15] [See suggestion 3 on page 210.]

The best way to teach our families to obey the Word of Wisdom is to obey it ourselves.

Fathers and mothers, if they will keep the Word of Wisdom, may transmit to their offspring virtues and strength that they could not otherwise give to them. I believe that the companionship of the Spirit of our Father will be in the hearts and homes of those who keep this law, and their desire to be obedient will be transmitted to their children. . . . It is a well known fact that the effect of tobacco upon the child brain is most harmful, destroying the memory and dulling the finer senses; also, that the effect of liquor upon the youthful brain is very deleterious: it breaks down the desire to be honorable and upright, and leads to vice and crime. . . . The Lord has given us this law in kindness and love, promising certain blessings if we will obey His counsel. I feel to exhort you, my brethren and sisters, to teach this in your homes. Call the attention of your growing children to it, and to the reward predicated on its observance.

Let me say to you that the best evidence of our faith in that law, that we believe it came from God, is a consistent observance of it in our lives. We may preach it all day long, but if we transgress it in practice, our example may be disastrous to those we love better than life, for they will feel that they can safely follow where we lead.[16]

Let me plead with you, search the Word of Wisdom prayerfully. Do not just read it; search it prayerfully. Discover what our Heavenly Father gave it for. He gave it to us with a promise of longer life and happiness, not if we fail to observe it, but if we observe it. Read the Word of Wisdom in the presence of your families and set the example. If we will do that Zion will continue to grow. If we will do that the Church of the Lamb of God will continue to become a power for good in the world.[17] [See suggestion 5 on page 210.]

Suggestions for Study and Teaching

Consider these ideas as you study the chapter or as you prepare to teach. For additional help, see pages v–vii.

1. On page 203, President Smith refers to the story of Daniel declining to partake of the king's meat and wine. Read Daniel chapter 1, and think about an experience you may have had when you were expected to partake of something that is forbidden in the Word of Wisdom. What are some appropriate ways to obey the Word of Wisdom in such circumstances while still being respectful to others?

2. Review the first section of teachings (pages 203–5). How could you use these teachings to help someone who is having difficulty obeying the Word of Wisdom?

3. Briefly review pages 205–8, in which President Smith discusses some of the blessings promised to those who obey the Word of Wisdom (see also D&C 89:18–21). How have these promises been fulfilled in your life? What other blessings have you received as you have lived this law?

4. On page 207, President Smith promises that obeying the Word of Wisdom brings a "disposition to obey." What does this phrase mean to you?

5. In your opinion, how does our obedience to the Word of Wisdom help the Church "become a power for good in the world"? (page 209). Prayerfully study section 89 of the Doctrine and Covenants, as President Smith suggests, and ponder what you can do to obey the Word of Wisdom more fully.

Related Scriptures: 1 Corinthians 6:19–20; Alma 34:36; Doctrine and Covenants 29:34; 130:20–21

Teaching help: "You can express love for those you teach by listening attentively to them and being sincerely interested in their lives. Christlike love has the power to soften hearts and help people be receptive to the whisperings of the Spirit" (*Teaching, No Greater Call,* 46).

Notes

1. "Boyhood Experiences," *Instructor,* Feb. 1943, 73.

2. In Conference Report, Oct. 1943, 44.

3. "Saints Blessed," *Deseret News,* Nov. 12, 1932, Church section, 5.

4. In Conference Report, Apr. 1907, 19–21.

5. "'Seek Ye First the Kingdom of God,'" *Improvement Era,* Oct. 1947, 688.

6. In Conference Report, Oct. 1935, 121.

7. In Conference Report, Apr. 1907, 21.

8. In Conference Report, Oct. 1923, 72–73.

9. In Conference Report, Apr. 1907, 19.

10. In Conference Report, Apr. 1907, 19.

11. In Conference Report, Apr. 1918, 40.

12. In Conference Report, Oct. 1908, 83–84.

13. In Conference Report, Apr. 1907, 19.

14. In Conference Report, Apr. 1905, 62.

15. In Conference Report, Oct. 1908, 84.

16. In Conference Report, Apr. 1907, 21.

17. In Conference Report, Apr. 1949, 191.

Temporal Salvation for Ourselves and Others

If we follow the Lord's counsel, we are better able to meet our own temporal needs and help those in need around us.

From the Life of George Albert Smith

George Albert Smith became President of the Church as World War II was ending. The war had left many nations devastated, and thousands of people were without food and other necessities. In a general conference address, President Smith described their plight and urged the Saints to help relieve their suffering: "They are all [God's] children. They need us; they need not only our moral support and our religious teaching, but they need food and clothing and bedding and help of all kinds because, in many cases, they haven't anything left. If you could see some of the letters that come into our office from some of the poor people over there, it would wring your hearts. People who have been taken away from their homes with the idea that they were going to be allowed to settle elsewhere, and all of a sudden deserted, and then when they returned to their homes, found them pillaged and robbed of what they had—everything— and left helpless, with no place to go."[1]

Because the Church had been in the practice of storing food for many years, it was prepared to help in these circumstances. Efforts to provide such help began near the end of 1945, when President Smith went to Washington, D.C., to make arrangements with the president of the United States, Harry S Truman, to send food and clothing to Europe. During their meeting President Truman said, "We will be glad to help you in any way we can. . . . How long will it take you to get this ready?"

George Albert Smith visiting a bishops' storehouse with other Church leaders. Because the Church had been storing food, it was prepared to help those in need in the aftermath of World War II.

President Smith surprised him by replying: "It's all ready. . . . We [have been] building elevators and filling them with grain, and increasing our flocks and our herds, and now what we need is the cars and the ships in order to send considerable food, clothing and bedding to the people of Europe who are in distress. We have an organization in the Church [the Relief Society] that has over two thousand homemade quilts ready."

President Smith reported to the Saints that as a result of these shipments, "many people received warm clothing and bedding and food without any delay. Just as fast as we could get cars and ships, we had what was necessary to send to Europe."[2]

Almost 15 years earlier, Elder Smith, then a member of the Quorum of the Twelve Apostles, addressed the Relief Society during another time of desperate need—the Great Depression. He taught that helping those in need goes beyond providing temporal assistance; it also requires true kindness and charity:

"There never has been a time, in my judgment, when kindness was needed more than now. These are the days when people's souls are being tried, and when their hearts are being wrung. These are the days when many are facing hunger and distress even among the Latter-day Saints. . . .

". . . I believe our Heavenly Father is giving us our opportunity for development. . . . We will discover now whether the love the Savior said should be in our hearts is among us."[3] [See suggestion 1 on page 221.]

Teachings of George Albert Smith

If we are wise with our means, we will be prepared for hard times.

It was the advice of [the] early pioneers under President [Brigham] Young to keep a year's foodstuffs on hand, so that if anybody did lose his crops, he could carry over until the next season. . . .

We may have hard times, brothers and sisters, but we can be prepared for them, if we think of the seven years of plenty and the seven years of famine in the days of Pharaoh and plan as they did [see Genesis 41]. Such conditions may come again. We do not know, but we do know that in the early days of the Church the Presidency and leadership of the Church advised the people to store sufficient food to meet an emergency. The result has been that since the people got thoroughly settled here and farms began producing, and herds and flocks increasing, there has been no real necessity for anybody to suffer for food.[4]

We are living in perilous times. The scriptures are being fulfilled, and as it appears to me this is the particular time when, if it were possible, the very elect would be deceived. It is remarkable how easy it is for those who desire to advance their financial interests in the world to find a reason for setting aside the plain teachings of the Lord with reference to our lives. And it is strange to me how many people fall into the habit of listening to those who say things that are contrary to the revealed will of our Heavenly Father. . . .

. . . This people have been advised to conserve their energies and their means. We have been taught by those whom the Lord has raised up to instruct us that we should live within our income, that we should not follow the fashions of the world and expend as rapidly and even more rapidly than we can earn the money that comes into our hands, to take care of ourselves and our families.

I fear that the Latter-day Saints, in many cases, are blinded by their own vanity, by their desire to be what the world is; and we have been told in such plain language by our Heavenly Father that we cannot live as the world lives and enjoy his Spirit.[5]

Some individuals . . . are disposing of their holdings and spending their money for unnecessary things, and if hard times come, they may find themselves unable to meet their obligations.

We might learn a lesson from the ant. He harvests his supplies when they are available and stores them up against the day when it would not be possible to obtain them. The result is that his larder is usually well stocked. The grasshopper, a much larger insect, does not operate that way. He does not lay up anything in store for hard times, but depends upon providence to provide him what he needs, and the result is that most grasshoppers starve to death.

"We may have hard times, brothers and sisters, but we can be prepared for them."

I fear that some human beings are like the grasshopper and do not take advantage of the opportunities that are theirs in a reasonable way. If they would take a lesson from the ant, they would lay up the food that they need and always have some on hand.[6] [See suggestion 2 on page 221.]

The Lord has directed us to work to earn our own livelihood.

The very fact that so much money has been made available to many people gives the youth in some instances the feeling that because money comes relatively easy, honest toil is not necessary or desirable. And yet I am satisfied that no people have ever lived upon the earth who, having failed to earn their livelihood by integrity and industry, have not gone to decay.

215

If our children grow up in idleness, we know that this is displeasing to the Lord.[7]

How much better off we are when we are occupied with some reasonable work.[8]

Our Heavenly Father . . . said long, long ago there were idlers in Zion, . . . and he said, "He that is idle shall not eat the bread nor wear the garments of the laborer." [D&C 42:42.] I am assuming that he did not mean those who cannot find employment, and who are legitimately trying to take care of themselves. I am assuming that he referred to the habit some people get into of leaning upon their neighbor. . . . I feel that there has been no justification given to any man in this world to feel that he can depend on somebody else to provide him a livelihood. I did not feel when I was a child that somebody would be compelled to provide me a means of living. The Lord gave me intelligence. He directed that I should work, and I began to work when I was twelve years of age, and I found joy in it, and have earned my living and helped others during more than fifty years.

I thank God for work, for the joy that comes from doing things in the world. I am not indicating any particular kind of employment except that it be honorable. But the Lord has indicated that we should be industrious. In ancient times he said that we should earn our living by the sweat of our face [see Genesis 3:19].[9] [See suggestion 3 on page 221.]

Neither the rich nor the poor should set their hearts upon riches.

"Wo unto you rich men, that will not give your substance to the poor, for your riches will canker your souls; and this shall be your lamentation in the day of visitation, and of judgment, and of indignation: The harvest is past, the summer is ended, and my soul is not saved!" (D&C 56:16.)

That is what the Lord says of the rich people who refuse to impart of their substance to those who are poor. But he says something just as serious to the poor man who is not doing his best. He says:

"Wo unto you poor men, whose hearts are not broken, whose spirits are not contrite, and whose bellies are not satisfied, and whose hands are not stayed from laying hold upon other men's goods, whose eyes are full of greediness, and who will not labor with your own hands!" (D&C 56:17.) . . .

. . . Then he said further, "But blessed are the poor who are pure in heart." There is quite a difference there, ". . . blessed are the poor who are pure in heart, whose hearts are broken, and whose spirits are contrite, for they shall see the kingdom of God coming in power and great glory unto their deliverance; for the fatness of the earth shall be theirs." (D&C 56:18.)

They are those who have not the wealth of the world but still have life and being and intelligence, and who are anxious to do the thing the Lord would have them do. . . .

Now, my brethren and sisters, we have both rich and poor in our organizations. If we are poor, we can be worthy just as the Lord indicates here. We can be pure in heart and do our best, and he will not permit those who do their best to suffer for the necessities of life among the people who are in the Church of Jesus Christ of Latter-day Saints. . . .

I hope we are not going to become bitter because some men and women are well-to-do. If we are well-to-do, I hope we are not going to be self-centered and unconscious of the needs of our Father's other children. If we are better off than they are, we ought to be real brothers and sisters, not make-believe. Our desires should be to develop in this world such an organization that others, seeing our good works would be constrained to glorify the name of our Heavenly Father. . . .

We must not fall into the bad habits of other people. We must not get into the frame of mind that we will take what the other man has. Refer back to the ten commandments, and you will find one short paragraph, "Thou shalt not covet." [Exodus 20:17.] . . .

We must not get into that frame of mind. Others may do that, but if we have the spirit of the gospel of Jesus Christ in our hearts, we will not be deceived in that regard.

We are told that we cannot serve God and some other master [see Matthew 6:24]. We have to make our choice, and if we want to be the servants of God and the children of our Heavenly Father and earn his blessings, we must do it by honoring him and by keeping his commandments. Our feelings, and our love, if I may use that expression, should go out to all the world as far as they will receive it. [10] [See suggestion 4 on page 222.]

Through tithing and other offerings, we assist in the work of the Church and bless those in need.

The Lord has given us the privilege of contributing one-tenth of our interest, for His Church, for the development of His work in the world. Those who pay their tithing receive their blessing. . . . We cannot expect to earn blessings without earnest effort. We will be required to make what appears to some to be sacrifices. I suppose people think when they pay their tithing that they are making a sacrifice, but they are not; they are making a real investment that will return an eternal dividend. Our Heavenly Father gives us all that we have. He places all in our hands, authorizing us to retain for our own use nine-tenths of it, and then He asks that we put His tenth where He directs, where He knows it will accomplish the most good in developing His Church.

When we heard the reports this morning of this great Church [during a session of general conference], the financial report impressed me much—to know that a great organization like this, with its multitudes of people, functioning in so many ways, in the midst of the world's turmoil and distress is in such a condition that one of the Presidency of the Church could stand here and truthfully say to us this Church is out of debt. With the nations and most of the people in debt, yet the Church has been so managed that it is out of debt. Let us think about it. Let us sustain the Church. Let us follow the active leadership of the Church. Let us so live that the Lord can bless us as He blesses the Church. [11]

If you have paid an honest tithing, I may say without hesitation the other nine-tenths has been a greater blessing to those who have

"The Lord has given us the privilege of contributing one-tenth of our interest, for His Church, for the development of His work."

paid than the one hundred percent has been to those who have not. It is the Lord's work. . . . Men could not have done this. With all your generosity and all your giving, all your missionary work, with your care of the poor, . . . with all that you have been giving as ordinary people, I testify that what you have left brings to you more happiness, more peace, more comfort and more assurance of eternal life than any other people in the world enjoy today.[12]

I am sure the Lord loves those humble, faithful souls who are willing to reach out and touch those who are in need whether it be with food or clothing or bedding or kindness because that is a part of the gospel of Jesus Christ.[13] [See suggestion 5 on page 222.]

If we are generous with our means, there is no need for anyone to go without.

There is no necessity for any man, woman, or child in the Church of Jesus Christ of Latter-day Saints to go without, for the Church is organized to help those who lack the necessities of life. There is plenty for all, and to spare. . . . God has permitted men to get wealth, and if they obtained it properly, it is theirs, and he will bless them in its use if they will use it properly. [14]

We are becoming so wrapped up with the world that we forget the people who are suffering that we could help, in many cases. [15]

Think of the men that have been out of employment and the women also. . . . Think of the number of our Father's children that he loves just as much as he loves us who will be in distress. Think of what the suffering will be if we who are more fortunate are not generous with the substance God has placed in our hands—not only the substance, but if we withhold from his children the word of encouragement and helpfulness and fail to visit in the homes where there are so many in need and give what it is possible for each one of us to give. Brethren and sisters, all these opportunities are given to us to enrich ourselves and develop our characters and that we may lay up for ourselves treasures in heaven where moth and rust do not corrupt, and where thieves do not break through and steal [see Matthew 6:20]. These opportunities are offered to us by an all-wise Father who knowing the end from the beginning has said: "This is the path, walk you in it."

Let us . . . look around us in our neighborhood—not leave it to the Bishop and the Relief Society, but let each of us be ministers of loving kindness to those who will need us so much. And whatever we do let us not make those who require assistance feel like paupers. Let us give what we give as though it belonged to them. God has loaned it to us. Sometimes we who have accumulated means [act] as though we think it belongs to us. Everything that we have, our food, our clothing, our shelter, our homes and our opportunities are all given to us as stewards in the Church and kingdom of our Heavenly Father, and if we will . . . impart of our substance even though it may be but the widow's mite, we will obtain from him who lives on high the blessings we need in our day here upon the earth, and when the time comes for us to go hence we will find awaiting us the blessing of a loving Father who has appreciated the efforts we have put forth.[16]

If we desire to be identified with the kingdom of our Lord, the celestial kingdom, this is our opportunity to prepare,—with love unfeigned, with industry, with thrift, with perseverance, with a desire to do all that is within our power to bless others, to give—not to be always feeling we must receive, but desire to give, for I say to you: "It is more blessed to give than to receive." [Acts 20:35.] The Gospel of Jesus Christ is a gospel of giving, not only of our substance but of ourselves, and I thank my Heavenly Father that I belong to such an organization that has been so instructed.[17] [See suggestion 6 on page 222.]

Suggestions for Study and Teaching

Consider these ideas as you study the chapter or as you prepare to teach. For additional help, see pages v–vii.

1. George Albert Smith told the Saints during the Great Depression, "I believe our Heavenly Father is giving us our opportunity for development" (page 213). What does this mean to you? In what ways do we "develop" as we serve those in need?

2. As you read the first section of teachings (pages 213–15), consider things you can do to begin or improve your storage of food and resources. What are some examples of emergencies or conditions for which you should prepare? What can priesthood quorums and Relief Societies do to help members prepare for these emergencies?

3. Review the section that begins on page 215 and read Doctrine and Covenants 68:31. Why do you think the Lord requires us to work for our livelihood? What are some effective ways to teach children the importance of work?

4. Read President Smith's warnings to the rich and the poor on pages 216–18. What are the consequences of setting our hearts upon riches? What can we do to avoid this?

5. Read the section that begins on page 218, in which President Smith discusses the blessings of paying tithing and other offerings. What are some effective ways to teach young people or new members about these blessings?

6. As you study the last section of teachings (pages 220–21), think of something specific you can do to help the bishop and other ward leaders meet the needs of people in your ward or community. What does it mean to you to give "not only of our substance but of ourselves"?

Related Scriptures: Ephesians 4:28; James 1:27; 2 Nephi 5:17; Jacob 2:17–19; Mosiah 4:22–25; Doctrine and Covenants 104:13–18

Teaching help: "Even when you teach many people at the same time, you can reach out to individuals. For example, you reach out to individuals when you greet each person warmly at the beginning of class. . . . You also reach out when you make participation inviting and safe" (*Teaching, No Greater Call,* 35).

Notes

1. In Conference Report, Apr. 1948, 181.

2. In Conference Report, Oct. 1947, 6.

3. "To the Relief Society," *Relief Society Magazine,* Dec. 1932, 706.

4. In Conference Report, Apr. 1947, 162, 165.

5. In Conference Report, Apr. 1929, 30.

6. In *Improvement Era,* Aug. 1946, 521.

7. "Some Warning Signs," *Improvement Era,* July 1948, 425.

8. In Conference Report, Oct. 1949, 171.

9. In Conference Report, Oct. 1934, 49–50.

10. In Conference Report, Oct. 1949, 170–72.

11. In Conference Report, Apr. 1941, 25, 28.

12. In Conference Report, Apr. 1948, 16–17.

13. In Conference Report, Apr. 1947, 162.

14. In Conference Report, Oct. 1949, 169, 171.

15. In Conference Report, Apr. 1948, 181.

16. "Saints Blessed," *Deseret News,* Nov. 12, 1932, Church section, 8.

17. In Conference Report, Oct. 1934, 52.

CHAPTER 21

The Power of Kindness

*By being kind and patient, we can soften hearts
and encourage others to live righteously.*

From the Life of George Albert Smith

George Albert Smith firmly believed in the power of kindness to soften hearts. He taught that we should "meet our problems in the spirit of love and kindness toward all."[1] His granddaughter told of how his kindness and consideration of others brought peace to a tense situation:

"Once on a hot summer day there was some problem happening under the street near Grandfather's home in Salt Lake City, and some workers from the city had come to fix it. It was hot outdoors, the sun shone fiercely, and the job at hand was a pick-and-shovel kind that made the sweat pour off the men's faces and backs as they dug into the roadway. The workers were not careful with their language, or maybe their mothers hadn't taught them any better, but they were swearing and using terrible language. Their words soon became offensive to many of the neighbors whose windows were open to catch any breeze that might help to cool them.

"Someone went out and asked the men to stop their foul talk, and in the process pointed out that Brother Smith lived right there—couldn't they show some respect and keep quiet, please? With that the men let loose a new string of bad words. Quietly, Grandfather prepared some lemonade and placing some glasses and the pitcher on a tray he carried it out to the struggling men with, 'My friends, you look so hot and tired. Why don't you come and sit under my trees here and have a cool drink?' Their anger gone, the men responded to the kindness with meekness and appreciation. After their pleasant little break they went back to their labor and finished their work carefully and quietly."[2] [See suggestion 1 on page 231.]

223

"Quietly, Grandfather prepared some lemonade and placing some glasses and the pitcher on a tray he carried it out to the struggling men."

One reason President Smith treated people with such kindness was his conviction that there is innate goodness in everyone. Just a few weeks before President Smith passed away, Elder Matthew Cowley, a member of the Quorum of the Twelve Apostles, visited him in the hospital. "I walked up to his bedside," he said, "and he reached out and took me by the hand, and gripping my hand firmly he said, 'Young man, remember all the days of your life that you can find good in everyone if you will but look for it.'"

Elder Cowley then said of President Smith:

"He loved everyone because he could see the good within them. He did not look upon sin with the least degree of allowance, but he loved the sinner because he knew that God was love [see 1 John 4:16], and that it is God's love that regenerates human souls and may, by that process, transform the sinner into a saint.

"Maybe there are sinners who mistook his love for respect. He didn't respect the sinner, but he loved him. I am sure that love found response in the hearts and lives of those whom he loved."[3]

Teachings of George Albert Smith

The Spirit of the Lord is a spirit of kindness, not harshness and criticism.

I feel sad sometimes when I hear the unkind things that are spoken, not only of people in our Church, but of people in the world. Unkind things are not usually said under the inspiration of the Lord. The Spirit of the Lord is a spirit of kindness; it is a spirit of patience; it is a spirit of charity and love and forbearance and long suffering; and there are none of us who do not need all these virtues that are the result of the possession of the Spirit of our Heavenly Father.[4]

Every influence for peace ought to be exercised. Lucifer is exercising every means to destroy the souls of the human family. He is more active than he has ever been and he works in such an insidious way. I will not take time to enumerate the many ways he employs but there is one way in which he operates, and has operated from the beginning of the world, and that is to tempt one individual to destroy the reputation of another by saying unkind things of them.[5]

It is so easy to criticize someone else, so easy to find fault, and sometimes we speak harshly of our neighbors and friends. Now this is what our Heavenly Father gave us . . . :

"Judge not, that ye be not judged.

"For with what judgment ye judge, ye shall be judged: and with what measure ye mete, it shall be measured to you again.

"And why beholdest thou the mote that is in thy brother's eye, but considerest not the beam that is in thine own eye?

"Or how wilt thou say to thy brother, Let me pull out the mote out of thine eye; and, behold, a beam is in thine own eye?" [Matthew 7:1–4.]

As a people we are advised not to be critical, not to be unkind, not to speak harshly of those with whom we associate. We ought to be the greatest exemplars in all the world in that regard. Consider the criticism today. Pick up your newspapers and see the unkind things that are being said by individuals about others, and yet many times the individual who is criticizing has a beam in his own eye and does not see at all clearly, but he does think his brother has a mote in his eye.[6] [See suggestion 2 on page 231.]

Aren't we rather prone to see the limitations and the weaknesses of our neighbors? Yet that is contrary to the teachings of the Gospel of Jesus Christ. There is a class of people who find fault and criticize always in a destructive way. There is a difference in criticism. If we can criticize constructively under the influence of the Spirit of the Lord, we may change beneficially and properly some of the things that are being done. But if we have the spirit of fault finding, of pointing out the weaknesses and failings of others in a destructive manner, that never comes as a result of the companionship of the Spirit of our Heavenly Father and is always harmful.[7]

We should look for the virtues in others and offer sincere praise.

I stand here tonight to speak of a man who has several years ago gone home. . . . I refer to Francis M. Lyman [of the Quorum of the Twelve Apostles] and I want to say to you that that great man was as tender as a baby, just as tender as a little child, and his desire to help and encourage was beautiful. I have heard him compliment his brethren many times when they have done something praiseworthy—one had delivered a fine address, another had borne a convincing testimony, another had done something else praiseworthy. I have seen him put his arm around them and say, "I am proud of you and the fine thing you have done." Is not that a commendable way to live? That is the way to make ourselves happy. If, instead of being jealous, we see and appreciate and commend the virtues and abilities of our fellows, if we see the power for good in [others], how much better it will be.

Many of us live in such an atmosphere that we are almost dumb when it comes to praising somebody else. We seem unable to say the things that we might say . . . to the blessing of others. Let us look for the virtues of our associates and observing them make them happy by commending them.[8]

I plead with you my brethren and my sisters, let us be generous with one another. Let us be as patient with one another as we would like others to be with us. Let us see the virtues of our neighbors and our friends and speak of those virtues, not find fault and criticize. If we will do that we will radiate sunshine, and those who know us best will love us.[9] [See suggestion 3 on page 231.]

Kindness has the power to lead people from their mistakes.

There are those who will make mistakes. There are those among us today that have gone astray, but they are the children of our Lord and he loves them. He has given to you and to me the right to go to them in kindness and love and with patience and with a desire to bless, seek to win them from the mistakes that they are making. It is not my privilege to judge some of these that have made mistakes and are still making mistakes, unless I am so called by reason of the authority that may be conferred upon me. But it is my privilege, if I see them doing the wrong thing, to in some way, if possible, turn them back into the pathway that leads to eternal life in the Celestial kingdom.[10]

Let us not complain at our friends and our neighbors, because they do not do what we want them to do. Rather let us love them into doing the things that our Heavenly Father would have them do. We can do that, and we cannot win their confidence or their love in any other way. [11]

What a joy, what a comfort, what a satisfaction can be added to the lives of our neighbors and friends through kindness. How I would like to write that word in capital letters and emblazon it in the air. Kindness is the power that God has given us to unlock hard hearts and subdue stubborn souls and bring them to an understanding of His purposes. [12] [See suggestion 4 on page 231.]

Love and kindness in our homes can lead our children to listen to our counsel.

It is our duty—I should say it is our privilege as well as our duty to take sufficient time to surround our children with safeguards and to so love them and earn their love that they will be glad to listen to our advice and counsel. [13]

Live in such a way, in love and kindness, that peace and prayer and thanksgiving will be in your homes together. Do not let your homes just be a place to hang your hats at night and get your meals and then run off some place else but let your homes be the abiding place of the Spirit of the Lord. [14]

I pray that we may be filled with that spirit that comes from [the Lord], and that is a spirit of love, of kindness and helpfulness and of patience and forbearance. Then, if we keep that spirit with us in our homes, our boys and girls will grow up to be what we would like them to be. [15]

I remember a few years ago I was on a train going north. I saw sitting in the day coach of that train a woman that I had known. . . . She recognized me as I passed down the aisle of the car. She spoke to me, and I asked: "Where are you going?" She said: "I am going to Portland, [Oregon]." I knew that the family were not well-to-do. I knew that this woman was the mother of a large family of sons, so I said: "What takes you to Portland?" She said: "I have a son there in the hospital."

"Live in such a way, in love and kindness, that peace and prayer and thanksgiving will be in your homes."

I was not aware that any of her children had moved away, so I questioned a little further, and then she opened her heart to me. She said: "My youngest boy, a few weeks ago, left home and did not tell us where he was going. We received no word from him, but he thought he would go out into the world no doubt and see it for himself, and the first intimation that we had of his whereabouts was when a telegram came from the Mercy hospital in Portland, stating that our boy was there sick in that hospital." She said: "Of course the message shocked us very much. There was only one thing to do, and that was to raise means and go at once to that boy."

. . . She was prepared to sit up during that long ride, day and night, not resentful of the unkindness and thoughtlessness of her boy, but only thinking that he was hers, that he belonged to her, that God gave him to her, and that our Heavenly Father expected her to use every possible means to enrich his life and prepare him for the opportunities that awaited him. So through the long hours of the night, as the train rumbled over the rails, this good woman sat there, yearning for her boy, every mile taking her just a little nearer to that lodestone that was tugging at her heart. Finally when she arrived, quickly as she could, she made her way to the hospital. It so transpired that the place where I was to remain was not far from the hospital so I went over there to see what had occurred.

There was that sweet mother sitting by the bedside of her boy who had been seized with a serious attack of pneumonia, and he was lying there in pain. She was not scolding him because he had been unmindful of her; she was not resentful of his thoughtlessness and of his carelessness, she was just thankful to be with her boy that God had given to her. She was now trying to nurse back the child for whom she had entered into partnership with her Heavenly Father, to bring him into this world. He, by the way, was about 16 years of age, but her baby. She was trying to encourage him by telling him the things that would make him happy and contented, holding out to him the opportunities that would be his when he was well. In the place of distress and anguish that filled that room prior to her entrance there, there was a perfect halo of light and of peace and happiness spread over the countenance of that boy as he looked up into the face of her who had offered her life that he might be, and who on this occasion had come that long distance to sit by his side and nurse him back to life.

I wonder sometimes if these mothers realize how wonderful they are in the eyes of their children in a case like that. That boy had resolved before his mother had been there many minutes that never again would he be recreant to her, never again would he be unmindful of what she had given to him, but determined that the name which had been given to him in honor would be kept by him in honor so long as life should last.[16] [See suggestion 5 on page 231.]

I pray that the love of the gospel of our Lord will burn in our souls and enrich our lives, that it will cause husbands to be kinder to wives, and wives to be kinder to husbands, parents to children, and children to parents because of the gospel of Jesus Christ, which is a gospel of love and kindness.[17]

Suggestions for Study and Teaching

Consider these ideas as you study the chapter or as you prepare to teach. For additional help, see pages v–vii.

1. Read the story about George Albert Smith preparing lemonade for weary workers (page 223). When have you seen an act of kindness soften someone's heart? What are some problems that you think could be solved with "the spirit of love and kindness toward all"?

2. President Smith taught that "we ought to be the greatest exemplars in all the world" in avoiding harsh criticism (page 226). What are some situations in which we can set such an example? In your opinion, why are harsh criticism and fault-finding so harmful?

3. Read pages 226–27, where President Smith tells of Elder Francis M. Lyman complimenting his brethren. How have you been affected by someone giving you sincere praise? Take a moment to think of someone whom you should compliment.

4. President Smith taught that "kindness is the power that God has given us to unlock hard hearts" (page 228). What stories can you think of from the scriptures that illustrate this principle? (For some examples, see Matthew 9:10–13; Alma 20:1–27.)

5. Review the story about the mother visiting her son in the hospital (pages 228–30). When a child goes astray, why is it sometimes difficult to react the way the mother in the story did? Prayerfully ponder how a spirit of kindness and patience could improve your relationship with members of your family.

Related Scriptures: Proverbs 15:1; Matthew 18:15; John 8:2–11; Ephesians 4:29–32; 3 Nephi 12:22–24; Doctrine and Covenants 121:41–46

Teaching help: Discussions in small groups "give a large number of people the opportunity to participate in a lesson. Individuals who are usually hesitant to participate might share ideas in small groups that they would not express in front of the entire group" (*Teaching, No Greater Call,* 161).

Notes

1. In Conference Report, Apr. 1941, 28.

2. Martha Stewart Hatch, in Susan Arrington Madsen, *The Lord Needed a Prophet* (1990), 130–31.

3. Matthew Cowley, in Conference Report, Apr. 1951, 166–67.

4. In Conference Report, Apr. 1937, 34.

5. "To the Relief Society," *Relief Society Magazine,* Dec. 1932, 704.

6. In Conference Report, Oct. 1949, 168–69.

7. In Conference Report, Oct. 1934, 50.

8. "To the Relief Society," 707.

9. In Conference Report, Oct. 1934, 50.

10. In Conference Report, Apr. 1937, 34.

11. In Conference Report, Oct. 1945, 174.

12. "To the Relief Society," 709.

13. In Conference Report, Apr. 1929, 33.

14. In Conference Report, Apr. 1948, 183.

15. In Conference Report, Oct. 1950, 9.

16. In *Deseret News,* May 15, 1926, section four, 6.

17. In Conference Report, Oct. 1948, 167.

C H A P T E R   2 2

Bringing Up Children in Light and Truth

*The Lord has given parents the responsibility to teach
their children the gospel by word and example.*

From the Life of George Albert Smith

Near the end of his life, President George Albert Smith reflected on his upbringing and the teachings of his parents:

"I was born in a humble home. . . . My parents were living in very humble circumstances, but I praise my Maker and thank him with all my heart for sending me into their home.

"I grew up in Salt Lake City. When eight years of age, I was baptized in City Creek. I was confirmed a member of the Church in fast meeting in the Seventeenth Ward, and I learned when I was a boy that this is the work of the Lord. I learned that there were prophets living upon the earth. I learned that the inspiration of the Almighty would influence those who lived to enjoy it. . . .

"I don't know of any man in all the world who has more reason to be grateful than I. I am thankful for my birthright, thankful for parents who taught me the gospel of Jesus Christ and set the example in their home. If I have done anything that I should not have done in my life, it would be something that I could not have learned in my mother's home. With a large family of children, it took a mother with a good deal of patience, but she was always patient with us. There were sweetness and kindness and love there always."[1]

In his own home, George Albert Smith tried to follow his parents' example of teaching with patience and love. His daughter Edith recalled an experience from her youth:

"He continually counseled us about our behavior, emphasizing honesty and fairness. I remember one day when on my way home

233

George Albert Smith's wife, Lucy, and their daughters,
Edith (left) and Emily (right).

from my piano lesson, the streetcar conductor overlooked collecting my fare. . . . Somehow he passed me by, and I reached my destination still holding my nickel in my hand, and frankly quite elated that I had made the trip free.

". . . I ran gleefully to Father to tell him about my good fortune. He listened to my story patiently. I was beginning to think I was a great success. . . . I was sure that the conductor did not know I had not paid for the ride, and therefore all was well.

"When I had finished my tale, Father said, 'But, darling, even if the conductor doesn't know about this, you know and I know and Heavenly Father knows. So, there are still three of us who must be satisfied in seeing that you pay in full for value received.'"

Edith went back to the street corner and paid her fare when the streetcar returned. She later expressed gratitude for the way her father handled the situation: "I am indeed thankful for a Father who was wise enough to kindly point out the error to me, because if it had been overlooked, I could have thought he approved, and I might have tried something similar another time."[2] [See suggestion 1 on page 244.]

Teachings of George Albert Smith

Parents have the primary responsibility to teach their children the gospel.

One of the greatest and richest of all your blessings will be that which comes if you teach as you should, and train as you should these choice spirits that our Heavenly Father is sending to the world in this latter day. . . . Do not leave the training of your children to the public schools. Do not leave their training to the Primary, to the Sunday School, to the [Church's youth organizations]. They will help you and make a fine contribution but remember what God himself has said, that parents who do not teach their children faith in God, repentance and baptism and the laying on of hands when eight years of age, the sin be upon the heads of the parents [see D&C 68:25–28]. This is not a threat, my brethren and sisters, that is the kind and loving advice of our Heavenly Father who knows all things and understands and realizes what it means when children are allowed to grow up without this training.[3]

What I am about to say I am exceedingly anxious that it should sink into the mind of every parent in Zion, and that is, that while the Lord has provided all these wonderful educational institutions, while science has contributed so much for our comfort and our blessing, while the Church has prepared places to which we may send our children to be taught the gospel of Christ, that does not relieve you or me of the responsibility and the obligation that is laid upon us by our Heavenly Father to teach our own children. . . . It is not sufficient that my children are taught faith, repentance and baptism, and the laying on of hands for the gift of the Holy Ghost in the auxiliary organizations. My Father in heaven has commanded that I should do that myself.[4]

Nobody else can perform the part that God has assigned to us as parents. We have assumed an obligation when we have been the means of bringing children into the world. We can't place that responsibility upon any organization. It is ours. . . . First and foremost the obligation is upon you and upon me to not only advise and counsel but to train, by setting an example, by spending sufficient time with our loved ones, these boys and girls, that they may not be led into . . . forbidden paths.[5]

Call your families about you, and if you have failed in the past to give them an understanding of the purposes of life and a knowledge of the Gospel of our Lord, do it now, for I say to you as a servant of the Lord, they need it now and they will need it from now on.[6] [See suggestion 2 on page 244.]

Other interests must not cause us to lose sight of our duty to teach our children.

We are told in Luke that there would be a time when men would be choked with the cares and the riches and the pleasures of life [see Luke 8:14]. I have in my mind . . . even now, men and women that I love, whose very spirituality is being choked by these very things, and the adversary is leading them along that easy pathway of pleasure and they are neglecting their duty as parents and as members of the Church of Jesus Christ.

. . . Now in the midst of confusion, excitement and all the plea-sures of life, . . . let us not lose sight of the duty that we owe these boys and girls who are created in the image of God. He is the Father of their spirits, and he will hold us responsible for the teaching that they receive. I hope and pray that we will so teach them that when the end shall come we can receive from him that blessing, "Well done, good and faithful servant, enter into the joy of thy Lord," and that we may have our loved ones with us eternally.[7]

I think I would like to tell you a story. A number of years ago, there lived in Indiana two boys, young fellows who worked on farms—farms five to seven miles apart. They worked hard each day doing their chores, milking cows, etc. The first boy went to his father one day when he was about 13 or 14 years of age and said, "Father, I would like to go into the city. I would like to see the bright lights. I wonder if I could not go in some evening early, if I worked hard and got my work done?" The father said, "You can not do that because you can not do your work." "If I am willing to get up at daylight and work all day, can I walk into the city? It is not very far, and I could be there for an hour or two and then come home early." The father said, "Well, of course if you will do all your chores, then you can go." Fathers, get this. The result was, he went in. He got in town when it was nearly dark. Stores and banks were closed. There were plenty of pool halls and gambling places open. All good people were indoors, most of them in their own homes. All the riff-raff was on the streets or in these places. They saw this young boy come in and they picked him up. It was not long until they had shown him some of the things no boy should see. That was his experience. It gave him a taste of something that was not good for him.

The second boy went to his father in the same way. He said, "Father, I would like to go into town sometime. Would you not like me to go and see some of the things I have never seen? I will have to go before dark to see anything." "My boy," replied the father, "I think you are entitled to go into town, and I think you are entitled to have your father go with you. You pick the day and I will help with the chores so we can go early enough that you can meet some of my associates."

It is the same state I'm talking about—the two farms were not far apart. Within a week he had chosen the day. They did the chores, and went into town. They arrived a little before four o'clock. They got there before the banks were closed. The boy was dressed in his good clothes. His father took him into the bank and introduced him to the banker, who took him by the hand and said, "When you are in town, come and see us and we will make you welcome."

His father took him to business houses where he had business, where people greeted him pleasantly. When they went home together, after they had remained to see a show, that boy had the acquaintance of some of the finest men in the community. The result was that when he grew older and went into town, his companionship was with fine people.[8] [See suggestion 3 on page 244.]

I want to suggest to you . . . , there is no time that you can spend, no way in which you can utilize your time that will be of greater advantage than training your boys and your girls to be worthy of the blessings of our Heavenly Father.[9]

A parent's example can lead a child to safety, righteousness, and happiness.

Let us be examples of righteousness to our children, have our family prayers and ask the blessing upon the food. Let our children see that as husbands and wives we are affectionate with one another. While there is yet time take the opportunity as husbands and wives to bless each other with your love, with your kindness and your helpfulness in every way. Take opportunity while there is yet time to teach your sons and daughters how to live to be happy. . . . Let our homes be sanctuaries of peace and hope and love.[10]

Only a few days ago I saw a letter from a man who had probably lived half his life. In writing to his father he said: "Your consideration for your loved ones, your teaching of me, the examples that you set me, have been an inspiration for me to do what the Lord would have me do. I have felt in following in your footsteps I would be safe." That was a wise father, that was a blessed father, who could plant in the mind of his son such confidence. . . . Because of the conduct of the father—at least he gave his father credit in his

"There is no time that you can spend, no way in which you can utilize your time that will be of greater advantage than training your boys and your girls to be worthy of the blessings of our Heavenly Father."

letter—because of the example set in his home, he is today one of the stalwarts of this Church. He can live in the world and keep the commandments of the Lord. His anxiety to do good was inspired by the home in which he lived. He did not discover selfishness in the home, but unselfishness. The parents were not anxious to get all that they could and hold it selfishly for their own, but they went about seeking those who needed them, encouraging and blessing them. All the talking in the world would not have put into that man's heart that which he has today, but it was the example that was set by his parents, by those who lived in the home in which he lived.

I have no doubt there are hundreds of men and women, thousands of them, perhaps, in the communities in which we live and in the world, who would say the same thing of the teachings of their fathers and their mothers. But I fear there are some of us who are influenced by the customs of the world and are obsessed with the idea that we have to follow the crowd regardless of what they believe or do. In that case our example will not be a blessing but may destroy the happiness of our children.[11]

Let us bear witness in our daily acts, as well as in our conversation, that we believe this is the Father's work and joy inexpressible will come to us, and the children that grow up in our homes will increase in faith and humility. They will be added upon, and be given power to turn aside the shafts of the adversary that are directed towards them, and in place of the distress that has afflicted the children of men, because of sinfulness, there will be comfort, peace and happiness, and . . . men and women will inhabit this earth who will have strength of character to put aside the evils of life.[12] [See suggestion 4 on page 244.]

By loving and teaching our youth, we can help safeguard them from evil.

Latter-day Saints, teach your children to observe the moral law. Surround them as by the arms of your love, that they may have no desire whatsoever to partake of the temptations to evil that surround them on every hand. . . .

What a privilege it is for parents to sit down in their own homes, surrounded by a family of pure boys and girls given to them by our Heavenly Father, their spirits begotten by our Father in Heaven! What a joy it is to have them mingle together partaking of the blessings of our Heavenly Father and rejoicing in the companionship of his Spirit, and to have them so trained in their younger days that while developing to maturity they have maintained the purity of their lives!

My brethren and sisters, I plead with you that with more earnestness, with more thoughtfulness, more patience than ever before, you safeguard the rising generation from the pitfalls that the adversary has laid for their feet. Many of our [movies], radio programs, magazines, books, etc., are unfit . . . , and unless we neutralize the influence of these things by wholesome teaching and environment, bringing to the youth the benefits derived from knowing the lives of good men and women, teaching them the virtues of the prophets and the meaning of the Gospel of Jesus Christ, some of those whom we love may slip away from us. . . .

Let us teach our children to be pure in their lives, to be upright. Teach your boys to safeguard the virtue of their sisters and their girl companions. Teach your daughters to safeguard the virtue of the boys they associate with. . . . Let us major, if we may use that term, in rearing our boys and girls under the influence of the Spirit of God, that the adversary will have no power to lead them astray. [13] [See suggestions 5 and 6 on page 244.]

Studying the gospel as a family will help us keep our children close to us.

In our homes, brethren and sisters, it is our privilege, it is our duty, to call our families together to enjoy and strengthen and sustain each other, to be taught the truths of the Holy Scriptures. In every home, children should be encouraged to read the word of the Lord as it has been revealed to us in all dispensations. We should read the Bible, the Book of Mormon, the Doctrine and Covenants, and the Pearl of Great Price; not only read it in our homes, but also explain it to our children that they may understand the . . . dealings of God with the peoples of the earth.

Let us see if we cannot do more of this in the future than we have done in the past. Let us commit ourselves to the principle and the practice of gathering our families around us in our own homes. Let each one of us ask himself: "Have I done my duty in my home in reading and in teaching the gospel, as it has been revealed through the prophets of the Lord? Have I kept my children close to me and made home a pleasant place and a place of reverence, love, understanding, and devotion?"

If we have not, let us repent of our neglect and draw our families around us and teach them the truth. . . .

"Have I set my house in order?" This should be the query in every heart. Not, has my neighbor done so? but, have *I* done what the Lord has required of me? [14]

Our children are the most precious gift that our Father bestows upon us. If we can guide their feet in the pathway of salvation, there will be joy eternal for us and for them. . . .

One way in which we can keep them closer to us is for us to meet together oftener in our homes. The Church has asked that there be set aside at least one home night each week for all the family to meet together and to enjoy each other's company, to enjoy the simple pleasures of the family fireside, and to discuss with each other those things which are of great and lasting worth.

. . . In 1915 the First Presidency wrote of this to "presidents of stakes, bishops, and parents in Zion," and I quote from what they then said:

"We advise and urge the inauguration of a 'Home Evening' throughout the Church, at which time fathers and mothers may gather their boys and girls about them in the home, and teach them the word of the Lord. . . . This 'Home Evening' should be devoted to prayer, singing hymns, songs, instrumental music, Scripture reading, family topics, and specific instruction on the principles of the gospel, and on the ethical problems of life, as well as the duties and obligations of children to parents, the home, the Church, society, and the nation."

And this was the promised blessing to those who would do what was asked:

"If the Saints obey this counsel, we promise that great blessings will result. Love at home and obedience to parents will increase. Faith will be developed in the hearts of the youth of Israel, and they will gain power to combat the evil influences and temptations which beset them."

These principles and promises are still before us. [15]

If the home evening could only be a fact among the Latter-day Saints, if during one evening a week we would live with our own, under the influence of the spirit of the Lord, at our own firesides surrounded by those whom the Lord has given unto us, and told us, particularly, that we should instruct them, how many happy

"If the home evening could only be a fact among the Latter-day Saints, . . . how many happy homes there would be."

homes there would be where today there is sorrow and discord and distress. . . .

. . . When we shut out the world and the things of the outside, and under the power of prayer and thanksgiving we give to our sons and daughters those rich truths that the Lord has deposited with us for our welfare and for theirs, a genuine development of faith will follow. I hope that it will be possible for us to return, if we have departed from that advice. Gather our children around us and let our homes be the abiding place of the Spirit of the Lord. If we will do our part, we may know and be sure that our Heavenly Father will do his.[16] [See suggestion 7 on page 245.]

Suggestions for Study and Teaching

Consider these ideas as you study the chapter or as you prepare to teach. For additional help, see pages v–vii.

1. Think about the story on pages 233–35. Why do you think George Albert Smith was able to teach his daughter Edith so successfully? Think about a time from your youth when a parent taught you something that was influential in your life. Why was that lesson so effective?

2. Study the first section of teachings (pages 235–36) and Doctrine and Covenants 93:37–40. Why do you think the Lord has given parents, rather than other organizations, the responsibility to teach their children the gospel? How can Church organizations help parents with this responsibility? How can extended family members help? If you do not have children of your own, consider ways you can be a righteous influence on the youth of the Church in a way that is supportive to parents.

3. Review the story on pages 237–38. How do children benefit when their parents spend time with them? What are some of "the cares and . . . pleasures of life" (page 236) that can cause us to neglect our responsibilities for our families? What can we do to overcome these distractions?

4. Read the section that begins on page 238. Think about your attitudes toward "the customs of the world" and how those attitudes may affect your children. What are some "daily acts" that bear particularly strong witness of our beliefs to our children?

5. What are some of the temptations that children and youth face in your community? Study the section that begins on page 240, looking for things parents, grandparents, and others can do to help the youth withstand temptation.

6. President Smith counseled that we should "major," or specialize, in rearing our children under the influence of the Spirit (see page 241). What does that mean to you? What kinds of things can parents do to specialize in raising their children in righteousness?

7. On pages 242–43, President Smith reviews some of the promises that are made to families who hold regular family home evenings. How have these promises been fulfilled in your family? What advice would you give to a family who has never held family home evening before but wants to begin?

Related Scriptures: Proverbs 22:6; Isaiah 54:13; Enos 1:1–3; Mosiah 4:14–15; Alma 56:45–48; Doctrine and Covenants 68:25–31; see also "The Family: A Proclamation to the World," *Ensign,* Nov. 1995, 102.

Teaching help: "Be careful not to end good discussions too soon in an attempt to present all the material you have prepared. Although it is important to cover the material, it is more important to help learners feel the influence of the Spirit, resolve their questions, increase their understanding of the gospel, and deepen their commitment to keep the commandments" (*Teaching, No Greater Call,* 64).

Notes

1. "After Eighty Years," *Improvement Era,* Apr. 1950, 263.
2. Edith Smith Elliott, "No Wonder We Love Him," *Relief Society Magazine,* June 1953, 367.
3. "To the Relief Society," *Relief Society Magazine,* Dec. 1932, 708–9.
4. In Conference Report, Apr. 1926, 145.
5. In Conference Report, Apr. 1933, 72.
6. In Conference Report, Apr. 1937, 36.
7. In Conference Report, Apr. 1926, 146–47.
8. "President Smith Gives Scouting Address," *Deseret News,* Feb. 22, 1947, Church section, 8.
9. In Conference Report, Oct. 1948, 181.
10. In Conference Report, Oct. 1941, 101.
11. In Conference Report, Apr. 1937, 35.
12. In Conference Report, Apr. 1913, 29.
13. In Conference Report, Oct. 1932, 24–25.
14. "The Family Hour," *Improvement Era,* Apr. 1948, 248.
15. "The Family Hour," 201.
16. In Conference Report, Apr. 1926, 145–46.

"Remember the example of the Divine Master, who, when suspended upon the cruel tree, said, 'Father, forgive them, for they know not what they do.'"

"Of You It Is Required
to Forgive"

*By forgiving others, we free ourselves from the burden
of hatred and prepare ourselves for eternal life.*

From the Life of George Albert Smith

In 1897, while still a young man, George Albert Smith enlisted in the Utah National Guard. At the encouragement of some of his companions, he ran for an elected office in the Guard, but during the weeks leading up to the election, a rival guardsman began spreading false rumors accusing George Albert Smith of unethical practices. As a result, Sergeant Smith lost an election that he felt he should have won. What made the situation more difficult was that the man who spread the false rumors had once been a friend.

Though he tried to brush it off, the offense filled George Albert Smith's heart with bitterness. He went to church the following Sunday, but he did not feel right about taking the sacrament. He prayed for help and realized that he needed to repent of the resentment he was feeling. He decided to seek out his friend and be reconciled with him.

George Albert Smith went directly to the man's office and said in a soft voice, "My brother, I want you to forgive me for hating you the way I have for the last few weeks."

Immediately his friend's heart softened. "Brother Smith, you have no need for forgiveness," he said. "It is I who need forgiveness from you." They shook hands, and thereafter they remained good friends.[1] [See suggestion 1 on page 253.]

A few years later, George Albert Smith made forgiving others one of his lifelong goals when he wrote in his personal creed: "I would not knowingly wound the feeling of any, not even one who may have wronged me, but would seek to do him good and make him my friend."[2]

A close associate of President Smith observed that the ability to forgive was indeed one of his defining attributes: "Truly he forgave all men. He was aware in all of his life of the commandment of God: God will forgive whom he will forgive. As for us, we must forgive all men. He could do that, and then refer the matter to God. As he forgave I am sure he forgot. When one who forgives can forget, then truly that man is an unusual man, indeed a man of God!"[3]

Teachings of George Albert Smith

If we understand the gospel of Jesus Christ, we are more disposed to forgive others.

There is one thing that we could well strive to cultivate, and that is, the disposition to forgive one another our trespasses. The spirit of forgiveness is a virtue without which we shall never fully realize the blessings we hope to receive.[4]

The people of the world do not understand . . . how the Savior felt when in the agony of his soul, he cried to his Heavenly Father, not to condemn and destroy these who were taking his mortal life, but he said:

". . . Father, forgive them; for they know not what they do." (Luke 23:34.)

That should be the attitude of all of the members of the Church of Jesus Christ of Latter-day Saints. That should be the attitude of all the sons and daughters of God and would be, it seems to me, if they fully understood the plan of salvation. . . . Anger and hatred in our hearts will not bring us peace and happiness.[5]

The Lord has given us great information, has revealed His mind and will unto us, has taught us things that the world knows not of, and, in accordance with the information we have received, He holds us responsible and expects us to live a higher life, a more ideal life than those who do not as fully comprehend the Gospel as we do. The spirit of forgiveness is something that the Latter-day Saints might with profit exhibit more fully among themselves. . . .

We must get into a condition where we can forgive our brethren.[6] [See suggestion 2 on page 253.]

When we forgive others, we show appreciation for the forgiveness Heavenly Father extends to us.

In connection with this matter [of forgiving others], I will read a few verses from the eighteenth chapter of St. Matthew, beginning with the twenty-first verse. It seems that the Apostles were with the Master upon this occasion, and Peter came to Him and said:

"Lord, how oft shall my brother sin against me, and I forgive him? till seven times?

"Jesus saith unto him, I say not unto thee, Until seven times but, Until seventy times seven." [Matthew 18:21–22.]

Then the Savior gave a parable . . . of two men. One of the men owed his lord a large amount of money, and he came to him and told him he could not pay what he owed, and asked that he might be forgiven the debt. The lord of that servant was moved with compassion, and forgave the debt. Straightway this man who had been forgiven went out and found a fellow-servant who owed him a small amount, and he demanded his pay. The poor man was unable to meet the obligation, and he in turn asked that he might be forgiven the debt. But he was not forgiven; on the contrary he was taken and cast into prison by the one who had already been forgiven by his lord. When the other fellow-servants saw what had been done they went to the lord of this man and told him, and he was wroth and delivered the one whom he had forgiven unto torment, until he should pay all that was due. His soul was not big enough to appreciate the mercy shown him, and because of that lack of charity he lost all. [See Matthew 18:23–35.]

At times we find little difficulties arising among us, and we forget the patience our Father in Heaven exercises towards us, and we magnify in our hearts some trivial thing that our brother or sister may have done or said concerning us. We do not always live that law which the Lord desires us to observe in regard to these matters. We forget the commandment He gave to the Apostles in the words of the prayer, wherein they were told to pray that they might be forgiven their debts even as they forgive their debtors [see Matthew 6:12]. I feel that we have to learn a great deal in this regard. We have not complied as completely as we should with the requirements of our Heavenly Father.[7] [See suggestion 3 on page 253.]

By choosing not to take offense, we can purge from our hearts all feelings of unkindness.

We have been taught to love our enemies, and to pray for those who despitefully use us and speak evil of us [see Matthew 5:44]. . . . When you are reviled, do not revile again. When others speak evil of you, pity them, and pray for them. Remember the example of the Divine Master, who, when suspended upon the cruel tree, said, "Father, forgive them, for they know not what they do."[8]

Sometimes a brother in authority has offended, in some way, one of the members of the Church, probably unknown to himself, and that child of our Father's silently continues to feel hurt, instead of doing as the Lord has commanded, going to the offending man and stating to him, in kindness, the feelings of his heart, and giving that brother an opportunity to say to him, "I am sorry I have offended you, and I desire that you shall forgive me." The result is that, in some instances, we find a resentful feeling existing that has been instigated by Satan.[9] [See suggestion 4 on page 253.]

We have no hard feelings toward any of our fellowmen; we have no occasion to. If they misunderstand us, misquote us, and persecute us, we should remember they are in the hands of the Lord. . . . So when we partake of the sacrament of the Lord's Supper, . . . let us purge from our hearts all feeling of unkindness toward one another and toward our brothers and sisters who are not of our faith.[10]

By forgiving others, we prepare ourselves for the celestial kingdom.

Let each of us live in such a way that the adversary will have no power over us. If you have any differences one with another, if there have been any disagreements between yourself and your neighbors, settle them just as soon as you possibly can, under the influence of the Spirit of the Lord, in order that when the time comes both

*"If there have been any disagreements between yourself and your neighbors,
settle them just as soon as you possibly can, under the
influence of the Spirit of the Lord."*

you and your descendants who may be following after you may be prepared to receive an inheritance in the celestial kingdom.[11]

In the Book of Doctrine and Covenants we find a reference made to this matter of forgiveness, wherein the Lord gives a commandment; it is contained in the sixty-fourth section, and refers to us in this day. It reads as follows:

". . . Verily I say unto you, I, the Lord, forgive sins unto those who confess their sins before me and ask forgiveness, who have not sinned unto death.

"My disciples, in days of old, sought occasion against one another, and forgave not one another in their hearts, and for this evil they were afflicted, and sorely chastened.

"Wherefore I say unto you, that ye ought to forgive one another, for he that forgiveth not his brother his trespasses, standeth condemned before the Lord, for there remaineth in him the greater sin."

The verse last read is the one I would emphasize.

"I, the Lord, will forgive whom I will forgive, but of you it is required to forgive all men;

"And ye ought to say in your hearts, let God judge between me and thee, and reward thee according to thy deeds." [D&C 64:7–11.]

If our lives were such that, when we differ with our neighbor, if, instead of setting ourselves up as judges one against another, we could honestly and conscientiously appeal to our Father in Heaven and say, "Lord, judge between me and my brother; thou knowest my heart; Thou knowest I have no feeling of anger against him; help us to see alike, and give us wisdom that we may deal righteously with each other," how few differences there would be, and what joy and blessings would come to us! But, little difficulties arise from time to time which disturb the equilibrium of our daily lives, and we continue to be unhappy because we cherish an improper influence, and have not charity. . . .

. . . "Now I speak unto you concerning your families; if men will smite you, or your families, once, and ye bear it patiently and revile not against them, neither seek revenge, ye shall be rewarded;

"But if ye bear it not patiently, it shall be accounted unto you as being meted out a just measure unto you." [D&C 98:23–24.]

This is also the word of the Master unto us. If we live according to this law, we will grow in grace and strength day by day, and in favor with our Heavenly Father. Faith will increase in the hearts of our children. They will love us for the uprightness and integrity of our lives, and they will rejoice that they have been born of such parents. I say to you that this commandment is not given in an idle way; for the Lord has declared that He does not give any law indifferently, but every law is given that it may be kept and lived up to by us.

We will be in this world only a short time. The youngest and strongest of us are simply preparing for the other life, and before we get into the glory of our Father and enjoy the blessings that we hope to receive through faithfulness, we will have to live the laws of patience, and exercise forgiveness toward those who trespass against us, and remove from our hearts all feelings of hatred toward them.

"And again, if your enemy shall smite you the second time, and you revile not against your enemy, and bear it patiently, your reward shall be an hundredfold.

"And again, if he shall smite you the third time, and ye bear it patiently, your reward shall be doubled unto you four fold." [D&C 98:25–26.] . . .

May we have the Spirit of the Master dwelling within us, that we may forgive all men as He has commanded, forgive, not only with our lips but in the very depths of our hearts, every trespass that may have been committed against us. If we do this through life, the blessings of the Lord will abide in our hearts and our homes.[12] [See suggestion 5 below.]

Suggestions for Study and Teaching

Consider these ideas as you study the chapter or as you prepare to teach. For additional help, see pages v–vii.

1. Ponder the story on page 247 and read 3 Nephi 12:22–24. Why do you think the Lord requires that we be reconciled with our brothers and sisters before we can come unto Him?

2. On pages 248–49 President Smith explains that our knowledge of the plan of salvation should help us be more forgiving. Why do you think this is so? How do we "get into a condition" (page 249) in which we can forgive others?

3. As you study the section that begins on page 249, think of a time when Heavenly Father forgave you. Why do you think failing to forgive others would make us unworthy of the forgiveness we seek?

4. Read the second full paragraph on page 250. What hinders us from being reconciled with a Church leader or someone else who has knowing or unknowingly offended us? What can we do to overcome these difficulties?

5. Review the last section of teachings (pages 250). How does our willingness to forgive prepare us for the celestial kingdom? In what ways are our families blessed when we forgive others?

Related Scriptures: Matthew 5:23–24, 38–48; 6:12, 14–15; 7:1–5; 18:15; 1 Nephi 7:16–21; Doctrine and Covenants 42:88

Teaching help: "When an individual asks a question, consider inviting others to answer it instead of answering it yourself. For example, you could say, 'That's an interesting question. What do the rest of you think?' or 'Can anyone help with this question?'" (*Teaching, No Greater Call,* 64).

Notes

1. See Merlo J. Pusey, "The Inner Strength of a Leader," *Instructor,* June 1965, 232.

2. "President George Albert Smith's Creed," *Improvement Era,* Apr. 1950, 262.

3. Matthew Cowley, in Conference Report, Apr. 1951, 167.

4. "The Spirit of Forgiveness," *Improvement Era*, Aug. 1945, 443.

5. In Conference Report, Oct. 1945, 169.

6. In Conference Report, Oct. 1905, 27.

7. In Conference Report, Oct. 1905, 27.

8. In Conference Report, Oct. 1904, 65–66.

9. In Conference Report, Oct. 1905, 27.

10. In Conference Report, Oct. 1906, 50.

11. Address given at Mexican mission conference, May 26, 1946, George Albert Smith Family Papers, University of Utah, box 121, page 288.

12. In Conference Report, Oct. 1905, 27–28, 30.

CHAPTER 24

Righteous Living in
Perilous Times

*Through our faithfulness to the gospel,
we can find safety from the perils of our day
and be a positive influence in the world.*

From the Life of George Albert Smith

George Albert Smith's service as a General Authority spanned most of the first half of the 20th century. During this period the world saw many devastating and tumultuous events, including the Great Depression and two world wars. These calamities, together with what he considered a general moral decline in society, led President Smith to say more than once, "This world is in a critical condition."[1] He saw in world events the fulfillment of prophecies about the last days, and he was convinced that the only hope for peace in the world was obedience to God's laws. At the height of World War I, he warned, "War will not cease and the strife in this world will not end until the children of men repent of their sins and turn to God and serve him and keep his commandments."[2]

In the midst of these difficult times, President Smith found that many people had become discouraged. He reported, "It has been my privilege to be in different parts of [the United States] and it is rare that one finds those who are not exceedingly pessimistic, because of conditions over which we seem to have no control."[3] While he acknowledged that war, natural disasters, and spiritual danger are part of living in the latter days, President Smith taught the Saints that they can escape much of the distress of these perilous times by living the gospel and resisting temptation.

He also found optimism in his belief that righteous Latter-day Saints could have a powerful influence on the world around them.

"Peace I leave with you, my peace I give unto you: not as the world giveth, give I unto you. Let not your heart be troubled, neither let it be afraid"
(John 14:27).

He taught that the Saints should not merely accept the condition of the world but should remain active in their communities and strive to make their influence felt, in spite of any opposition they might face. "We are all under the obligation of making this world a happier place for our having lived in it," he said.[4]

Sister Belle S. Spafford, general president of the Relief Society, shared an experience in which President Smith taught her this principle. Shortly after being called to her position, Sister Spafford was notified of a meeting to be held in New York City by the National Council of Women. The Relief Society had been a member of that council for many years, but recently several other members of the council had been antagonistic toward the Church and had embarrassed Latter-day Saint delegates at its meetings. Because of this, Sister Spafford and her counselors felt that the Relief Society should terminate its membership in the council, and they drafted a recommendation expressing their views. Sister Spafford later recounted:

"By appointment one morning, I went alone to see President George Albert Smith, taking the recommendation with me, together with a list of the reasons why the recommendation was being made. The President carefully read the typed material. Then he inquired, 'Isn't this the organization which the sisters joined before the turn of the century?'

"I said, 'Yes, sir.'

"He said, 'Am I then to understand that you now wish to terminate that membership?'

"I said, 'Yes, sir.' Then I added, 'You know, President Smith, we don't get anything from the Council.'

"The President looked at me with surprise. He said, 'Sister Spafford, do you always think in terms of what you get? Don't you think it is well at times to think in terms of what you have to give? I believe,' he continued, 'that Mormon women have something to give to the women of the world, and that they may also learn from them. Rather than have you terminate your membership, I suggest that you take several of your ablest board members and go back to this meeting.'

"Then he said with emphasis, 'Make your influence felt.'"[5]

257

Sister Spafford obeyed this counsel and was later appointed to leadership positions in the National Council of Women, eventually being elected its president. [See suggestion 1 on page 264.]

Teachings of George Albert Smith

Serious difficulties have been predicted for the latter days.

We have been told that in the last days serious difficulties would arise. . . . We have not only been warned by the scriptures that were given in the days of the Savior and prior to his time, and those that were given after him, but in our own day and age the Lord has spoken and the revelations of our Heavenly Father are found in the Doctrine and Covenants. If we will read these revelations we will learn that the experiences through which we are passing were predicted. . . .

. . . The daily press brings to us accounts of disasters that are everywhere—the sea being tempestuous and loss of life upon it, earthquakes, great tornadoes, such as we have been told would occur in the last days—and it does seem to me, brethren and sisters, if men are thinking seriously, if they are reading the scriptures, they must know that the happenings that the Lord said would occur in the last days are occurring. The fig tree surely is putting forth its leaves [see Joseph Smith—Matthew 1:38–39], and those who are thoughtful must know that the summer is nigh, that those things that the Lord has predicted as preceding his second coming are now coming to pass.[6]

We are not out of the woods. This world is in for a housecleaning unless the sons and daughters of our Heavenly Father repent of their sins and turn to him. And that means the Latter-day Saints, or the members of the Church of Jesus Christ of Latter-day Saints, along with all the rest, but we, first of all, ought to be setting the example.[7] [See suggestion 2 on page 264.]

The only way to peace is the gospel of Jesus Christ.

There is only one remedy for the universal distress—a panacea for the sickness of the world. It is the gospel of Jesus Christ; the perfect law of life and liberty, which has been restored again in fulfilment of the Scriptures.[8]

"Peace I leave with you, my peace I give unto you: not as the world giveth, give I unto you. Let not your heart be troubled, neither let it be afraid." (John 14:27.)

These are reassuring words from the Prince of Peace to his faithful followers. Surely there is nothing men need more than the blessings of peace and happiness and hearts free from fear. And these are offered [to] all of us if we will but be partakers of them.

When the gospel was restored to earth in this dispensation, the Lord repeated what he has said so many times in the Old and New Testaments, that the price of peace and happiness is righteousness. Notwithstanding this knowledge, there are many who appear to think that we can obtain happiness in some other way, but we should all know by this time that there is no other way. And yet by his cunning craftiness Satan has persuaded the majority of mankind from walking in the way that will insure happiness, and he is still busy. The adversary of righteousness never sleeps.

But by following the teachings of the Lord, by turning unto him and repenting of sin, by going about doing good, we may have peace and happiness and prosperity. If mankind will love one another, the hatred and the unkindness that have existed so much in the world will pass away.[9]

In these days of uncertainty when men are running to and fro seeking for some new plan by which peace may be brought into the world, know this: that the only way to peace for this world is the pathway of the Gospel of Jesus Christ our Lord. There is no other. . . . To possess a knowledge of the truth is worth all the wealth of the world, to know that we are on the safe highway when we are in the pathway of duty as defined by our Heavenly Father, and to know that we can continue there if we will, regardless of the influences and inducements that may be offered by those who have not been appointed to be our leaders, is a blessing that is priceless.[10]

We live in a day when the scripture is being fulfilled among the nations wherein the Lord said through one of his prophets, that in the latter-day, ". . . the wisdom of their wise men shall perish, and the understanding of their prudent men shall be hid." (Isaiah 29:14.) With all the wisdom of the world, no group thus far has been able to point the way for peace with the certainty that it is the way. We . . . are fortunate to know that there is a way for peace that alone will produce results, and that way is to keep the commandments of God as revealed to the children of men anciently and in our day. If that way were followed, all the problems that are so serious in the world could be solved, and peace would come to this unhappy earth. [11]

Though the world may be filled with distress, and the heavens gather blackness, and the vivid lightnings flash, and the earth quake from center to circumference, if we know that God lives, and our lives are righteous, we will be happy, there will be peace unspeakable because we know our Father approves [of] our lives. [12] [See suggestion 3 on page 264.]

We need have no fear if we do what the Lord has asked us to do.

We need have no fear if we do what the Lord has asked us to do. This is His world. All men and women are subject to Him. All the powers of evil will be controlled for the sake of His people, if they will honor Him and keep His commandments. [13]

If we have the confidence of our Heavenly Father, if we have His love, if we are worthy of His blessings, all the armies of the world cannot destroy us, cannot break down our faith, and cannot overcome the Church that is named for the Son of God.

Read in the nineteenth chapter of II Kings how Sennacherib the Assyrian king sought to overthrow Jerusalem. Hezekiah, the king who represented Israel pleaded with the Lord for deliverance while Sennacherib mocked him, saying, "Don't think that your prayers to your God can help you. Every place that I have been and taken already, they have been praying. You are helpless," and the next morning a large part of the Assyrian army was found dead upon the ground, and Jerusalem had been preserved by the Lord. [See 2 Kings 19:10–20, 35.] He is our strength, . . . your Father and mine, the Father of all; if we will only be worthy He will preserve us as He did Helaman's sons [see Alma 57:24–27], and as He preserved Daniel from the lions [see Daniel 6], and the three Hebrew children from the fiery furnace [see Daniel 3], and six hundred thousand of the descendants of Abraham when he brought them out from Egypt under the leadership of Moses and drowned Pharaoh's army in the Red Sea [see Exodus 14:21–30]. He is the God of this universe. He is the Father of us all. He is all-powerful and He promises us protection if we will live worthy of it.[14]

No matter whether the clouds may gather, no matter how the war drums may beat, no matter what conditions may arise in the world, here in the Church of Jesus Christ of Latter-day Saints, wherever we are honoring and keeping the commandments of God, there will be protection from the powers of evil, and men and women will be permitted to live upon the earth until their lives are finished in honor and glory if they will keep the commandments of our Heavenly Father.[15] [See suggestion 4 on page 264.]

Our homes can be peaceful, holy places even in the midst of calamities.

I think that with the distress everywhere, with the prediction that the Lord made in the first Section of the Doctrine and Covenants, that "peace should be taken from the earth," [D&C 1:35] we must feel that that time has come. Surely we ought to take stock of ourselves, and our homes should be the abiding place of prayer and gratitude and thanksgiving. Husbands should be kind to their wives, and wives considerate of their husbands. Parents should hold the love of their children by their righteous living. Our homes would then not only be the abiding place of prayer and thanksgiving, but would be the place where our Father could bestow His choicest blessings, because of our worthiness.[16]

I pray that our homes may be sanctified by the righteousness of our lives, that the adversary may have no power to come there and destroy the children of our homes or those who dwell under our roofs. If we will honor God and keep his commandments, our

*"Make your homes the abiding place of the spirit of the Lord;
let them be holy places."*

homes will be sacred, the adversary will have no influence, and
we will live in happiness and peace until the winding-up scene in
mortality and we go to receive our reward in immortality.[17]

Conform your lives to the teachings of the gospel of Jesus Christ
and when calamities threaten you will feel the support of his all
powerful arm. Make your homes the abiding place of the spirit
of the Lord; let them be holy places, where the adversary cannot
come; listen to the still small voice prompting you to works of righteousness. It is my prayer for one and all that you be not swerved
from the path that leads to the knowledge and power of God, the
heritage of the faithful, even life everlasting.[18]

I pray that in our hearts and in our homes there may abide that
spirit of love, of patience, of kindness, of charity, of helpfulness
that enriches our lives and that makes the world brighter and better
because of it.[19] [See suggestion 5 on page 264.]

We can be a positive influence in the world.

I want to plead with you, . . . be as anchors in the community in which you live that others may be drawn to you and feel secure. Let your light so shine that others seeing your good works will have a desire in their hearts to be like you. [20]

It is our duty to set the example; it is our duty to hold aloft the banner of truth. It is our duty to encourage our Father's other children to listen to his advice and counsel and so adjust things that wherever we are we will find the spirit of God burning in our souls and our influence will be for good. [21]

The Lord has not required something that is impossible. On the contrary, he has given us commandments and advice and counsel that it is possible for all of us to follow in this day and age in which we live. . . .

. . . Brethren and sisters, we ought to be faithful. The land that we live in should be sanctified by our lives of righteousness. . . . All that we need is to repent of our sins, turn from the error of our ways, cleanse our lives of impurity, and then to go about doing good. It does not require that we shall be set apart for that purpose. Every man, woman and child in the Church of Jesus Christ may go about doing good and receive the blessing that results therefrom. [See suggestion 6 on page 264.]

. . . Let us set our hands to the work that he has entrusted to our care, let us bless our Father's children wherever they may be, and our lives will be enriched and this world will be made happier. This is the mission that has been placed upon our shoulders. Our Heavenly Father will hold us responsible for the manner in which we fulfil it. God grant that in the humility of our souls we will go about with the desire in our hearts to do good to all people wherever they may be, and bring to them the joy that can only come through observing his laws and keeping his commandments. That peace may abide in our hearts and in our homes, that we may radiate sunshine and cheer wherever we may go, that we may prove to the world that we do know that God lives, by the lives that we lead, and receive his blessings therefor, I humbly pray. [22]

Suggestions for Study and Teaching

Consider these ideas as you study the chapter or as you prepare to teach. For additional help, see pages v–vii.

1. Read the story about Belle S. Spafford receiving counsel from President Smith (pages 257–58). In what ways can you "make your influence felt"?

2. In the first section of teachings (page 258), President Smith tells of the difficulties that have been predicted to precede the Second Coming (see also 2 Timothy 3:1–7; D&C 45:26–35). Why do you think it is important to know that these difficulties were predicted in the scriptures?

3. Review the section that begins at the bottom of page 258. What are some of the problems in the world that could be solved by obedience to the restored gospel of Jesus Christ? How has the gospel brought peace to your personal life? to your family? to your relationships with others?

4. On pages 260–61 President Smith gives examples from the scriptures of the Lord protecting His people. In what ways has He protected you and your family? How does obedience help us overcome fear?

5. What are some of the dangers that threaten the spiritual safety of our homes today? What can we do to make our homes "holy places, where the adversary cannot come"? (For some ideas, review the section that begins on page 261.)

6. Read the first and fourth paragraphs on page 263. How are faithful Latter-day Saints like "anchors" in their communities? Why does "[cleansing] our lives of impurity" make us better able to "go about doing good"? Prayerfully consider what you should do to cleanse your own life of impurity.

Related Scriptures: Isaiah 54:13–17; Matthew 5:13–16; John 16:33; 2 Nephi 14:5–6; Doctrine and Covenants 87:6–8; 97:24–25; Joseph Smith—Matthew 1:22–23, 29–30

Teaching help: Consider inviting class members to read the headings in "Teachings of George Albert Smith" and select a section that is meaningful to them or their family. Invite them to study President Smith's teachings in that section, including any corresponding questions at the end of the chapter. Then ask class members to share what they learned.

Notes

1. In Conference Report, Apr. 1948, 162.
2. In Conference Report, Apr. 1918, 41.
3. In Conference Report, Apr. 1932, 41.
4. "Some Thoughts on War, and Sorrow, and Peace," *Improvement Era,* Sept. 1945, 501.
5. Belle S. Spafford, *A Woman's Reach* (1974), 96–97.
6. In Conference Report, Apr. 1932, 42–44.
7. In Conference Report, Oct. 1946, 153.
8. "New Year's Greeting," *Millennial Star,* Jan. 1, 1920, 2.
9. "'At This Season,'" *Improvement Era,* Dec. 1949, 801.
10. In Conference Report, Oct. 1937, 53.
11. In Conference Report, Apr. 1946, 4.
12. In Conference Report, Oct. 1915, 28.
13. In Conference Report, Apr. 1942, 15.
14. In Conference Report, Apr. 1943, 92.
15. In Conference Report, Apr. 1942, 15.
16. In Conference Report, Apr. 1941, 27.
17. In Conference Report, Oct. 1946, 8.
18. "New Year's Greeting," *Millennial Star,* Jan. 6, 1921, 3.
19. In Conference Report, Oct. 1946, 7.
20. In Conference Report, Oct. 1945, 117–18.
21. In Conference Report, Oct. 1947, 166.
22. In Conference Report, Apr. 1932, 43–45.

List of Visuals

Cover: *George Albert Smith,* by Lee Greene Richards, © IRI.

Page 4: *The Sermon on the Mount,* by Carl Heinrich Bloch, used by permission of the National Historic Museum at Frederiksborg in Hillerød, Denmark.

Page 12: *Christ Healing a Blind Man,* by Del Parson, © 1983 IRI.

Page 20: *Christ's Image,* by Heinrich Hofmann, courtesy C. Harrison Conroy Co., Inc.

Page 25: *Behold My Hands and Feet,* by Harry Anderson, © IRI.

Page 27: *Behold Your Little Ones,* by Robert T. Barrett, © 1996 IRI.

Page 37: *Joseph Smith's First Vision,* © 1988 Greg K. Olsen, do not copy.

Page 40: *Joseph Smith,* courtesy of the Community of Christ Archives, Independence, Missouri.

Page 49: *The Melchizedek Priesthood Restored,* by Walter Rane, © 2010 IRI.

Page 56: Photo courtesy of the Church History Library and Archives.

Page 62: *One before God,* by Joseph Brickey, © 2010 IRI.

Page 65: Photo © 2000 Steve Bunderson.

Page 68: Photo © 2006 Robert Casey.

Page 75: *Jesus Said to Her, "Mary,"* by William Whitaker, © 1999 IRI.

Page 127: *Go Ye Therefore, and Teach All Nations,* by Harry Anderson, © IRI.

Page 154: Photo © 2000 Steve Bunderson.

Page 180: *Elijah Contends against the Priests of Baal,* by Jerry Harston, © 1978 IRI.

Page 183: *Moses Parting the Red Sea,* by Robert Barrett, © 1983 IRI.

Page 185: *Arrival of Brigham Young,* © 1986 VaLoy Eaton, courtesy of Zions Bank, do not copy.

Page 190: *Christ and the Rich Young Ruler,* by Heinrich Hofmann, courtesy C. Harrison Conroy Co., Inc.

Page 202: *Daniel Refusing the King's Meat and Wine,* by Del Parson, © 1983 IRI.

Page 224: *Lemonade on a Hot Day,* by Michael Malm, © 2010 IRI.

Page 246: *The Crucifixion,* by Harry Anderson, © IRI.

Page 256: *Peace I Leave with You,* © 2004 Walter Rane, courtesy of the Church History Museum.

Index

A

Aaronic Priesthood. *See* Priesthood

Adversary
tries to deceive us, 194–97
we can resist, 197–99

Apostasy
Heavenly Father restored the gospel in response to, 39
in the meridian of time, 47
priesthood authority lost during, 48

Atonement. *See* Jesus Christ; Resurrection

B

Baptism
of Jesus Christ, 24

Bible
testimony of Jesus Christ, 24–25
See also Scriptures

Book of Mormon
George Albert Smith shares, with others, xxii, xxxiv
testimony of Jesus Christ, 25–26
See also Scriptures

C

Callings
responsibility of members to fulfill, 160–62

Charity. *See* Love

Church leaders
are chosen by the Lord, 58–59
the Lord guides His people through, 59–60, 115–16
safety in following, 60

we should not criticize, 63–64
See also President of the Church

Church of Jesus Christ
directed by Jesus Christ, 59, 115–16
possesses divine authority, 50–51
progress of, 42, 157–59, 162–66

Commandments
God gives, because He loves us, 193–94
keep us on the Lord's side of the line, 192
safety comes from obeying, 260–61

Covetousness
warning against, 217

Criticism
contrary to the gospel of Jesus Christ, 226
look for virtues in others instead of criticizing, 226–27
of Church leaders, 63–64

D

Daniel
faith of, 182–83
obeyed the Lord's law of health in his day, 201–3

Death
gospel helps us understand, 67–70, 75–77

Devil. *See* Adversary

E

Elijah
faith of, 183